THE STRIKE

THE STRIKE WINGS

Special Anti-Shipping Squadrons
1942–1945

Roy Conyers Nesbit

London:HMSO

By the same author:

Woe to the Unwary
Torpedo Airmen
Target: Hitler's Oil (with Ron C. Cooke)
Arctic Airmen (with Ernest Schofield)
Failed to Return
An Illustrated History of the RAF
RAF Records in the PRO (with Simon Fowler, Peter Elliott and Christina Goulter)
The Arnold Rovers

Cover painting by Frank Wootton depicts the attack on a German convoy made by the North Coates and Langham Strike Wings on 15 June 1944.

In Memory of
the nine squadrons
of the Strike Wings
COASTAL COMMAND

143	236	404(RCAF)
144	248	455(RAAF)
235	254	489(RNZAF)

with their outriders in
333 (Norwegian) Squadron

The Author

Roy Conyers Nesbit joined the RAFVR in September 1939. Commissioned as an air navigator, he flew with a squadron of Bristol Beauforts, completed forty-nine operational sorties, and was mentioned in despatches. Following a spell as an instructor in Africa, he volunteered for the Far East and flew in a Dakota squadron over India, Burma and South-East Asia.

After demobilisation he graduated from London University and pursued a business career until taking early retirement. He is President of the Beaufort Aircrews Association and has written nine books as well as numerous articles on aviation history. He is on the editorial staff of a German aviation magazine and is an author of the Public Record Office's guide to RAF research.

In recent years he has appeared on television news programmes and has frequently been interviewed on radio on matters relating to aviation history.

Contents

List of Maps and Diagrams

List of Illustrations

Foreword

by
Air Chief Marshal Sir Neil Wheeler, GCB, CBE, DSO,
DFC and bar, AFC, FRAeS, RAF(retired)

To have been a member of one of the Strike Wings was an unforgettable experience. They were momentous days, over forty years ago, and I was pleased to tell Roy Nesbit all the details of them that I could remember. But I was greatly honoured when he asked me to contribute a foreword to his impressive book. It had been such a privilege as a very young Wing Commander to lead men of skill and great courage into battle that I readily agreed.

There has been such an abundance of books about the Royal Air Force in World War Two that it is surprising to find that the story of the Strike Wings has not been told until now. Yet this area of conflict and the part played by Coastal Command was of great significance. By the autumn of 1944, nearly 200 front-line Beaufighters and Mosquitos of Coastal Command were employed in the Strike Wings.

In general, there still seems to be little awareness of the role and purpose of strike aircraft of Coastal Command during the war. Nevertheless, the nine squadrons of the Strike Wings fought in some of the bitterest and bloodiest attacks of the war, all at low level and at close quarters. As the author shows, they suffered heavy casualties, in the same proportion as Bomber Command, but they inflicted far greater damage on the enemy in relation to their losses. The main reason why the British public was only vaguely aware of these dramatic and ferocious events is that anti-shipping attacks came under conditions of strict secrecy; the results were known quite accurately at the time, but only scrappy details were released to the Press and the BBC.

Since the war, with the release of many documents at the Public Record Office under the Thirty Year Rule, it has been possible for researchers to trace the history of the nine squadrons of the Strike

Wings in their Operations Record Books and other sources. The story is very complex, however, requiring much unravelling and a good deal of esoteric knowledge. It is fortunate that the author flew, as a junior officer, in strike aircraft of Coastal Command and retains an understanding of the technicalities of the aircraft, ships and armament, as well as his personal experience of flying in these conditions. Moreover, he has not relied wholly on British records but has painstakingly examined many German war diaries, considerably helped by the Naval Historical and Air Historical Branches of the Ministry of Defence. The results, combined with the recollections of many of the aircrews involved, form a compelling, accurate and detailed account of those events.

As could be seen during the recent Falklands conflict, the weapons employed in air/sea warfare have evolved considerably since the days of the Strike Wings, although some of the tactics used from 1943 to 1945 could still be studied with advantage by modern air forces. What have not changed, however, are the degrees of resolution and courage required by the participants. If the reader wishes to learn more of these qualities, he will find that they are vividly portrayed in this book.

Acknowledgements

I am very grateful for the help given to me, when researching the material for this book, by officials and staff of the following organizations:

Aeroplane Monthly, International Publishing Corp., Sutton.
BBC Written Archives, Reading.
British Aerospace, Weybridge-Bristol Division.
Commonwealth War Graves Commission, Maidenhead.
Deutsche Dienststelle, Berlin.
Imperial War Museum, Lambeth.
Ministry of Defence, Air Historical Branch, Holborn.
Ministry of Defence, Naval Historical Branch, Fulham.
National Maritime Museum, Greenwich.
National Meteorological Archive, Bracknell.
Public Record Office, Kew.
Royal Aeronautical Society, Hamilton Place, London.
Royal Air Force Museum, Hendon.

My thanks are also due, for assistance with research, to:

Major Pierre Lorain, in France.
Mrs Annie Ross, widow of Flight Lieutenant David Ross.
Per Skaugstad, skin-diver and author, in Norway.
Gerrie J. Zwanenburg, Identification and Recovery Officer, Royal Netherlands Air Force.

Several friends have encouraged and helped me with technical advice, translations, and improvements in the narrative. They are:

Wing Commander Arthur H. Aldridge, DFC and bar, MA, RAFVR.
Ron C. Cooke, MSc(Econ).
Flight Lieutenant J. Dudley F. Cowderoy, BSc(Eng), FICE, AIAS, MSoc.E(France), RAFVR.
Squadron Leader Norman Hearn-Phillips, AFC, DFM, RAF(Ret'd).
Flight Lieutenant Eddie G. Whiston, RAFVR.

I should also like to thank my brother, Michael H. Nesbit, for improving old and faded photographs by the photo-mechanical transfer process; my nephew Peter Nesbit for designing the cover; Colin Rose for drawing the maps and diagrams; and Frank Wootton for allowing me to use his splendid painting on the cover.

This book relates the story of those who flew in the Strike Wings. Those who have helped me with their recollections, advice and encouragement are:

Flight Lieutenant P.R. Bassett, DFC, RAFVR.
Flight Lieutenant M.C. Bateman, DFC, RAF(Ret'd).
Group Captain R.E. Burns, CBE, DFC and bar, BSc, C.Eng, MRAeS, RAF(Ret'd).
The Late Wing Commander F.E. Burton, OBE, DFC, RAF(Ret'd).
Flying Officer T.A. Cochrane, RAFVR.
Group Captain W.A.L. Davis, CBE, DFC, AFC, RAF(Ret'd).
Air Chief Marshal Sir Christopher N. Foxley-Norris, GCB, OBE, DSO, MA, RAF(Ret'd).
Wing Commander A. Gadd, DFC and bar, RAF(Ret'd).
Group Captain A.K. Gatward, DSO, DFC and bar, RAF(Ret'd).
Flying Officer F.L. Hinks, RAFVR.
Flying Officer F.S. Holly, RAFVR.
Air Commodore P.A. Hughes, CBE, DFC, RAF(Ret'd).
Group Captain S.R. Hyland, OBE, DFC, AFC, RAF(Ret'd).
Flight Lieutenant R.A. Irving, DFC and bar, RAFVR.
Flight Lieutenant R.E. Jones, DFC, RAFVR.
Master Navigator D.M. Kennedy, RAF(Ret'd).
Wing Commander D.O.F. Lumsden, DFC, RAF(Ret'd).
The Late Flying Officer D.H. Mann, DFC, RNZAF.
Flight Lieutenant D. Marrow, DFC, RAFVR.
Warrant Officer W.G.S. Parfitt, RAFVR.
Flight Lieutenant G.E.E. Peckover, RAFVR.
Squadron Leader H. Shannon, DFC, RAF(Ret'd).
Flight Lieutenant S.S. Shulemson, DSO, DFC, RCAF.
Wing Commander A.H. Simmonds, DFC, RAF(Ret'd).
Flying Officer P.C. Smith, DFC, RAFVR.
Flight Lieutenant H.R. Spink, DFC, RAAF.
Air Commodore E.W. Tacon, CBE, DSO, MVO, DFC and bar, AFC and bar, RAF(Ret'd).
Air Chief Marshal Sir H. Neil G. Wheeler, GCB, CBE, DSO, DFC and bar, AFC, FRAeS, RAF(Ret'd).
Flight Lieutenant J.H. White, RAFVR.
Squadron Leader G.W.E. Woolley, DFC, RAF(Ret'd).

and a man who did much to keep them in the air:
Flight Sergeant H.A.S. Dearman, RAF(Ret'd).

CHAPTER ONE

Historical Background

The men who flew the hundreds of sorties against ship
targets were required to make do with aircraft of unsuitable types, which were ill-defended and ill-equipped. It
is their unflinching acceptance of the new duty required
of them, in full knowledge of the deficiencies from which
their aircraft and weapons suffered, which is the brightest
feature in the scene here depicted.

S.W. Roskill. *The War at Sea*

When Hitler invaded Denmark, Norway and the Low Countries in
the spring of 1940, he was not motivated solely by a desire to con-
quer small nations and to impose the evil doctrines of his National
Socialism on subjugated peoples. If Germany was to wage war
against the more powerful countries of Britain, France and Russia,
her armaments and munitions factories would be largely dependent
upon the Swedish iron ore which was transported from Scandinavia
to her industrial centres. Of course, iron ore was mined in many
areas of Europe, including Germany, but the Swedish deposits
included vast quantities of the highest grade of phosphorous con-
tent, called magnetite. Germany's iron and steel industry, the
largest in the world apart from the USA, consumed over ten million
tons annually of this Swedish ore, the richest and least adulterated
of all the iron ores. Her industrial processes were geared to its use
and could not easily be adapted to the lower grades of ore.

The high-grade ore was mined in the districts of Kiruna and
Gällivare in northern Sweden and transported to Germany by two
main routes. The Swedish route was by rail to the port of Luleå on
the Gulf of Bothnia and thence by sea to the German ports in the
Baltic or through the Kiel canal to Emden, but the northern part of
this route was frozen up for as long as six months of the year; the ore
could be transported further overland by rail to the ice-free port of
Oxelsund, near Stockholm, but this small Swedish port could handle
only about a fifth of Germany's requirements. The more important and more economical route from the ore mines was across a
short though mountainous rail link to the ice-free port of Narvik in

Norway. From here it was shipped down the long and indented coastline of Norway, and then directly across the North Sea to the bustling and well-equipped port of Rotterdam in Holland. Enormous barges then carried the ore up the broad waters of the Rhine to the blast furnaces, smelting works and steel factories of the Ruhr and the Saar. In return, Germany exported millions of tons of coal and coke, by the same routes.

It was to protect these lifelines to Sweden that Hitler launched his invasion; in doing so, he believed that he was forestalling naval and military action by the British. On 16 December 1939, Winston Churchill – then First Lord of the Admiralty – had sent a note to the British Cabinet which recommended the laying of mines in Norwegian territorial waters; this included the words:

> If Germany can be cut off from all Swedish ore supplies from now onwards until the end of 1940, a blow will be struck at her war-making capacity equal to a first-class victory in the field or from the air and without any sacrifice of life. It might indeed be immediately decisive.

Churchill seemed to hope that Germany would retaliate by invading Norway, thus giving Britain an excuse for a counter-invasion which would result in the military control of Scandinavia and incidentally bring help to the Finns in their desperate war against the Russians. During this period the Russo-German non-aggression pact was in force and British sympathies were with the Finns. The Cabinet did not immediately adopt Churchill's recommendations but prepared contingency plans, Operation Wilfred for the minelaying and Plan R4 for the counter-invasion.

Meanwhile, Admiral Raeder, the Commander-in-Chief of the German Navy, informed Hitler on 23 February 1940:

> What must not be permitted is the occupation of Norway by Britain. That could not be undone; it would entail increased pressure on Sweden, perhaps the extension of the war to the Baltic, and cessation of all ore supplies from Sweden.

Hitler could not remain idle under such a threat. On 1 March 1940, he issued a directive for the invasion of Norway under the code-name Operation Weserübung, which included these words:

The development of the situation in Scandinavia requires the making of preparations for the occupation of Denmark and Norway by a part of the German armed forces. This operation should prevent British encroachment on Scandinavia and the Baltic; further, it should guarantee our ore base in Sweden and give our Navy and Air Force a wider start-line against Britain.

Germany's invasion of Norway began on 9 April 1940. Forewarned of the action, Britain began mine-laying a day earlier but did not land troops until 15 April; these men fought a bitter action for several weeks but were forced to withdraw when the German blitzkrieg left Britain isolated in Europe.

There was a rich haul for victorious Germany in the resources of Norway. Nickel, used for armour-plating and armour-piercing shells, was mined in significant quantities in Norway, an important source now that Germany was denied the vast output of Canada. Further supplies of nickel were mined near Petsamo in Finnish Lapland, by the northern border of Norway; Germany assumed, quite correctly, that Finland would be allied with her in the forthcoming war against Russia. Other resources included Norwegian molybdenum for hardening steel, iron pyrites for producing sulphuric acid, and aluminium produced by the power from Norwegian hydro-electric stations. These resources were invaluable to Hitler in his bid for world domination.

In a few brief weeks, Germany's blitzkrieg extended her coastline from the Arctic Circle to the Franco-Spanish border. This coastline harboured threats to Britain, but it also required defence. Its length was enormous. The Norwegian coastline alone was 2,100 miles long, disregarding indentations; if long inlets and large islands were included, the length was 16,500 miles, half the circumference of the globe. Along the whole of her new coastline, Germany plied captured merchant vessels from France, Holland, Denmark and Norway, almost with impunity in 1940.

Responsibility for attacking enemy vessels from the air rested mainly with RAF Coastal Command and the Fleet Air Arm. In September 1939, the strike force available to Coastal Command consisted of only two squadrons of the Vickers Vildebeest torpedo bomber, an obsolete bi-plane that was already ten years old and quite inadequate for its allotted task. In addition, there were eight squadrons of Avro Ansons, a reliable twin-engined monoplane that was useful for general reconnaissance and anti-submarine duties but quite unsuitable for the role of strike aircraft which it was sometimes called upon to perform. There were also two squadrons of Lockheed Hudsons, the military version of the Lockheed Electra airliner – a twin-engined monoplane that was to assume the unsuitable task of bombing enemy surface vessels.

So inadequate was the strike force of Coastal Command in the early part of the war that the RAF was forced to transfer to it three squadrons of Bristol Blenheims; these were 53 Squadron from Army Co-operation, 59 Squadron from Bomber Command, and 254 Squadron from Fighter Command. Also transferred was a Swordfish squadron, number 812, from the Fleet Air Arm. During 1940, the ancient Vildebeest was replaced with the Bristol Beaufort, a twin-engined monoplane designed for torpedo and low-level bombing, and Coastal Command began to assume a more aggressive role against enemy shipping. The Ansons were steadily replaced with Hudsons or Beauforts, whilst Handley-Page Hampdens adapted for torpedo bombing began to appear.

The crews of Coastal Command's hodge-podge strike force performed prodigies of valour in 1940–42, but their anti-shipping tactics were ill-defined, fighter escort was seldom available, their aircraft were inadequate in numbers and performance, whilst some of the aircrew were insufficiently trained. The results were disappointingly meagre. A post-war analysis reveals that during the period 1940 to March 1943, all Commands of the RAF sank only 107 enemy vessels, totalling 155,076 tons, at sea by direct attack in north-west Europe. In the process, the RAF lost 648 aircraft, giving an average of 239 tons per aircraft lost. This was hardly a worthwhile return for the sacrifices made by the young airmen. These were indeed the dark days for the strike aircrews of Coastal Command. By contrast, aerial electro-magnetic mines sank 369 vessels totalling 361,821 tons for the loss of 329 aircraft, giving an average of 980 tons per aircraft lost. The undramatic work of the mine-laying aircraft was proving far more effective than direct attack on ships at sea.

These shipping losses were irritating to Germany but they did not seriously impair her flow of coastal traffic. Supplies of iron ore and other minerals continued to pour into Rotterdam and the German ports. Nevertheless, Hitler continued to worry about Norway and, in his conferences on naval affairs, returned again and again to the possibility of an Allied invasion of the Scandinavian country. Norway was, he reiterated, the 'zone of destiny'. If the Allies contrived to cut supplies of Swedish iron ore, Germany would be unable to prosecute a full-scale war once her reserves were exhausted. On Hitler's insistence, the battleships *Scharnhorst* and *Gneisenau** and the cruiser *Prinz Eugen* daringly and successfully dashed up the Channel from Brest in February 1942 in order to join in the defence of Norwegian waters. The armament on the coastal merchantmen and their escorts was increased to such an extent that Coastal Command began to lose one in four aircraft on low-level attacks and was compelled to increase the bombing height to medium-level, with a consequent reduction in the casualty rate but also a steep decline in the results achieved.

Hitler was quite correct in his assessment of the British intention of invading Norway. Precisely such a plan had been hatched, and approved by Winston Churchill. Code-named Operation Jupiter, it envisaged an expedition into Norway in 1942. It was hoped that this would be accompanied by a revolt on the part of the Norwegians and that it might win the Swedish government over to the Allied cause. The stages of the plan were first to establish several squadrons of Allied fighters and bombers near Murmansk in Russia. Then a division of troops would be landed in the Petsamo region of Finland, which was occupied by Russia, with a further brigade at Parsangerfjord in Norway. The air forces would then establish themselves in the northern aerodromes of Norway whilst the Russians would intensify their attacks from northern Finland, with the aid of additional supplies by sea from Britain. The Allied troops would then be reinforced and advance southwards down Norway, 'unrolling the Nazi map of Europe from the top', in the words of Winston Churchill. However, Churchill's eloquence for his favourite scheme did not win over Roosevelt. In July 1942, the two leaders sanctioned Torch, the Anglo-American invasion of North Africa but Jupiter, which Churchill had hoped would also be carried out, was shelved.

Whether Jupiter would have been successful must remain in the realm of speculation. But in the absence of a direct attack, the British sought to hit hard at the coastal traffic to and from Scandinavia. The concept, belated in its arrival, was based on the experiences of aircrews and envisaged the creation of specialized

---

*   The Royal Navy referred to the *Scharnhorst* and the *Gneisenau* as battle-cruisers, but the German word was *Schlachtschiff*, battleship.

anti-shipping Strike Wings. The lesson that had been learnt slowly and painfully over the previous three years was that it was almost useless to send ill-armed and unescorted torpedo bombers singly or in small formations against heavily defended convoys. Some method of suppressing the enemy flak and providing fighter protection had to be found. Two major developments made these objectives possible.

The first requirements were for an effective anti-flak aircraft and for an improved torpedo bomber. Both of these were found in the Bristol Beaufighter. The powerful and versatile 'Beau' was not a new aircraft in 1942, for it had been designed in 1938. The first production version, the Mark IF, came into service in Fighter Command as early as August 1940. In March 1941, Coastal Command began to employ the Mark IC as a long-range fighter; in 1942 it took deliveries of the Mark VIC, the first version to be used by the Strike Wings. The Mark VIC, with a dihedral instead of a straight tailplane, was a more stable aircraft than the Mark IC and could be trimmed to fly steadily for long distances at low level, but it was less manoeuvrable and always at a disadvantage in an encounter with single-engined fighters.

The Beaufighter was a development of the underpowered Beaufort. It retained the wings, tailplane and rear fuselage of its predecessor, but two 1,650 hp Hercules radials powered the Beaufighter Mark VIC in contrast to the inadequate 1,150 hp Taurus engines of the Beaufort Mark I. The front part of the Beaufort was redesigned to a much shorter nose in the Beaufighter. The Beaufort's crew of four were reduced to two in the Beaufighter Mark VIC, the pilot and a navigator who assumed the additional functions of wireless operator and rear gunner. The weight saved in the shorter nose and the two crew members was taken up in extra armament. The anti-flak Beaufighter Mark VIC possessed an enormous forward fire-power, four Hispano-Suiza 20 mm cannon mounted in the fuselage underneath the pilot and firing through the nose, and six Browning .303 machine guns, four in the port wing and two in the starboard wing. There was also a single backward-firing .303 Vickers K or Browning machine gun mounted in the mid-upper cupola above the navigator. The Beaufighter had a wing span of 57'10", a length of 41'8" and a height of 15'10". The cruising speed at Coastal Command's normal operational height of under 1,000 feet was around 200 mph; the maximum speed at this height was a reassuring 350 mph. Under ideal conditions

The first Beaufighters in Coastal Command were the Mark IC with two Bristol Hercules engines of 1,400 h.p. each. This version had a straight tailplane; it was manoeuvrable but considered insufficiently stable for low-level flying.

The Beaufighters in use by Coastal Command when the first Strike Wing was formed in November 1942 were the Mark VIC. This version had two Hercules engines of 1,650 h.p. each, and a tailplane with a dihedral of twelve degrees. This aircraft is firing rockets in practice in April 1943.

The Beaufighters of Coastal Command were eventually standardised as the TFX with two Hercules 1,772 h.p. engines. Later, this version was modified with a dorsal fin extension towards the navigator's cupola, reducing the tendency to swing on take-off. This is the torpedo-carrying TFX, or Torbeau.

and with a drop tank, a range of 1,500 miles could be achieved, but operationally this was not possible; the Beaufighter seldom ranged more than 1,000 miles, the return trip from, say, north-east Scotland to Trondheim fjord in Norway.

In the Beaufighter Mark VIC, Coastal Command possessed an excellent and robust anti-flak aircraft for the formation of the proposed Strike Wings, but a torpedo bomber of equivalent performance was required to destroy the enemy merchant vessels. It was but a short step to adapt some of the Beaufighters for this additional role. This version of the Mark VIC was known as the Torbeau, and it carried the four cannon as well as a torpedo. However, the aerial torpedo in use during the first three years of the war, the Mark XII with a diameter of 18″ and a weight of 1,610 lb, was not strong enough for dropping at the higher speed of the Torbeau. The second technical advance which made possible the creation of the Strike Wings was the modification of this weapon. The work was carried out at the Aircraft Torpedo Development Unit (ATDU) at Gosport. Torpedoes were scarce and valuable, but ATDU was given six Mark XIIs to 'test to destruction if necessary'. The engineers and pilots set about their task with a will. The torpedoes were dropped at progressively higher speeds and greater heights, being stripped down and examined for weaknesses after each drop. Pipes were re-routed, attachment points were strengthened and a new after-body was built, producing the Mark XV torpedo. It was also necessary to improve the performance of the torpedo during its flight in the air, so that it entered the water like a dart, within a couple of degrees of its trajectory. For this purpose a gyroscopically-controlled air tail was built, known as the Monotane Air Tail (MAT) Mark IV. Whereas, in the Beaufort, the Mark XII torpedo had to be dropped at about 80 feet and at a speed of 160 mph, the new torpedo could be dropped from up to 1,000 feet and at a speed of up to 350 mph, although in practice the Torbeau usually dropped from about 175 feet and at about 210 mph. This new torpedo also contained the underwater explosive Torpex instead of TNT, giving an increase in explosive power of around 25%.

The first of the Strike Wings was formed by 16 Group in November 1942, at North Coates on the coast of Lincolnshire. It consisted of two squadrons of the Beaufighter Mark VIC; 236 Squadron armed with cannon, machine guns and bombs, and 254 Squadron armed with cannon and torpedoes. In early 1943, these two squadrons were joined by 143 Squadron, which by then had been re-equipped with the Beaufighter Mark XIC, a version of the Mark VIC with two 1,772 hp engines, used in the anti-flak role. The intention was that the squadrons of the Strike Wings should live and work together, operating as a single co-ordinated unit. When they flew on a strike, they would be protected by at least two squadrons of single-engined aircraft of Fighter Command, a role that was at first allocated to Spitfires; this restricted the operational range of the new North Coates Wing to the Dutch coast as far as the Frisian Islands. The primary task of the new wing was thus to destroy enemy shipping along this vital coastline.

The opposition that the wing faced in November 1942 was both ferocious and formidable. As with the British, the German convoys contained vessels from their merchant marine and from their navy. The previous May, the activities of the merchant marine had been brought under a single authority headed by Karl Kaufmann, the Gauleiter of Hamburg, his title being Reichskommissar for Schifffahrt. Kaufmann assumed control of 504 vessels in north-west Europe, totalling 946,598 tons, and he was responsible only to Hitler. With intense dedication, he sat about rationalizing port facilities, reorganizing port labour, improving pay and conditions for his ships' crews, arranging shorter turn-round times, utilizing the space more efficiently in each ship and speeding up voyage times. His cargo vessels ranged from 1,000 to 10,000 tons, the average being about 3,000 tons carrying petroleum and lubricants to the occupying forces in Norway. All these vessels were armed, the weapons often being served by well-trained naval gunners.

These merchant vessels were protected by the German navy, or Kriegsmarine. The most ubiquitous escorts were converted trawlers, usually of around 500 tons, jammed with flak guns of all calibres; the Germans called these *Vorpostenboote* and the RAF authorities referred to them as 'trawler-type auxiliaries', whilst to the aircrew they were simply 'flak-ships'. There was a larger and more feared version of the *Vorpostenboot* called the *Sperrbrecher*, meaning literally a 'barrier-breaker'; these were ex-merchant vessels of up to 8,000 tons, specially reinforced for exploding mines and for general work, packed with flak defences – the most dangerous escorts of all. Then there were purpose-built mine-sweepers or escorts that usually sailed just ahead of the convoys; these were *Minensuchboote* to the Germans and 'M-class mine-sweepers' to the RAF. Smaller and more agile minesweepers sometimes buzzed around the convoys, averaging only 125 tons but still dangerous with their cannon; they were *Räumboote*, or 'R-boats' to the RAF. Of course, the defences might include German destroyers, or torpedo-boats the size of small destroyers, and sometimes naval patrol vessels called *Geleitboote*. Sometimes the Beaufighters would be called upon to attack the German equivalent of the motor-torpedo boat, 'E-boats' to the British and *Schnellboote* to the Germans.

Fully aware of the growing threat to their convoys, the Germans increased their defensive fire-power and reinforced the protective umbrellas of their Me 109s and FW 190s. A convoy was usually protected in the ratio of two or three escort vessels to one merchant ship. It could put up an intense and accurate defensive fire, often co-ordinated by a Kriegsmarine gunnery officer in the Commandant's ship. The heavier flak would consist of 105 mm, 88 mm, 40 mm and 37mm shells, pockmarking the sky with black and white puffs, the first peril for the attackers. Then would follow the deadlier streams of tracer fire from 20 mm cannon and 7.92 mm machine guns, the equivalent of the Beaufighters' weapons but usually in greater quantity, aimed by determined gunners.

Most of these actions took place in daylight. Attacks by the Beaufighters and later the Mosquitoes of the Strike Wings on German surface vessels must be classed as some of the most dangerous and ferocious encounters of the war. The sky would be full of shells, bullets and missiles travelling in all directions, with the opponents in full view of each other. Inevitably, casualties were extremely heavy. Such battles continued to the end of the war, fought by Allied airmen and German sailors of great skill and courage.

Recently, the author, as an ex-flyer in strike aircraft of Coastal Command, together with two pilots of the same vintage, was permitted to enter and renew acquaintance with a Beaufighter TFX, the version that followed the Mark VIC later in 1943. The aircraft stood there, blunt and business-like, still in its camouflaged livery of the 'Temperate Sea Scheme', wavy patterns of slate grey and dark sea-grey, with bluey-white undersurfaces. Using the toe-holds in the opened entry hatches and the hand grips above, we climbed somewhat stiffly into the ancient but well-preserved warplane, to awaken memories of forty years before.

There was still an impression of violent power. The four cannon boxes, each with space for 240 explosive shells, were still there, set

The pilot's cockpit in a Strike Wing Beaufighter. In the windscreen, the reflector gunsight locked into its central position.

The effect of a 20mm cannon shell on the armoured windscreen of Beaufighter TFX, serial JM 343, of 248 Squadron on 2 August 1943. The aircraft was flown by Flying Officer J.F. Green; he was blinded temporarily by dust and splinters but managed to land the Beaufighter safely at base, Predannack in Cornwall.

Medium-calibre flak protecting a convoy near Den Helder on 25 September 1944. Although this 88mm and 37mm flak was a serious hazard for the attacking Beaufighters, the 20mm tracer fired from the vessels at close range was even more dangerous.

athwart the fuselage behind the hinged double doors of armoured plate that protected the pilot's back in his commanding position in the nose. It seemed remarkable that the pilots of those days could have mastered the complexity of the fifty-six dials, sights, wheels, buttons, switches and levers that surrounded them, but after a few minutes the old knowledge began to flood back again. Nevertheless, it would be difficult for the uninitiated to believe that those young Beaufighter pilots could have operated all those controls, skilfully and without hesitation, under conditions of extreme stress with the ever-present possibility of sudden death.

The view from the pilot's position was superb. The helmeted head would have been just a few inches below the perspex top hatch when sitting on a parachute pack. On either side, the great Hercules XVII 1,772 hp engines jutted forward, emphasizing the brute strength of the warplane. Behind the cannon boxes, the navigator's position was set well back down the cramped and almost claustrophobic fuselage. A hinged plotting table swung down from the right, whilst further back were the brackets for the Marconi T1154/R1155 wireless set and the Gee radar. A tail drift sight was set in the floor on the left, and there were positions for the Aldis lamp and the Very pistol. In the perspex cupola above were the brackets for the backward-firing Vickers K or the Browning machine gun.

This was the aircraft which was to change the course of the war in the coastal waters of German-occupied Europe.

CHAPTER TWO

Courage is not enough

Courage is not enough – in technical warfare of this
nature we must also have the best possible weapons and,
above all, be so well trained as to be able to use those
weapons effectively.

General Douglas McArthur, 1880–1964

Pilot Officer Mark Bateman grasped the hand rails in the roof of the
fuselage of his Beaufighter Mark VIC and swung nimbly into the
pilot's seat. Like many other aircrew, he was not a large man, a
medium-sized 5'8". A wartime volunteer now aged twenty-five, he
could count himself an experienced pilot, with thirty-one operational
sorties in Beaufighters to his credit. Some of these flights had been
uneventful, but he had taken part in several dangerous attacks in
the previous five months. On one sortie, an air-sea rescue search,
he had fought a desperate battle with two Me 109s* until the German fighters had apparently run out of ammunition or fuel and
Bateman had been able to nurse his badly crippled Beaufighter
back to Wattisham, making a successful belly landing with a wounded
navigator on board. Today, however, this strike would be different
from all the others, for 236 Squadron was to combine with the Torbeaus of 254 Squadron; protected by long-range Spitfires, they
would make a joint attack on a German convoy off the Dutch coast.
It was 20 November 1942, the date of the first attack of the new
North Coates Strike Wing.

Bateman strapped himself into the pilot's seat, sitting on a
parachute pack that was connected by a short lanyard to a 'K type'
dinghy pack. He would be unlikely to bale out when flying at the
wave-top height of Coastal Command's strike aircraft, but a ditching in the sea was an ever-present possibility. The small dinghy was
an essential part of his safety equipment if he had to scramble out of
the top hatch of a heavy Beaufighter that usually sank within
thirty seconds.

---

* The author uses the RAF designation of Me 109 rather than the more correct
Bf 109.

The pilot's position was crowded, but the controls were conveniently arranged so that he could reach all of them with a minimum of movement. Quickly and automatically, Bateman checked that the ignition switches were off, that the hydraulic lever was on, and that the air supply registered 220 lb per square inch. The undercarriage selector lever was down, with the locking pin engaged. Switching on the electrical services, he checked that the undercarriage position indicators registered 'down' and that the fuel gauges showed 'full'. With both hands, he moved the control column forwards and backwards, and the handles up and down, ensuring that the movements were completely free. It was time to start up and go into the standard cockpit drill.

All pilots used mnemonics in their drill and in the Beaufighter the first was FTPSCG – fuel tanks 'on' for inner tank, throttles open by ¾ inch, propeller speed controls fully forward, supercharger control to low gear, carburetter control to cold, and gills fully open. It was simple when one had done it a hundred times before.

The ground crew were waiting attentively as Bateman nodded to them. The airmen began to turn the engines by hand and to operate the priming pumps. The starter battery was plugged in and an NCO looked up at Bateman, who gave him a thumbs-up sign. There was no point in trying to shout through the closed canopy of the Beaufighter, and the sign meant, 'Contact'.

Bateman switched on the ignition and pressed the port starter button and then the starboard. The ground crew disconnected the battery whilst the engines were slowly ticking over, and they screwed down the covers of the priming pumps in the engine nacelles. Bateman gradually increased the revolutions to 1,000 per minute, checking temperatures, pressures, magnetos and the vacuum pumps. When the engine cylinders had warmed to 120°C and the oil to 15°C, he opened the throttles to zero 1b per square inch and began the next series of checks – the rpm, the generator on the starboard engine, the propellers from fine pitch to coarse, and the throttles at both 'rated gate boost' and 'static rpm'. Then came the critical point of all cockpit drills – magneto drop; if the drop in either engine exceeded 50 rpm, the aircraft would not be flown, and Bateman's part in the operation would be cancelled.

On this occasion, the magneto drops were within the limit and Beaufighter Mark VIC, serial 5258, letter B for Bertie, was ready to taxi out. Bateman waved his hands crosswise above his head, palms outwards, and the ground crew pulled out the undercarriage locking pins, displaying them to the pilot before passing them to the navigator, Sergeant Charles Easterbrook. The two entry hatches in the belly of the Beaufighter, pilot's and navigator's, were slammed shut, and the chocks were pulled away.

There were twenty-six Beaufighters on the strike, their engines combining in a steady roar as the pilots taxied round the perimeter track to the end of the single concrete runway at North Coates. Bateman was in the anti-flak section, comprising fourteen aircraft of 236 Squadron, led by Wing Commander H.D. Fraser, who was also leading the entire Wing. The remainder of the Beaufighters were part of 254 Squadron: two in the anti-flak role and ten Torbeaus armed with Mark XV torpedoes, led by Wing Commander R.E.X. Mack. One of the Torbeaus did not taxi, with a faulty selector gear, but the remaining twenty-five aircraft moved forward to the runway.

Bateman was the first to take off. At the end of the runway, he went rapidly through the final checks, using the mnemonic HTMPFFGC – hydraulic power on, trimming tabs to 'take-off', mixture to rich, rudder and aileron to neutral, propeller pitch to fully fine, fuel with inner tank on, flaps 15° down, gills one third open, and carburetter to 'cold'. All was well.

The Beaufighter had a tendency to swing to starboard on take-off. Bateman aligned his aircraft on the runway and opened up the throttles against the brakes, throttling back within a few seconds. He then released the brakes and opened up again slowly, the starboard throttle slightly in advance of the port. The heavy aircraft rolled forward and gathered speed, nearly ten tons of warplane with its load of two men, four cannon, seven machine guns, ammunition, and two 250 lb general-purpose bombs. Bateman raised the tail as quickly as possible and pushed both throttles through the 'rated gate' position, at 6 lb boost and 2,900 rpm. The Beaufighter left the runway after about 600 yards. Bateman quickly retracted the undercarriage, building up speed to 170 knots. He adjusted the throttles to 2,400 rpm, raised the flaps at about 300 feet, closed the cowling gills, climbing at 150 knots and looking around for the following Beaufighters. He had taken off for his thirty-second operational flight, an attack on a German convoy. Within ten minutes, the entire formation of Beaufighters was in the air; at 15.15 hours, the aircraft wheeled south to the fighter aerodrome of Coltishall in Norfolk, ninety miles away.

3 June 1942. Mark Bateman's Beaufighter IC serial X8037 after his air battle with two Me 109s.

Two views of North Coates in 1943. The aerodrome was L-shaped, with only one concrete runway. Only two or three Beaufighters could take off together from the longer concrete runway but six or seven could take off from the shorter but wider grass section.

The formation reached the fighter aerodrome half an hour later and circled anti-clockwise over nearby Ludham, the rendezvous for the Spitfire escort. It was a cold, clear day over East Anglia, with a fresh, westerly wind. The Wing Leader was anxious to set off for the Dutch coast without delay, for reconnaissance had reported that their target was steering towards the Hook of Holland and Rotterdam, nearing the shelter of formidable shore batteries. When the Spitfires failed to appear, Wing Commander Fraser impatiently set course for the target. Most of the Beaufighters formed up behind him, in a goose-like gaggle, but four of the anti-flak aircraft missed the formation and headed off independently before returning fruitlessly to North Coates.

'All OK, Charlie?' said Bateman to Easterbrook over the intercom.

'OK, skipper', replied the navigator, who was trying to work out the course and speed of the Wing Leader. 'The track's around 110° and the ETA should be 16.02 hours.'

The flight time to the Hook, the anticipated point of interception of the convoy, was a bare thirty minutes' flying time away with the following wind. The pilots kept down low, barely thirty feet above the white flecks in the grey sea below, and they kept a strict R/T silence, hoping to keep under the German radar screen and achieve a surprise attack. One anti-flak aircraft drew alongside Fraser and waggled its wings before turning back to North Coates; an engine was giving trouble and the pilot was compelled to return. The Wing was now reduced to eleven anti-flak and nine torpedo aircraft.

Fifteen miles from the target, Fraser began to climb, leading the anti-flak section to 2,000 feet. Below, Wing Commander Mack brought the Torbeaus up to their dropping height of 175 feet.

'Target in sight', Bateman informed Easterbrook. 'It's a big one!'

Easterbrook looked down the fuselage past his pilot. About five miles off the Dutch coast, just north of the Hook of Holland, were about ten enemy vessels. There was one large merchantman and the remainder seemed to be flak-ships.

Leutnant zur See der Reserve Lucht looked carefully through his binoculars at the approaching aircraft. There seemed to be about thirteen of them, all twin-engined, maybe Blenheims or Bostons, or perhaps Beauforts, coming at them from the south-west. The formation was splitting into two, some of them continuing straight ahead whilst another section lower down banked around to attack them from the coast. Well, they'd get more than they bargained for this time! There were six *Vorpostenboote* protecting a single merchant vessel and they were all heavily armed with 88 mm, 40 mm and 37 mm flak guns, as well as the quick-firing 20 mm and light machine guns. The vessel they were protecting was called *Schiff 49* by the Kriegsmarine. Originally launched as the *Amerskerk* at Minerva Haven in Amsterdam, the Germans had re-named her the *Coburg* and now she was being acquired by the Kriegsmarine as a *Versuchsschiff*, or experimental vessel. She was still incomplete and was riding high out of the water, under tow by *BS4*, a former Dutch tug of 449 tons which was also called the *Indus*. The convoy had left Ijmuiden barely eight hours before, bound for the Hook and then Rotterdam. It had been making only about four knots. Since a force eight gale was forecast, Lucht was about to put a line on the tug from his own vessel; he was the Commandant of the convoy, in *Vp 1304*. By coincidence, another three vessels were approaching on a reciprocal course; these were three more *Vorpostenboote*, commanded by Leutnant zur See der Reserve Schwarting, and they had just rounded the approach buoy outside the Hook, in time to add their considerable fire power to Lucht's escorts. Moreover, there were FW 190s about. The 'Tommis' were in for a hot reception!

'Cock cannon. Close doors', Bateman instructed his navigator. Easterbrook clambered over the ammunition boxes and pulled back the levers of the four Hispano-Suiza 20 mm cannon; these were not usually cocked before take-off for fear of spraying destruction if the Beaufighter accidentally swung and crashed. He slammed shut the two folding armoured doors between himself and the pilot. Then he went back to his position and pulled back the cocking handle of his Vickers K gun; craning his head around he could see the convoy ahead.

'God, there are fighters about!' snapped Bateman. 'FW 190s! Keep your eyes on our tail!'

Bateman had good reason to fear the German fighters. His encounter earlier in the year with the two Me 109s had taught him that, although the Beaufighter packed an enormous punch with its fire power, its turning circle was much wider than that of a single-engined aircraft. A German fighter in the hands of a skilful pilot could out-manoeuvre him every time.

'Attack attack attack!' The voice of Wing Commander Fraser

ATTACK BY NORTH COATES STRIKE WING
16.10 HOURS 20 NOVEMBER 1942 OFF HOOK OF HOLLAND

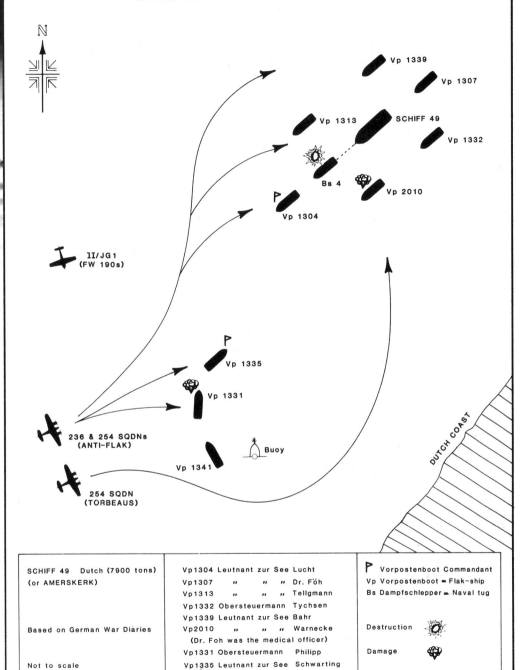

SCHIFF 49 Dutch (7900 tons)	Vp1304 Leutnant zur See Lucht	⚑ Vorpostenboot Commandant
(or AMERSKERK)	Vp1307 „ „ „ Dr. Föh	Vp Vorpostenboot ▬ Flak-ship
	Vp1313 „ „ „ Tellgmann	Bs Dampfschlepper ▬ Naval tug
	Vp1332 Obersteuermann Tychsen	
Based on German War Diaries	Vp1339 Leutnant zur See Bahr	Destruction
	Vp2010 „ „ „ Warnecke	
	(Dr. Foh was the medical officer)	
Not to scale	Vp1331 Obersteuermann Philipp	Damage
	Vp1335 Leutnant zur See Schwarting	
	Vp1341 Obersteuermann Breiler	

came urgently over the R/T. The enemy vessels were straight ahead. Black and white puffs surrounded the Beaufighters. The escort vessels had opened up with their heavier-calibre armament.

Then the flak ceased. Two FW 190s of II/JG1 (2nd Wing of the 1st fighter group) from Schipol, near Amsterdam, dived on the anti-flak Beaufighters. Smoke streamed from the aircraft of one of 236 Squadron's Flight Commanders, Squadron Leader G.A. Edney, bursting into a red glare as the Beaufighter dived uncontrollably into the sea, raising a furrow of white foam before the petrol tanks exploded. The German fighters banked steeply to attack Flight Sergeant Turton of 236 Squadron, closing in on his port quarter whilst his navigator, Flight Sergeant Alexander, rattled away defiantly with his single Vickers K gun. Turton, his aircraft badly damaged, was forced to dump his bombs and head for home, shaking off his pursuers with corkscrew turns at low level. Next, Warrant Officer Bonnett of 236 Squadron was attacked and also jettisoned his bombs, diving low over the water to escape. Then the German fighters wheeled away out of range as intense light-calibre flak began to stream up from the convoy.

The remaining Beaufighters were now split into two sections, the eight anti-flak aircraft diving to attack the flak-ships and the nine Torbeaus below banking to starboard in the beginning of an S manoeuvre to attack the merchant vessel from the land. In the anti-flak section, Pilot Officer Sergeant of 254 Squadron picked *Vp 1331*, the middle flak-ship of the three coming from the Hook and rounding the buoy. He hit it with cannon fire and his stick of bombs fell on both sides of the vessel, but his Beaufighter received the full force of the defences and crashed into the sea 200 yards beyond his target. Another Beaufighter followed him and raked *Vp 1331* with cannon shells, but the flak-ship was only lightly damaged, one German sailor being killed.

Six anti-flak Beaufighters continued north to the main convoy. Amongst them, Bateman had put the nose of his aircraft down into a 20° dive. Tracer curved up from the convoy and whipped past his wings. He aimed at the merchant vessel, *Schiff 49*, opening up with the six .303 Brownings in his wings, carefully ranging his fire until he could see the splashes in the sea reaching the vessel and then pressing the cannon-firing button. The four cannon thudded in unison like pneumatic drills and an acrid smoke filled the fuselage, smelling of cordite. The Beaufighter seemed to slow down as the 20 mm explosive shells poured out of its nose and converged on

20 November 1942. The first strike of the North Coates Wing. The large vessel is the incomplete hull *Schiff 49* under tow by the tug *BS 4*. (*Right*): Mark Bateman, photographed as a Flight Lieutenant in 1944. The rather blurred photograph below shows the tug being blown up by bombs.

the enemy. Bateman pressed the release switch of his two 250 lb bombs and flew directly over the ship towards the shore, followed by long lines of tracer as he broke away to port, skidding just above the surface of the sea. To his starboard, another Beaufighter had scored bomb hits on the tug *BS4*, which blew up and began to sink. Another Beaufighter straddled *Vp 2010* with bombs, on the landward side of the convoy.

'Are you OK, Charlie?' Bateman enquired over the intercom.

'OK, skipper', replied the navigator. 'Bit hot, isn't it?'

'Are we damaged?' asked the pilot, testing the controls.

'Nothing visible', replied Easterbrook. 'Some of those ships are smoking.'

Then shells exploded once more around the Beaufighters. The anti-flak attackers had flown right over the convoy and had come within range of the shore batteries.

'Someone's gone in!' said Bateman, as he saw a tremendous splash in the water on his port bow. It was Wing Commander Fraser, the Wing Leader. At this moment, one of the anti-flak Beaufighters of 254 Squadron, flown by Flying Officer Cameron, was also hit and turned on one engine for the English coast. Still under fire, Bateman circled Fraser's sinking Beaufighter, hoping vainly to see the crew scramble out of the top hatches.

'It looks as though they've had it', said Easterbrook ruefully as his pilot headed out to sea.

Meanwhile, the nine Torbeaus had completed their S manoeuvre. One of them, flown by Pilot Officer Hodge, suffered an engine cut on the run-up and had to jettison, but the remaining eight aimed and dropped their torpedoes at the main convoy. The Germans spotted the tracks of four torpedoes, three of which hit the sea bed and exploded, whilst the fourth passed harmlessly right underneath the keel of the Commandant's vessel, *Vp 1304*. Obviously, the water was too shallow for torpedo dropping and the torpedo settings were too shallow for the draught of the escort vessels. One of the Torbeaus, flown by Flying Officer Parson, was hit by 20 mm flak and flew back to make a belly landing at North Coates. As the remainder flew over the convoy and out to sea, they found that the FW 190s were waiting. The New Zealander Squadron Leader 'Bill' Sise was attacked repeatedly and suffered many hits on his wings and fuselage, but he flew back to make a frightening but successful landing in a field near Frinton-on-Sea in Essex. All the other Beaufighters reached England, although three of the Torbeaus had used up so much petrol in evasive action that they could not reach North Coates and had to land at the nearest aerodromes.

It was a very chastened gathering at North Coates that evening. Three crews had been lost, all of whom were later confirmed as killed, two Beaufighters had crashed on return and were beyond repair, whilst five more aircraft had been badly shot up. The Wing had failed to make contact with its fighter escort and had somehow lost contact with four anti-flak Beaufighters on the way out. The whole attack had been a costly shambles and no one could work out what had gone wrong. The new Wing had tried, been blooded, and had failed.

The Germans had good reason to be pleased with their performance, as they duly recorded in their war diaries. *Schiff 49* was almost unscathed and two *Vorpostenboote* had been slightly damaged; the only real loss was the tug *BS4* which had sunk with some loss of life. At least three of the attackers had been shot down and many others hit. The captains of the escorts reported that they had fired 20 shells of 20 mm, 60 of 40 mm, 25 of 37 mm, 1,998 of 20 mm, 180 of 13.2 mm, and 1,993 rounds of machine gun ammunition. Their gunners had put up a very effective defence. The 'Tommis' would think long and hard before they tried that again!

Squadron Leader H. Neil G. Wheeler had not quite completed his conversion course on Beaufighters at the Operational Training Unit at Catfoss in Yorkshire when he was called urgently to the Station Commander's office. To his surprise, he was told to assume command of 236 Squadron. He hurriedly packed his kit, put up the stripes of a Wing Commander, and rushed to North Coates. Full of enthusiasm himself, he was disappointed to find his new squadron and most of the station personnel sunk in despondency. The loss of their CO and one of their Flight Commanders coupled with the crippling of several aircraft on the disastrous strike a few days ago had weakened the confidence of the crews of 236 Squadron.

'If we try that again, we'll be wiped out!' This was the grim message being passed around North Coates.

The new CO had to face up to a series of problems and it was fortunate that he brought with him a wealth of operational experience and the energy of youth as well as a steely determination to succeed. Then aged twenty-six, he was an ex-Cranwell entrant who had graduated in 1937. He had served in Bomber Command before the

war, flying Fairey Gordons and then Vickers Wellesleys in 207
Squadron. By the time war broke out, his squadron had been re-
equipped with Fairey Battles but Wheeler was posted away as an
instructor at the OTU at Benson in Oxfordshire. This job gave him
additional flying experience but was not to his liking in wartime. He
pestered the Air Ministry for a posting to an operational squadron
and in the summer of 1940 was able to join the Photographic
Development Unit at Heston, near the site of today's London Air-
port. This was the unconventional but enormously successful unit
that later became the famous Photographic Reconnaissance Unit.
For the most part in this *corps d'élite*, Wheeler flew stripped-down
and unarmed Spitfires deep into enemy territory, bringing back
vital photographic evidence that was interpreted by the Central
Interpretation Unit in Medmenham. Awarded a DFC in August
1941, Wheeler continued to fly in PRU until he was injured as a
passenger in a car accident. After recovering, he spent some time
test-flying the new de Havilland Mosquito. He had almost completed his OTU on Beaufighters when the posting arrived that was
to prove such a milestone in his career and to play such a vital part
in the development of the Strike Wings.

It was evident to the new CO of 236 Squadron that there was little
wrong with the basic qualities of the aircrews under his command.
The pilots and navigators had more than the normal share of skill,
experience and courage. The trouble sprang from the defective tactics
employed in the first strike; Wheeler thought that he had the answer
to these problems. In his views he had the collaboration of Wing
Commander W.O.V. Bennett, the CO of 143 Squadron, another
squadron of anti-flak Beaufighters that had joined the new Wing at
North Coates. A new Station Commander also arrived, Group Captain O.I. 'Giles' Gilson, who shared in the belief that the three
squadrons could be welded together so as to operate successfully.
The CO of the Torbeaus of 254 Squadron, Wing Commander
R.E.X. Mack, was an experienced pilot from the days of the Bristol
Beaufort, but was to lose his life before the Strike Wing went into
action again; he was replaced temporarily by Squadron Leader
G.D. Sise, one of the most courageous and effective leaders who
flew in the Strike Wings, until the enthusiastic Wing Commander
C.S. Cooper took over.

The three Beaufighter squadrons at North Coates did not fly
together as a Wing for nearly four months. Individual sorties and

reconnaissances took place. Some aircraft were lost, but for the most part the Beaufighter crews underwent a period of intense training. Again and again, the three squadrons practised forming up together and then flying low over the sea. They discussed tactics endlessly, and Wheeler expressed his conviction that a Wing attack on an enemy convoy could be successful if several conditions were met:

1) Prior reconnaissance or accurate intelligence was essential.

2) The anti-flak sections must protect the Torbeaus from the enemy fire. Where possible, three cannon-firing Beaufighters should be detailed to attack each escort in the convoy. All their diving attacks should be simultaneous but from slightly different angles, synchronized to confuse the enemy gunners and keep their heads down at the time when the Torbeaus were flying in steadily at low level to drop their torpedoes and sink the merchant vessels.

3) The Torbeaus should operate in 'fluid pairs', each pair being allocated in advance a definite target in the convoy.

4) The torpedoes should usually be dropped from sea to land in the shallow waters off the Dutch coast, in not less than ten fathoms. The initial 'plunge depth' of a torpedo dropped from about 175 feet was about 50 feet, so that there was a strong danger of the weapon striking the sea bottom or a sandbank at a lesser depth.

5) Above all, no Wing strikes should take place without protection from single-engined fighter escorts. The Beaufighters would usually be outfought by FW 190s or Me 109s and would be either shot down or diverted from their tasks. Wheeler vowed to his squadron that, no matter what pressure was put on him, he would refuse to lead a Wing strike without fighter escort.

Wheeler's firm views brought an enthusiastic response from his crews. They liked and respected their new and vital CO, whilst the ground crews at North Coates could also recognise a natural leader. Wheeler soon became known as a strict but fair man. Some of his human touches are still remembered by his crews, such as his suggestion that the one day off per week allocated to each flier could be accumulated into four successive days, enabling some of the men to go home and see their families. Morale improved gradually and a mood of cautious optimism began to replace the gloomy atmosphere at North Coates. However, a decisive operational success was needed to confirm that the new theories and methods of training were correct and indeed to ensure that the Strike Wing would survive in its present form. Wheeler knew that if he met with another débâcle such as that of the previous November, the whole concept of the Strike Wing would be abandoned. Fraser had been courageous but foolhardy in not waiting for his fighter escort, he decided. Eleven Spitfires had taken off from Coltishall but had missed their rendezvous with the Beaufighters over Ludham by only a few minutes. Wheeler would not make that mistake.

The Beaufighter squadrons at North Coates formed part of 16 Group, commanded at that time by Air Vice Marshal Brian E. Baker from his headquarters at Chatham near London. By 1943 there was no absence of accurate information concerning the movement of the German coastal convoys. The Hydra code used by these convoys had been decrypted by the Government Code and Cipher School at Bletchley Park in Buckinghamshire, following the seizing of cipher material in the captured U-boat *U-110* on 8 May 1942. From that time on, British Intelligence knew almost as much about the proposed movements of the convoys as the Germans themselves. The decrypted German messages were augmented by fragmentary information provided by the Dutch and Norwegian Resistance movements and were confirmed by aerial reconnaissance. These dangerous sorties were undertaken by Beaufighters from North Coates equipped with cameras, or sometimes by Spitfires and Mustangs of Fighter Command; the operations were known as Lagoons and later as Jim Crows.

All these reports were fed into the Admiralty's Operational Intelligence Centre in the bowels of the stark building known as the Citadel, built in 1941 near Admiralty Arch in London. The information was studied intently and conferences took place daily on scrambler telephone with the Senior Air Staff Officer of Coastal Command, Air Vice Marshal A. Durston, and the Naval Liaison Officer, Captain D.V. Peyton-Ward. The Station Commander at North Coates, Group Captain Giles Gilson, was alerted if enemy vessels were expected to pass through his designated area, which was the Dutch coast and the North Sea as far as the south of Norway. Hurried conferences then took place with the COs of the three Strike Wing squadrons.

In the early morning of 18 April 1943, two Mustangs of 613 Squadron shadowed a north-bound convoy leaving the Hook. A few hours later, a Beaufighter of 236 Squadron, flown by Flight Sergeant A.S. Shimmin, spotted the same convoy off Ijmuiden; he thought that the largest vessel was around 5,000 tons and that there were at least four flak-ships. Shimmin landed back at North Coates and his photographs were quickly developed. The three squadrons of Beaufighters, already standing by, were briefed to attack.

For Wheeler, the prospect of the Wing strike came as a relief. Like all intelligent men, he was not immune from fear and knew that as Wing Leader he would be in an especially dangerous position, but at least the period of training and worrying would be over and his theories could be put to the test. His squadron had recently made a flight to Scotland, where the crews had practised simulated attacks on the battleship *King George V* and her accompanying destroyers. The crews seemed to be in peak form. It was a fine and warm day, with a light westerly wind and a few white strato-cumulus clouds, but with the prospect of a deep depression and gale force winds in the evening. There was just time to attack the enemy convoy before this bad weather closed in.

Twenty-one Beaufighters taxied out to take off from the runway at North Coates. There were nine Torbeaus from 254 Squadron, led by Squadron Leader Sise, whilst the anti-flak sections contained six from 143 Squadron, led by Wing Commander Bennett, and six from 236 Squadron, with Squadron Leader G.H. Denholm as Wheeler's Number Two. The Wing took off and formed up smoothly at around 13.30 hours, setting off for Coltishall with Wheeler leading. Mark Bateman formed up on the port quarter of his CO. The Beaufighters of 254 and 236 Squadrons were still the Mark VIC with the 1,650 hp Hercules engines, but 143 Squadron had been re-equipped with the Beaufighter Mark XIC with the 1,772 hp Hercules engines. The two anti-flak sections were armed with cannon and machine guns, and each carried the usual load of two 250 lb general-purpose bombs. The Torbeaus carried cannon and Mark XV torpedoes.

This time, there was no mistake. Twenty-two long-range Spitfires of 118 and 167 Squadrons rose from Coltishall to escort the Strike Wing, accompanied by eight beautiful new Mustangs from 613 Squadron. As arranged, the Fighter Leader, Wing Commander H.P. Blatchford, positioned his Mustang slightly above Wheeler's starboard quarter, his fighters spread in an arc protecting the rear of the formation. The R/T call sign for the Beaufighters was 'Rostrum' whilst that for the fighter escort was 'Useful', but the two leaders had arranged to signal to each other visually on the way out, thus avoiding the danger of their R/T conversation being picked up by the Germans.

Wheeler led his impressive formation of fifty-one aircraft north-west to the Dutch Frisian Islands on a course given to him by his navigator, Flying Officer Robert A. Irving. In a squadron that included many remarkable men, Irving was one of the most unusual. A musician of distinction before the war, he was a popular and adept navigator. The previous January, he had flown on a dangerous reconnaissance off the Norwegian coast, hunting for the battleship *Scharnhorst* which was believed to have slipped out of Kiel and to be heading north. In appalling weather, Irving and his pilot, Flying Officer Edmund H. Jeffreys, had spotted and reported the battleship, which promptly turned back to German waters. Jeffreys and Irving had each been awarded a DFC, but after a few months Jeffreys had pressed for a transfer to a Mosquito squadron, in which he was later to meet his death. Irving decided to remain in 236 Squadron, where he was a natural choice for the navigator of the new CO.

Crossing the English coast, Wheeler brought the Strike Wing down to thirty feet above the waves. The air disturbance from the propellers of the aircraft rippled the surface of the sea, leaving a broad wake that faded in a straight line towards the coast of Norfolk. The formation was flying towards the tail of the convoy, about forty minutes flying time away. The fighters weaved just above the Beaufighters, reducing speed to avoid flying ahead of their charges. Not a word was said over the R/T and very little within the Beaufighters. Some of the navigators had been designated to listen continuously to the receivers of their 1154/1155 wireless sets for any recall signal. Irving concentrated on his navigation, taking drifts and watching the wind lanes in the sea. Once, he gave a minor change of course to his pilot. Wheeler kept looking over his shoulders at the disposition of the formation. The clouds began to thicken until they formed a continous layer at about 3,000 feet. Visibility was no more than about five miles. The crews, all senses alert, scoured the horizon for the smoke of ships and the clouds above for the black dots of enemy fighters.

Fifteen minutes from the enemy coast, Irving cocked the four cannon and closed the armoured doors. Eight minutes later he broke the silence between himself and his pilot:

'Climbing in five minutes, sir.'

'Right, Bob', replied Wheeler.

The calculation for the start of the climb was vitally important. Too soon, and the German radar would pick them up and the fighters would stream out of Holland; too late and they might not be able to see the convoy until they were almost upon it and there would be confusion in arranging dispositions for the attack.

'Start climbing now, sir', said Irving.

Wheeler motioned to Blatchford, who was still in position above his starboard wing. The Fighter Leader rose in the air, followed by his three squadrons, and moved ahead. Gently, Wheeler pulled back his control column, listening intently to his R/T for the tell-tale yowling noise that would indicate that the German radar had plotted their position. Below and slightly behind, the Torbeaus brought up the rear of the Wing, with Spitfires weaving protectively above them. Ahead, the sea was innocent of enemy vessels and some of the pilots began to fidget uncomfortably. Had something gone wrong?

Convoy 1105, which had left the Hook at 06.00 hours that morning bound for the Elbe and then for Norway, was an impressive sight. There were eight merchant vessels disposed in two columns, mostly carrying cargoes of coal, the largest being the Norwegian *Hoegh Carrier* of 4,906 tons. Every merchant vessel was flying a balloon to deter low level attacks, and two of them were armed with 37 mm and 20 mm flak guns. Protecting them were eight escorts, four M-class minesweepers armed with 105 mm, 37 mm and 20 mm guns, and four *Vorpostenboote* flak-ships armed with 88 mm, 37 mm and 20 mm guns. Some of the 20 mm were the deadly 'quad guns' capable of firing 750 shells per minute. Every vessel carried light machine guns.

With such formidable defences the Germans must have felt fairly confident of their ability to repel any likely attack from the air. For the past ten months, the RAF had proved ineffectual off the Dutch coast, for they had sunk only four vessels by direct attack, two of them being under 500 tons. There was far more danger from the magnetic mines that they dropped in the shipping lanes, and the *Minensuchboote* steamed ahead to clear the waters of this danger. The Commandant of the convoy, Kapitänleutnant Prager, in the minesweeper *M-33* at the head of the vessels, had watched the two Mustangs of 613

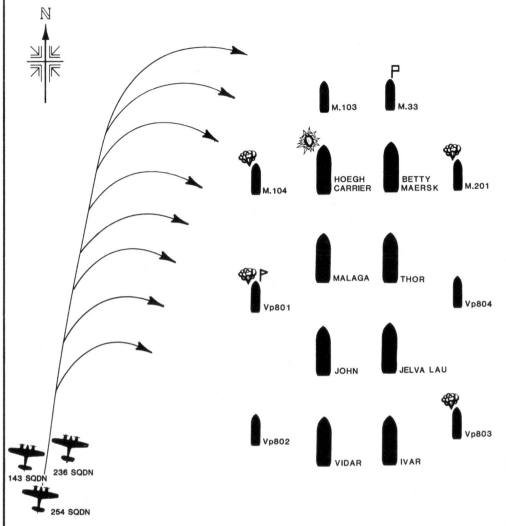

ATTACK BY NORTH COATES STRIKE WING
14.30 HOURS 18 APRIL 1943 OFF TEXEL

N

P
M.103   M.33

M.104   HOEGH   BETTY
         CARRIER MAERSK   M.201

P
Vp801   MALAGA   THOR   Vp804

         JOHN   JELVA LAU

Vp802   VIDAR   IVAR   Vp803

143 SQDN
236 SQDN
254 SQDN

HOEGH CARRIER	Norwegian	(4906grt)	Vp801	Oberleutnant zur See	Reyers		P	Minensuchboot Commandant
MALAGA	German	(2146 ")	Vp802	Leutnant	" "	Kleiner		
JOHN	Swedish	(3121 ")	Vp803	Oberfähnrich	" "	Dillman	P	Vorpostenboot Commandant
VIDAR	"	(2104 ")	Vp804	Oberleutnant	" "	Dörwaldt		
BETTY MAERSK	Danish	(2357 ")	M.33	Kapitänleutnant		Prager	M	Minensuchboot = Minesweeper
THOR	"	(1561 ")	M.103	"		Fock	Vp	Vorpostenboot = Flak-ship
JELVA LAU	"	(2257 ")	M.104	Oberleutnant zur See		Meyer		
IVAR	"	(2145 ")	M.201	"	" "	Hoenck		Destruction
								Damage
Based on German War Diaries								
Not to Scale								

Squadron shadowing him after leaving the Hook. He thought that they were reconnaissance Spitfires and anticipated an attack, prudently ordering two of his minesweepers to haul in their gear and close up to join the *Vorpostenboote*. However, the convoy was making good time, well ahead of schedule, and he hoped to be off Borkum by nightfall, with the prospect of a peaceful night's run along the German Frisian Islands to the mouth of the Elbe.

When Wheeler saw the convoy, it was a good fifteen miles further along the coast than had been calculated, off the island of Texel. Most of these convoys made about eight knots, but sometimes they were a little slower or even faster. It looked huge, the eight merchant ships in two parallel lines of four apiece, with two mine-sweepers ahead and three escorts on either flank. There were no enemy fighters about, so far as he could see, but Blatchford and his boys could take care of any that appeared. He led his Beaufighters along the seaward side of the convoy, looking over his starboard wing at the vessels. His anti-flak boys would be picking out their allotted targets, just as they had been briefed. The Torbeaus were in position now, able to turn to their best angle of 60° off the bows of their targets. Now for it!

'Rostrum Leader to Strike Wing. Attack attack attack!'

Twenty-one Beaufighters turned in well-drilled unison towards the convoy, the anti-flak sections diving from 1,500 feet and the Torbeaus flying in steadily at 150 feet, all from the same direction.

The Germans thought that they could count as many as forty bombers, which they identified as a mixture of Beaufighters and Beauforts, for they were probably unaware of the existence of the new Torbeau. Above the bombers, they counted twenty Spitfires. They opened fire at long range, firing 6 shells of 105 mm, 21 of 88 mm and 130 of 37 mm, none of which scored hits. The anti-flak Beaufighters dived through the exploding barrage and swept towards the minesweepers and flak-ships. Tracer fire arced up to them, but the speed and ferocity of their attack confused the defenders.

On the seaward side of the convoy, a burst of cannon fire raked the superstructure of *M-104*, some of the shells penetrating her bunker and boiler rooms and wounding four men; a few seconds later, a stick of bombs straddled her. In *Vp 801* behind her, the Commandant of the *Vorpostenboote*, Oberleutnant zur See Reyers,

29 April 1942. *(Left, top):* A general view of an attack by the North Coates Wing.
18 April 1942. *(Left, centre):* Bombs straddle an escort which cannot be identified.
18 April 1942. *(Left, bottom):* An M-class minesweeper under attack.

(Facing page, top left): 18 April 1943. An M-class minesweeper, probably *M-104*, raked by cannon fire. *(Top right and bottom):* 18 April 1943. Two views of the *Hoegh Carrier* after being hit by three torpedoes. Note the balloons and the torpedo track.

had the unpleasant experience of a stick of bombs exploding alongside whilst his vessel was badly hit with 20 mm shells. On the landward side of the convoy, bombs badly damaged the boilers of *M-201* and she lost her steering, leaking badly; cannon fire hit her forecastle and bridge, one of the shells bowling over two men behind a gun shield whilst another hit her store of 105 mm ammunition, which exploded and wounded another five men. Behind her, cannon shells hit *Vp 803* in the superstructure and mast and wounded one of her crew.

Following the anti-flak Beaufighters, the Torbeaus droned steadily towards the convoy. They released their torpedoes from 1,000 yards and continued ahead to attack with their cannon. Nine torpedoes plunged into the water and sped at 40 knots towards the convoy. The alarmed Germans thought that they could count as many as fifteen tracks. Suddenly, the largest ship and main target, the *Hoegh Carrier*, exploded. Columns of smoke and debris rose a hundred feet into the air. Both the Germans and the British estimated that at least three torpedoes struck her. Her engine room was hit and she began to sink.

The entire attack was over within four minutes and the Germans were left in shock and bewilderment at its effect. From the rear of the convoy, *Vp 802* and *Vp 803* steamed up to the oily patch left by the *Hoegh Carrier* and picked up a few of her crew; nine men and her cargo of coal had gone to the bottom, leaving her balloon still flying incongruously above the waves. The shattered *M-201* was taken in tow by the damaged *Vp 803* and the two vessels turned for the nearby harbour of Den Helder, where their appearance gave grim satisfaction to the Dutch. The remainder of the convoy closed up and carried on, welcoming the approach of twilight. The escorts recorded that they had expended a total of 2,575 shells of 20 mm and 1,201 rounds from their machine guns. They claimed to have shot down three of the attackers and to have hit two others, but their fire was wild and inaccurate, for the only effect was that two Beaufighters sustained light damage.

'Well done, Rostrum', said Blatchford over the R/T as the formation headed for home. They were all there, the same number that had set out. Eight Typhoons of 56 Squadron met them, acting as 'rear cover' in case the Luftwaffe put in a belated appearance. The RAF fighter pilots were disappointed to find that there was no opposition to them, for at this stage in the war they had already gained the upper hand over their adversaries. Some of the Mustang pilots had had a squirt or two at the flak-ships, but they had to admit that the Strike Wing was the star of the day's performance.

As the Beaufighters touched down at North Coates, the fliers were met with an astonishing and unexpected sight. All the ground crews, with WAAFs, motor mechanics, sick-bay attendants, operations room staff, and indeed the majority of the 1,000 personnel of the station, were lined up outside the crew rooms in front of the hangars. Each time a Beaufighter landed, they waved and cheered thunderously, counting in the aircraft. It was as though the fliers had won the Cup at Wembley or had each flown the Atlantic single-handed. The crews piled into trucks driven by smiling young WAAF drivers, jubilant, laughing and chaffing each other. They had done it at last! They had given the Jerries a bloody nose and they'd give them a few more in the future. There'd be a bit of a party that night. They were the North Coates Wing, the best unit in the RAF!

The first successful attack of the Wing was a significant defeat for the Germans. It represented the turning point of the fortunes of the strike squadrons of Coastal Command. The *Hoegh Carrier*, 4,903 tons and 393 feet long, was a useful vessel, built in 1935 in Copenhagen. There were not many ships like her to carry iron ore and coal, and the Germans did not want to divert resources into building merchant vessels, any more than they wanted to allocate additional fighter support to their convoys. More important than the loss of the ship, however, was the deadly precision and speed with which the attack had been carried out and what this boded for the future. 18 April 1943 was Hitler's fifty-fourth birthday, but he had little to celebrate with the loss of an army in Stalingrad and another crumbling in North Africa. His birthday present from Coastal Command was the first taste of a new force that would eventually obliterate his coastal convoys.

Author's Note: The conversations over the intercom and the R/T are based on the recollections of the aircrews concerned. The action taken and the views expressed by the Germans are taken from their lengthy war diaries. See Bibliography and Sources.

CHAPTER THREE

Rocket Projectile

To knock a thing down, especially if it is cocked at an arrogant angle, is a deep delight to the blood.

George Santayana, 1863–1952

U-418 was returning from her first war cruise. A brand-new type VIIC U-boat, she had left Kiel on 24 April 1943 and now, five weeks later, was bound for the bomb-proof shelters of Brest on the west coast of France. With a displacement of 769 tons when surfaced, she had a length of 220 feet and carried fourteen torpedoes as well as an 88 mm gun and a 20 mm cannon. Her captain, Leutnant zur See Lange, commanded a crew of 47 officers and men. He had last sent a message to his headquarters on 23 May and now, on 1 June, was 130 sea miles west of the peninsula of Brittany on his homeward run. It had not been a successful cruise, for the increased protection given to convoys and the improved methods of detection utilized by the naval escort and carrier-borne aircraft had tipped the scales of war in the Atlantic in favour of the Allies. Nearly sixty U-boats had been lost during April and May. During the latter month, Admiral Dönitz had been compelled to order the withdrawal of his entire force from the North Atlantic.

Keeping watch from the conning tower of a surfaced U-boat required a continuous concentration that was difficult to maintain. The sea was rough and the boat was pitching and rolling. The noise of an approaching aircraft was drowned by the drone of diesel engines and the hissing of water from bows cutting through the heaving sea at a speed of fifteen knots. A lookout could see the black dot in the dome of the sky only if he was looking in the right direction with his eyes focussed to the correct distance. The diving Beaufighter was barely 5,000 yards away when she was spotted below the grey clouds.

'*Alarm! Flugzeug backbord voraus!*' (Alarm! Aircraft port bow!) yelled the lookout. The urgent ringing of an electric bell sounded throughout the U-boat. The two men in the conning tower slid frantically down the metal ladder, their hands and feet curved round the uprights. The handwheel of the upper lid was spun around, securing the hatch.

'*Fluten!*' (Dive! Dive! Dive!)

The control room crew pulled open the vent levers and sea water rushed into the main ballast tanks. The well-drilled crew were quick but not quick enough. All of them were to die in the next few minutes.

Lieutenant-Commander Francis J. Brookes lowered his binoculars and tapped Mark Bateman on the shoulder. He pointed ahead and shouted above the noise of the engines.

'U-boat! Can you see it?'

Bateman reacted instantly. He was flying a Beaufighter VIC, serial T5258, and had set off at 09.10 hours from Predannack, an aerodrome near the Lizard in Cornwall. A detachment of 236 Squadron from North Coates had flown there a few days before, armed with a new and secret weapon. His passenger was a naval specialist in U-boat warfare who had just returned from a lecture tour of Coastal Command stations. It was almost midday and the Beaufighter was at 3,500 feet with the U-boat ten miles away when Bateman began to dive, his quarry continuing serenely on its easterly course as it loomed larger in his gunsight. Bateman selected four of his new weapons, in pairs. The U-boat began to dive but her conning tower and stern were still above the surface when Bateman fired the first pair, 800 yards from her port bow, followed by the second pair a moment later. He did not aim directly at the hull but at the sea twenty-five yards his side of the target, just as he had been taught. Four stick-like objects left the undersurfaces of the wings of his Beaufighter, slowly at first and then gathering speed as bluey-white smoke trailed behind them.

Three seconds after firing, the projectiles hit the sea by the side of the U-boat and their trajectories curved upwards as density changed from air to water. They struck the cigar-shaped object with terrible force, puncturing holes in the pressure hull. The warheads broke off and smashed through the other side of the U-boat, leaving the motor tubes flaming and spinning inside the hull.* Great jets of sea-water spurted uncontrollably into the perforated and stricken U-boat. The men inside could not blow her quick-dive

---

*   The behaviour of this weapon is taken from eye-witness reports of survivors from other vessels.

tanks and the extra five tons of water inside them propelled the vessel downwards, taking her maimed and drowned crew to lie forever inside a steel coffin.

A green patch rose to the surface amidst the swirl left by the U-boat, followed by a larger patch a hundred yards ahead. Bateman turned and flew back to Predannack. His attack was recorded as 'U-boat probably sunk' followed by the deliberately false statement 'by depth charges'.

The rocket projectile was by no means an unknown weapon at the outset of the Second World War. Rockets were used, at least as fireworks, by the Chinese in ancient days. During the war with Mysore in 1799, the troops of the East India Company were alarmed when rockets were used against them at the siege of Seringatam. Soon afterwards, Sir William Congreve, the son of the Comptroller of the Royal Laboratory at Woolwich, became a keen advocate of the use of rockets and introduced them into the British Army as artillery weapons. A Rocket Corps was formed in 1814, but the early weapons proved unreliable and unpopular; interest in them faded by the 1870s. By the 1930s, however, it became apparent that the Germans were making substantial progress with long-range rockets as strategic weapons, and the British set up a Rocket Advisory Committee. Thereafter, development in the UK was confined to smaller rockets designed for tactical use.

By the outbreak of war, a three-inch rocket had been devised, intended primarily for use by ground defences against low flying aircraft, or by aircraft against armoured fighting vehicles. With the enormous extension of the German-controlled coastline and her fleet of captured merchant vessels, it soon became apparent that a version of this new weapon should be used in an anti-shipping role.

The three-inch rocket was introduced into Coastal Command and the Fleet Air Arm at the beginning of 1943. It was about six feet long overall. The main body, or motor, was simply a steel tube containing the propellent, an 11¼ lb stick of cordite. Originally this propellent had weighed 12½ lb and was tubular, filling the entire motor. However, the tubular charge was found to have an upper firing limit of only 86°F air temperature, above which it would burst. This was considered dangerous and the charge of cordite was altered to one in cruciform section, so that four air gaps ran down the length of the motor, giving a safe firing limit of 135°F. The new

ROCKET PROJECTILES

60lb HIGH EXPLOSIVE HEAD

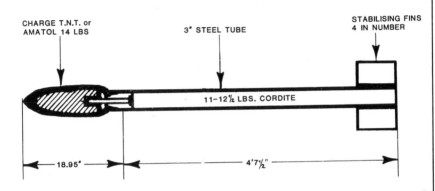

25lb SOLID SHOT HEAD

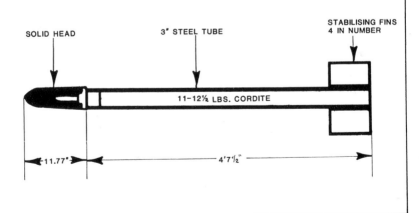

charge also incorporated a small percentage of cryolite, a substance which helped reduce the blinding effect of the jet on the pilot during firing at night. However, the smaller charge of cordite resulted in a reduced velocity and an increased curvature of trajectory, introducing special problems in aiming some of these rockets, as we shall see later.

The warhead of the rocket threaded into the front of the motor. Two types were used operationally, a 60 lb head with a diameter of six inches filled with high explosive, and a 25 lb head of 3.44 inch diameter made from solid steel and armour-piercing. Originally the 60 lb head had been intended for use against ships' gunners and the 25 lb solid shot against armoured vehicles, but trials during 1942 had established that the 25 lb head was capable of inflicting lethal damage on a submarine. The rockets used by Mark Bateman to sink *U-418* on 1 June 1943 had 25 lb heads made of mild steel, the first time that such a weapon was used by the RAF in the North Atlantic.* Of course, the 60 lb high explosive head exploded on impact, so that the pilot had to score a direct hit to achieve results, another problem that was to dog the operational success of this warhead.

On the rear of the motor, four stabilizing fins were slotted. The rocket was fired electrically by the pilot, a 'pigtail' or electric wire being plugged in before take-off. The Beaufighter carried eight rockets, four under each wing, and the pilot could fire them in pairs or select a complete salvo. In training, the pilots often fired pairs of rockets at ranges of 1,200 yards, 1,000 yards, 800 yards and 600 yards, but operationally this procedure could be highly dangerous and pilots sometimes released all eight rockets in a salvo.

The device from which the rocket was launched fitted underneath the wing and was called a projector, the rocket being held in place by two metal clamps called saddles. When rockets were first fitted experimentally to aircraft, blast plates were installed underneath the wings from which were suspended guide rails, but this early form of projector was too heavy and clumsy, causing drag and loss of aircraft speed. By 1943, a modified form of projector was introduced, a single guide rail 7'10½" long made from extruded

---

*   Two U-boats had been sunk by aerial rockets before Mark Bateman's success on 1 June 1943. The first was by a Swordfish flown by Sub-Lieutenant Horrocks from the escort carrier HMS *Archer*, when *U-752* was sunk north of the Azores on 23 May 1943. The other was by a Hudson flown by Flying Officer G.A.K. Ogilvy from Blida in Algeria, when *U-594* was sunk north of the Balearic Islands on 28 May 1943.

light alloy. This suspended the rocket about ten inches from the undersurface of the wing, sufficient to prevent damage from blast and eliminating the need for heavy blast plates in the Beaufighter.

By April 1943, rocket rails had been fitted to all the Beaufighters of 236 Squadron and work had begun on those of 143 Squadron. The new weapon was not yet used operationally, but it was intended that it should replace the machine guns and bombs of the anti-flak squadrons, so that the pilots would use a combination of rockets and cannon in their attacks. Of course, the pilots needed practice with their new weapon, and training took place against a target provided by the Royal Navy. This was a destroyer called HMS *Sherwood*, one of the four-funnel warships built in 1919 and transferred from the USA to the UK under the agreement of 2 September 1940. This ancient destroyer had originally seen service as the USS *Rodgers* and was now considered expendable by the Admiralty. She was moored about a mile off the coast near North Coates and the pilots made diving attacks on her, using practice 60 lb warheads made of concrete instead of high explosive to avoid reducing their target to a shambles.

Meanwhile the squadrons at North Coates continued to operate with their old weapons, for the rocket rails could easily be removed once the fittings were in place. Reconnaissances were flown on most days, either singly or in pairs. On 29 April, Wheeler led the Wing out again, to the Dutch island of Terschelling, where the Beaufighters sank three vessels, the Dutch *Aludra* of 4,930 tons, the Swedish *Narvik* of 4,251 tons and the flak-ship *Vp 807* of 385 tons. It was a successful strike on the pattern of 18 April, although on this occasion a Beaufighter of 143 Squadron was lost, flown by Flying Officer J.H. Wilsdon.

On 1 May, Wheeler's insistence that the Wing should not go out without fighter escort was grimly justified when thirty-one aircraft from the three squadrons were sent out to hunt the cruiser *Nürnberg* and three destroyers reported moving towards Germany along the coast of south-west Norway. This area was outside the range of the fighters available, and the unescorted Wing found no enemy vessels, but the FW 190s and Me 109s found them, shooting down three Torbeaus of 254 Squadron and two anti-flak Beaufighters of 143 Squadron, which tried desperately to stave off the attack but were easily out-manoeuvred by the agile single-engined fighters. The whole Wing was forced to jettison torpedoes and bombs. The

Beaufighters corkscrewed and skidded violently to avoid the deadly Germans, and twenty-six aircraft landed at Wick in north-east Scotland, the crews in a chastened and dispirited mood. On this occasion, the Wing was led by Squadron Leader G. H. Denholm of 236 Squadron.

The next attack, on 17 May, produced valuable results. Wheeler led the Wing, heavily escorted, to the island of Texel, and there they sank the German merchant vessel *Kyphissia* of 2,964 tons, the M-class minesweeper *M-414* of 775 tons, and the flak-ship *Vp 1110* of 523 tons. There was no loss to the attacking force, and the results demonstrated that the tactics were correct if carried out carefully. The next strike, on 24 May, did not succeed owing to poor weather and faulty reconnaissance.

By now, the activities of the new Wing were attracting interest in the RAF and there were signs that the Germans were becoming alarmed. The sinking of irreplaceable ships was bad enough for the Germans but even worse was the effect of the loss of the ship's cargoes on their war economy, for a merchant vessel could carry almost its own weight in vital supplies. On 27 May, the RAF station at North Coates received a royal visit when King George V and Queen Elizabeth arrived, primarily to look at the strange new weapons that were fitted to the anti-flak Beaufighters but which the crews had not yet fired in action. It is probably true to say that before the War the majority of the British public was somewhat lukewarm towards the monarchy, but the royal couple and their two daughters had endeared themselves by remaining in London during the Blitz and by their unflagging interest in the armed forces and the war effort of their people. Although the visit to North Coates meant a formal parade, the aircrews felt honoured to be introduced to the royal pair. A few days later, the visit was followed by another from Sir Archibald Sinclair, Secretary of State for Air, who duly made a speech of encouragement to the assembled squadrons.

Meanwhile, a small detachment of 236 Squadron had been sent to Predannack. Then followed the first use of the rocket projectile on sweeps against U-boats and Mark Bateman's successful encounter with *U-418*. His passenger, Lieutenant-Commander Brookes, had only a couple of days to celebrate his part in that sinking. On 3 June, he accompanied Flight Lieutenant H. 'Mike' Shannon of 236 Squadron in Beaufighter 'W', serial JL819, on another sweep from Predannack. Shannon, a pre-war officer born twenty-five years

7 May 1943. King George V and Queen Elizabeth walk out of a hangar at North Coates. Behind them is Air Vice Marshal Baker. Looking at his watch is Group Captain 'Giles' Gilson.

7 May 1943. The King shakes hands with Flying Officer Brewer, a Canadian. 236 Squadron. Looking on, with his back turned, is Wing Commander Wheeler. Standing stiffly to attention in the foreground is Flying Officer Bob Irving. Behind him is Pilot Officer Jack White.

The Secretary of State for Air visits North Coates. Left to right: Wing Commander Bennett, Group Captain Gilson, Sir Archibald Sinclair, Wing Commander Wheeler, Wing Commander Cooper, Wing Commander Sir Louis Greig (ADC to Sinclair), Wing Commander Davis. Soon afterwards, both Cooper and Bennett were killed in action.

before in Northern Ireland, was a highly experienced pilot with 119 operational sorties to his credit. He took off soon after 09.00 hours.

Nearly two hours later, the crew were appalled to see that eight Ju 88s had formated on their Beaufighter. The Germans had come out of the sun, three above each beam about a mile away, with another on each quarter, like wild dogs surrounding their victim before closing in to savage it. The Beaufighter was at 3,500 feet when two Ju 88s dived down and opened fire, one from each side. The first burst caught the navigator in the shoulder. Pilot Officer Idwal S. 'Wally' Walters, a Rugby enthusiast from Wales, spun round as the bullet hit him; semi-conscious, he was unable to fire his rear gun. Shannon heard a bullet smack into the armoured door behind him. The two Ju 88s returned to their positions whilst another two dived down, evidently in some pre-arranged drill. Shannon also dived, down to sea level, and began to twist and turn violently. A bullet cracked past his ear and Brookes collapsed, struck in the head. Shannon thought that the Ju 88s were able to range on him by watching the splashes of their gunfire in the sea, just as he was accustomed to do himself, and he began to climb once more.

Again and again, the eight Germans attacked. One came in for a head-on attack, and Shannon was able to loose off a short burst with his cannon, which may have had a discouraging effect even if no hits were scored. He resisted the temptation to fire his rockets, for he did not wish to disclose the nature of this secret weapon to his tormentors. He managed to turn north, with one Ju 88 pressing on his tail, probably in an attempt to make him turn. For several dreadful minutes, the pursuers kept pace with the Beaufighter, but gradually Shannon drew away and the Ju 88s turned back to France.

Shannon kept his sturdy machine in the air. Walters recovered sufficiently to put out a fire in his wireless transmitter, but Brookes was dying. Despite hits in one of his starboard petrol tanks, holes in both mainplanes, hydraulics shot up and with no flaps or undercarriage, Shannon contrived to make a good belly-landing at Predannack. Brookes had died, but Walters was taken to hospital and eventually made a good recovery. That evening, German radio made the false claim that one Beaufighter had been destroyed over the Bay of Biscay. Shannon continued to fly in 236 Squadron until he was badly wounded when going in to an attack on a convoy off Texel on 23 November 1943; he completed the attack and then flew back to North Coates with twenty-six pieces of shrapnel embedded in his body, assisted by his navigator. He was awarded a somewhat belated DFC.

The Strike Wing made one more attack with its old weapons before using the new rocket projectile in its combined actions. This was on 13 June, when Wheeler led the three squadrons, with strong fighter escort, to attack a north-bound convoy off Den Helder, the main naval base of Holland. There were three merchant vessels, escorted by five M-class minesweepers and four flak-ships. The higher protection given to this convoy was taken as an indication of the effectiveness of the Strike Wing in its previous attacks. The curtain of flak was tremendous, rising up like red rain to meet the Beaufighters. An anti-flak Beaufighter flown by one of the Flight Commanders of 143 Squadron, Squadron Leader P.J.E. Ritchie, was shot down and the crew lost their lives. Nevertheless, the Wing made its usual determined attack and sank the largest merchant vessel, the German *Stadt Emden* of 5,180 tons, as well as one of the flak-ships, *Vp 1109* of 487 tons.

The first strike using the rocket projectile against a German convoy took place on 22 June, with Wheeler once again in the lead. The Wing consisted of ten Beaufighters of 236 Squadron, each armed with four cannon and eight 60 lb rockets, twelve Beaufighters of 143 Squadron similarly armed, and twelve Torbeaus of 254 Squadron armed with cannon and 18 inch torpedoes. The target was a large convoy moving south off Vlieland. This had been spotted and photographed in the early morning but the attack could not take place until the late afternoon when three squadrons of Spitfires and two of Typhoons became available to join in a large-scale strike. The convoy was number 445, consisting of five Swedish merchant vessels ranging from 1,274 to 2,030 tons, escorted by seven flak-ships and five M-class minesweepers. They had left the Elbe during the previous morning and were bound for the Hook of Holland. When off Texel, they were joined by three more flak-ships, providing in total an enormously powerful escort.

The Strike Wing caught up with this convoy at 17.08 hours off the seaside resort of Scheveningen and attacked from the seaward side. Twenty-two Beaufighters dived down from 1,500 feet and fired 176 rockets, each pilot selecting his flak-ship or minesweeper from a careful briefing that had been accompanied by some excellent photographs of the convoy. The return fire was light and inaccurate

ATTACK BY NORTH COATES STRIKE WING
17.08 HOURS 22 JUNE 1943 OFF SCHEVENINGEN

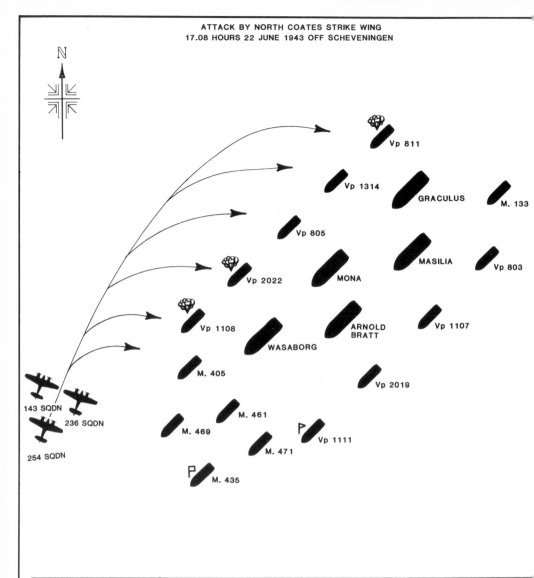

GRACULUS	(1941 grt)	SWEDISH	M.133 Oberleutnant zur See Berghausen
MONA	(2030 grt)	"	M.405 Oberleutnant " " Külper
WASABORG	(1274 grt)	"	M.435 Kapitänleutnant Junker
MASILIA	(1631 grt)	"	M.461 Oberleutnant zur See Mengel
ARNOLD BRATT	(1430 grt)	"	M.469 Oberleutnant " " Schlink
			M.471 Oberleutnant " " Auer
			Vp803 Oberleutnant " " Dillman
			Vp805 Leutnant " " Asskamp
BASED ON GERMAN WAR DIARIES			Vp811 Oberleutnant " " Fielder
			Vp1107 Leutnant " " Schnabel
			Vp1108 Leutnant " " Luddeneit
NOT TO SCALE			Vp1111 Kapitänleutnant Nitsch

P Minensuchboot Commandant

P Vorpostenboot Commandant

M Minensuchboot = Minesweeper
Vp Vorpostenboot = Flak-ship

Damage

Senior officer was in
Vp1111,Korvettenkapitän Loewer

at first, some measure of surprise having been achieved, and none of the anti-flak aircraft was hit. The flak intensified when the Torbeaus made their attack, however, for the torpedo crews had been briefed to delay their run slightly to avoid the risk of being hit by the new rockets. The ship's gunners were able to concentrate a hail of fire on the Torbeaus and two were shot down, the crews being killed. Four more Torbeaus were hit and three crash-landed at North Coates or other bases; of these, the Beaufighter flown by Flight Sergeant W.H. Hood survived not only flak damage but a collision with a balloon cable. It was a black day for 254 Squadron.

A post-war examination of the German records of this convoy shows that the damage inflicted was slight. Three of the flak-ships on the seaward side of the convoy were hit by rockets. One rocket hit the leading flak-ship, *Vp 1108*, on the forecastle and wounded three of the gunners manning the 88 mm gun. Behind her, *Vp 2022* was hit on her aft 37 mm gun platform, killing seven men and wounding two more. The next flak-ship in line, *Vp 805*, was hit by machine-gun fire and one man was wounded. The last flak-ship in the column, *Vp 811*, was hit by three rockets that failed to explode, although one destroyed her wireless. Several other vessels were hit by cannon and machine-gun fire, causing splinter damage. All the torpedoes missed. The slight interval between the anti-flak and the torpedo attack enabled the vessels to turn neatly and simultaneously to starboard and thus to 'comb the tracks'. The torpedoes passed by harmlessly.

The defence expended an enormous amount of ammunition, 105 mm, 88 mm, 20 mm and machine-gun. The Germans claimed nine Beaufighters shot down, inclding one which struck and severed the cable of the balloon flown by the leading merchant vessel, the *Wasaborg* of 1,274 tons; this must have been the Beaufighter flown by Flight Sergeant Hood. As usual, the German claims were grossly exaggerated.

It is interesting to note that the escort vessels were also using new weapons during the attack of 22 June. One of these was a rocket launcher that fired a device similar to one that had already been developed for use in British defences. The Germans called this a *Drahtseilrakete* whilst the name for the British version was a 'Parachute and Cable' rocket. The German rocket contained a parachute fitted with a cable 100 metres long, timed to unfold at a range of 400 to 1,000 metres after firing from the launcher. The idea was that a low-flying aircraft would become entangled in the slowly-descending cable, and in fact this form of defence did bring down several aircraft in the course of the anti-shipping war, both Allied and German. Later, both sides in the conflict fitted explosive mines to the cables, so that the devices became even more dangerous.

The other new weapon used by the Germans on this day was the *Flammenwerfer* or flame-thrower. Of course, flame-throwers had been used as weapons for several years, both by infantry and by static defences, but the Germans developed the idea for use on escort vessels. It consisted of a tank containing about 1.5 cubic metres of diesel oil, to which was attached a long pipe and nozzle running up a mast. The oil was ignited electrically by remote control using spark plugs or combustion cartridges. The device could throw a jet of burning oil to a distance of up to 40 metres, having the capacity of about 50 squirts of three seconds duration apiece. Fearsome though this might seem, it was not a very effective weapon. Tests in the UK disclosed that an aircraft could fly through a jet of burning oil with little damage to its fabric and none to its occupants, in the same way that one can pass one's hand fairly slowly over a candle flame. The defect was recognized by the Germans who stated in their manuals that the purpose of the flame-thrower was to force the pilot to fly higher and to spoil his aim. The ships' crews disliked the weapon. Sometimes it would fail to ignite and smother them with oil whilst on other occasions burning oil would run down the mast and create an additional hazard.

The flyers at North Coates were naturally disappointed with the lack of confirmed results following the first rocket attack of 22 June, but they were only vaguely aware that things had not gone well. In combat of this sort, the air-sea battle was a kaleidoscope of quickly-moving events, with each airman's attention concentrated on the small part that he played in it. He could not be sure from his personal observation whether the strike as a whole had been successful, and relied on being informed by higher authority. The men were not told that the first attack with rocket projectiles had been a failure, and there was little discussion about improving the tactics and weapons employed.

Three days later, the Strike Wing was saddened by the deaths of Wing Commander W. O. V. Bennett, the CO of 143 Squadron, and his navigator, Flying Officer H. Emmerson; they were lost on a

2 June 1943. The first rocket attack. 60lb high-explosive rockets and cannon shells narrowly miss a flak-ship.

2 June 1943. The rockets are exploding in the sea. In the centre, a flak-ship is squirting its flame-thrower at a Beaufighter.

2 June 1943. The torpedoes have been dropped too late; the enemy convoy manoeuvres so as to 'comb the tracks'. The explosion top left is probably the funeral pyre of a Torbeau.

reconnaissance sortie. This crew had led the squadron with pan-
ache for the past few months, and a new CO Wing Commander
R.N. Lambert, was appointed. Although Wheeler was recognized
as the natural leader of the Strike Wing at North Coates, it would
have been difficult for him to have led the Wing on every occasion
and indeed dangerous to have relied on one man exclusively. Any
of the three COs could be called upon to fulfil this function, or
perhaps any of the Flight Commanders in each squadron, so that
several men had to study the tactics involved.

There was another person who understudied Wheeler at North
Coates, someone without a squadron who was given the title of
Wing Commander Flying. This post became similar to that of a
Wing Leader in Fighter Command. It was given to an experienced
Wing Commander for whom there was no squadron available to
command, but it rapidly developed into a position where the occu-
pant could lead the whole Wing on a strike. This person was Wing
Commander W.A.L. 'Willy' Davis, a 26-year-old officer who had
joined the RAF in 1935 and had spent most of his time as an
instructor, although for two dangerous months he had commanded 217 Squadron in their attacks with Beaufort torpedo bombers
whilst based at Malta.* His navigator was Pilot Officer John H.
'Jack' White, a 29-year-old navigator who became 'spare' when his
pilot, Flying Officer Myles Scargill of 236 Squadron, broke his leg in
the unwarlike activity of playing tennis. Davis and White had flown
in the abortive strike of 22 June and were now to take their turn in
leading the Wing. The first strike led by Davis was on 27 June. On
this occasion there were no Torbeaus, the Wing consisting of nine
Beaufighters of 236 Squadron and twelve from 143 Squadron, all
armed with 60 lb rocket projectiles. They attacked a south-bound
convoy off the Hague, consisting of four merchant vessels, five M-
class minesweepers and seven flak-ships. The attackers faced a
torrent of flak but dived down and released 168 rockets. The attack
did not succeed and there were no casualties on either side.

Davis led the Wing out again on 18 July. On this occasion, there
were twelve Torbeaus from 254 Squadron and twenty-three anti-
flak Beaufighters of 236 and 143 Squadrons only eight of which
were fitted with rockets. Heavily escorted, they swept out to attack a
large convoy near Den Helder but were thwarted when they found
that their target had reached the haven of the harbour and the pro-

---

*   See *Torpedo Airmen* by the author, published by William Kimber in 1983.

tection of the shore batteries. The Wing was compelled to return to North Coates but, nothing loath, Davis led out twelve aircraft of 236 and 143 Squadrons later in the day, all equipped with rockets. They caught the convoy coming out of Den Helder and an air battle ensued between the escorting Spitfires and enemy fighters. Two Beaufighters were shot down and the crews were killed. Once again, the rockets caused little damage to the convoy.

Towards the end of July 1943, 236 Squadron was the first to be re-equipped with the Beaufighter TFX, a version specially designed for the low-flying squadrons of Coastal Command. Even more powerful engines were fitted in this new Beaufighter, two 1,772 hp Bristol Hercules XVIIs. Eventually, all squadrons of the Strike Wings converted to the Beaufighter TFX, other than those that were equipped with Mosquitoes. There were minor variations in the TFX over the next two years – for instance in some the armoured doors were placed to the rear of the navigator whilst in others the doors remained between the pilot and the navigator. The later Beaufighter TFX incorporated a dorsal fin extension, reaching almost as far forward as the navigator's cupola, which improved stability in flight.

The first major strike with the new Beaufighters of 236 Squadron took place on 2 August. A reconnaissance Beaufighter of 254 Squadron, flown by Squadron Leader F.T. Gardiner, spotted a large enemy convoy off the island of Terschelling, at 06.23 hours. Two minutes later, the German gunners saw the Beaufighter and opened fire, their heavy flak being wide of the mark but their light flak passing uncomfortably close. Gardiner flew back to North Coates, bearing photographs that were rapidly developed. The convoy was number 453, consisting of three columns. They were carrying iron ore. Four M-class minesweepers sailed in front, whilst seven flak-ships and a harbour defence vessel provided close escort on the flanks. An R-boat tender called the *Alders* guarded the rear. The Commandant was Oberleutnant zur See Eggers, in *Vp 1111*, the leading flak-ship on the starboard flank. The convoy had left Cuxhaven at 11.00 hours on the previous morning, bound for Rotterdam. It was running late, since the *Fortuna*, a German vessel of 2,700 tons, had developed engine trouble. Eggers had been forced to reduce speed to three knots whilst repairs took place, although by the time Gardiner saw the convoy a speed of eight knots had been resumed. The German Commandant reported the Beaufighter

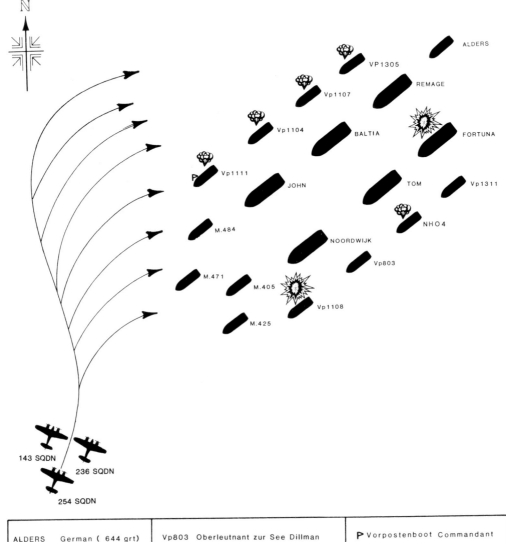

ATTACK BY NORTH COATES STRIKE WING
13.35 HOURS 2 AUGUST 1943 OFF TEXEL

N

ALDERS

VP1305

REMAGE

Vp1107

Vp1104

BALTIA

FORTUNA

Vp1111

P

JOHN

TOM

Vp1311

M.484

NHO4

NOORDWIJK

Vp803

M.471

M.405

M.425

Vp1108

143 SQDN

236 SQDN

254 SQDN

ALDERS German (644 grt)	Vp803 Oberleutnant zur See Dillman	Vorpostenboot Commandant
FORTUNA " (2700 grt)	Vp1104 Leutnant " " Hennings	
NOORDWIJK " (3679 grt)	Vp1107 Leutnant " " Schnabel	M Minensuchboot = Minesweeper
REMAGE " (1830 grt)	Vp1108 Leutnant " " Luddeneit	
BALTIA Swedish (1169 grt)	Vp1111 Oberleutnant " " Eggers	Vp Vorpostenboot = Flak-Ship
JOHN " (3148 grt)	VP1305 Oberleutnant " " Kasper	
TOM " (2109 grt)	Vp1311 Leutnant " " Reuter	NH Harbour defence
	M.405 Leutnant " " Kupler	
BASED ON GERMAN WAR DIARIES	M.425 Leutnant " " Beuschler	Destruction
	M.471 Oberleutnant " " Schlink	
NOT TO SCALE	M.484 Oberleutnant " " Sievers	Damage

and a *Schwarm* of four Me 109s swept out to protect the vessels, being replaced at set intervals. The Germans were on the alert.

The North Coates Wing lost no time. By 10.30 hours, twelve Torbeaus of 254 Squadron were in the air, with ten Beaufighters of 143 and fourteen of 236 Squadrons providing anti-flak protection. Wheeler led the formation, the anti-flak aircraft being armed with 60 lb rockets and the usual cannon. On this occasion, their fighter escort consisted of no less than fifty-one long-range Spitfire Vs of 118, 402(RCAF), 416(RCAF) and 611 Squadrons, led by the Wing Commander Flying at Coltishall, L.V. Chadburn. In all, eighty-seven aircraft headed for convoy number 453.

Wheeler saw the enemy at 11.34 hours, off the island of Texel. The Germans spotted the aircraft at the same time; they thought at first that they were friendly fighters, but were soon to be disillusioned. The Beaufighters and the convoy were converging on a reciprocal course, but Wheeler swung his formation out to sea, attacking from the west. Twenty-four Beaufighters dived down in a copy-book attack, through a curtain of fire towards the balloon carrying merchantmen and their escorts. The pilots had become more proficient with their tricky rockets. All four flak ships on the starboard of the convoy were hit, as was *NH 04*, the harbour defence vessel on the port flank. Seven seamen were killed and twenty-eight wounded, some seriously.

Then the Torbeaus released their torpedoes. According to the Germans, four of these struck the sea bed in the shallow waters, but two found their marks. The unlucky *Fortuna* was hit; weighted down with her cargo of iron ore, she went to the bottom in thirty seconds, with her captain and five of his crew. The *Vp 1108* was hit and exploded, with the loss of thirteen of her crew. Meanwhile, the Spitfires pounced on four Me 109s, who fought a desperate air battle against impossible odds. Unteroffizier Gotthard Obst was shot down and killed, whilst Feldwebel Werner Sadrina was wounded but baled out to safety. These fighters were part of III/JG54, the 3rd Gruppe of Jagdgeschwader 54, based at Leeuwarden in Holland. The Spitfires claimed four Me 109s.

The convoy turned into Den Helder with her dead and wounded, with *Vp 1108* in tow. The vessels had expended 244 heavier shells, 2,109 of 20 mm, 1,911 machine gun bullets and 18 rockets. The Germans made wild claims in their reports: the four Me 109s had destroyed five aircraft, whilst the escort ships had shot down another ten. In fact, none of the attackers was lost and no one was

(*Left*):
2 August 1943. The peaceful sight of the enemy convoy before the attack. In the background, the Dutch island of Texel.

2 August 1943. During the attack. An M-class mine-sweeper in the van of the convoy.

(*Top right*): 2 August 1943. A flak-ship explosion. This is *Vp 1108*, hit by a tor-pedo, before sinking.

(*Bottom right*): 2 August 1943. In the thick of it. Rockets explode around flak-ships and mine-sweepers. The intense return fire cannot be seen in this photograph.

(*Left*):
2 August 1943. The Torbeaus have dropped their torpedoes. In the centre background, the *Fortuna* is hit; she sinks immediately afterwards.

wounded, although five Beaufighters were hit and one made a belly landing at Coltishall.*

In spite of the successful attack of 2 August, the whole of the future of the Strike Wing was suddenly thrown into doubt. On 8 August, the Air Officer Commanding-in-Chief of Coastal Command, who at that time was Air Marshal Sir John C. Slessor, sent a letter to the Air Ministry saying that he could not justify the continuation of the North Coates Wing in the light of the results achieved. He pointed out that the Wing tied down 60 front-line aircraft and their crews, as well as ground staff totalling 72 officers and 1,309 other ranks, but that the Beaufighters had sunk only ten enemy vessels since 18 April. He was perturbed at the inability of the Wing to attack on enough occasions. He had originally envisaged five Wing strikes per month, but the average was working out at just over two, the main reason being the lack of suitable fighter cover. Fighter Command was so heavily occupied with protecting American bombers flying to and from the European mainland that it had no squadrons to spare for Coastal Command. In consequence, Slessor thought it might be advisable to divert the squadrons of the Strike Wing to operations over the Bay of Biscay where they could join in the hunt for U-boats and also provide extra protection against marauding Ju 88s in that area. He asked the Air Ministry for guidance in this matter.

Slessor's letter produced a flurry of activity. A meeting was convened on 20 August, consisting of top-ranking representatives from the Admiralty, the Air Ministry, Fighter Command, Coastal Command, the Ministry of Economic Warfare, and the Nore Command, the latter being the naval command concerned with operations off the Dutch coast. After intensive discussions, it was agreed that the North Coates Strike Wing should continue. A strong argument was presented by the Commander-in-Chief, Nore. He pointed out that the daylight attacks of the Wing were complementary to the night bombing of the German ports and the night mine-laying of Bomber Command. Above all, the attacks were compelling many of the German convoys to sail at night, giving his motor-torpedo boats and motor gunboats from Felixstowe, Lowestoft and Yarmouth the opportunity to attack them under cover of darkness.

---

*   German claims against Strike Wing aircraft were so consistently exaggerated that the author thinks that the gunners may have been genuinely mistaken. A Beaufighter evading at low level with full throttle left a trail of smoke, perhaps giving the impression of crashing.

The most powerful argument in favour of continuing was presented by the Ministry of Economic Warfare, which pointed out that the activities of the Strike Wing were having a remarkable effect on the German coastal trade, even though they were falling short of expectations. In the summer of 1942, the average tonnage of enemy shipping observed in Rotterdam was 100,000 whilst that in the German port of Emden was 39,000. By the summer of 1943, Rotterdam had declined drastically and the respective tonnages were almost reversed.

In January 1943, Germany had concluded her annual Iron Ore Freight Agreement with Sweden, holding out many financial inducements for Swedish vessels to sail as far as Rotterdam, but now the Swedes were becoming increasingly apprehensive and there were reports that insurance cover had been withdrawn for vessels sailing beyond Emden. This made matters very awkward for the Germans, since barges of only 1,500 tons could ply along the Dortmund-Ems canal from Emden to the Ruhr, through a system that included many locks, whilst barges of 4,000 tons carried the iron ore from Rotterdam up the Rhine. The Ministry of Economic Warfare stressed the vital importance of Swedish iron ore to the German armaments industry and recommended that not only should the Strike Wing continue but that the port of Emden should be flattened by Bomber Command in the same way as Hamburg. The result of this meeting was an instruction to Fighter Command to provide an escort of three squadrons of fighters for the Strike Wing on all but exceptional occasions. From that date the future of the Strike Wing was assured and it continued to operate for the remainder of the war.

With hindsight, however, it is possible to identify a defect in the operations of the Strike Wing which was not discussed at this meeting. This was the failure of the higher command to recognize the weaknesses as well as the effectiveness of the new weapon being used by the Strike Wing – the rocket projectile.

There were two problems in scoring hits with this weapon. The first was that ideally it should be fired from a stable platform, and a Beaufighter diving into attack was rarely stable. When a bullet, shell or rocket leaves an aircraft, the velocity of the aircraft is imparted to it in addition to the forward velocity of the missile itself. If an aircraft is skidding, banking or jinking up or down, the missile will be deflected from its aiming point even when the target is squarely in the pilot's gunsight. Where the missile leaves at a high speed, such as a cannon shell at a muzzle velocity of 2,800 feet per second, the deflection is less marked than if the missile leaves the aircraft very slowly, such as a rocket at an initial velocity of only 150 feet per second. Thus, if a pilot was to have any chance of hitting a target with the rocket, he had to steady his aircraft and fly in a completely controlled dive, regardless of enemy fire. This required almost superhuman nerves when tracer was snaking towards him.

The second problem concerned the trajectory of the rocket. It is obvious that a rocket is affected by the forward thrust imparted by gases escaping from the rear of its motor and by the drag created by the air resistance around the warhead. The rocket accelerates steadily at first and then decelerates as the charge in its motor begins to burn out, the force of gravity then producing a curved trajectory towards the sea or ground. The trouble with the rocket supplied to the Strike Wing was that its motor was not powerful enough. It worked reasonably well with the lighter and more streamlined 25 lb warhead, but there was far too much air resistance around the 60 lb warhead, so that this weapon often plopped in the sea and exploded before it reached the target. When using their old weapons, the Beaufighter pilots were accustomed to open fire first with their longer-ranging .303 machine-guns, watching the splashes in the water 'walking' towards the target, and then opening up with their four cannon. This method of aiming was not possible with the 60 lb warhead of the new rocket. The trajectory was so curved that the pilots had to pull up the nose, wait for a moment, and then almost lob the rocket towards the target. It proved impossible to match the trajectory of the 60 lb rocket with that of the 20 mm cannon, at any distance. It is small wonder that the introduction of the rocket projectile led to a loss of effectiveness in the Strike Wing. Yet eventually the rocket was to prove the most lethal and devastating weapon in the armoury of the Strike Wings, when it was used with the 25 lb warhead as a weapon for sinking ships and not with the 60 lb warhead for anti-flak purposes.

Thirty-seven years after leaving 236 Squadron, Robert Irving was re-introduced to Queen Elizabeth the Queen Mother at Covent Garden. He reminded her that they had met at North Coates all those years before. The Queen Mother thought for a moment.

'Something to do with rockets?' she asked.

'Good Lord, yes!' replied the astounded Irving.

'I remember, I was nervous in case they went off!' said the royal lady, leaving Irving captivated by her charm and astonished at her remarkable memory.

Irving did not mention the effect that the rocket projectile had on the enemy. The weapon may have made the Queen Mother nervous but before long it was to terrify the ships' gunners. The time would come when the Beaufighter airmen would sometimes see the ships' gunners dive over the side rather than face those burning projectiles converging towards them.

CHAPTER FOUR

The Good Shepherd

*That man deserves the highest honours who does not ask
for them, but performs worthy deeds.*

Talmud 'Kiddushin'

Twenty thousand years ago, a great ice-cap covered the country
which we now know as Norway. Thrusting out from the Arctic, the
ice had scoured the land mass, rounding and polishing boulders,
forming beneath it U-shaped and hanging valleys. It had pushed
the surface of clay, sand and boulders in front of its path, leaving
deposits on the coast and carrying the remainder further, even to
the North European Plain. When the ice-cap receded, the sea-level
rose and fell several times, leaving thin layers of marine deposits in
banks along the coast. In the Norway of today, a complex string of
islands borders the length of her coast, stretching from the very
north to the south-west tip. The Norwegians call these islands the
Skjaergard whilst to the British they are the 'great skerry-fence' or
simply the Skerries. They are of hard crystalline rock, with rounded
summits and sparse vegetation. The outer islands are only 25–100
feet in height but they are higher towards the mainland, where
some rise to 1,000 feet. Between this string of islands and the
mainland is a convoluted sea passage which British mariners call
the 'Leads'. The glaciated valleys piercing the coast of the mainland
are called fjords; they are long, narrow, and often straight. From
these fjords, deep gorges stretch upwards into the mountainous
interior, often shrouded with cloud.

To the airman, these islands and fjords are often difficult to dis-
tinguish one from another. The Leads are so narrow in places that
during the war torpedoes could not always be used against the
enemy vessels plying along their length.* The Allied squadrons
operating over this impressive coastline were usually based in
north-east Scotland. Sometimes detachments were sent to Sumburgh in the Shetlands, but even from this aerodrome Beaufighters

---

*   Winston Churchill called the Leads 'the covered way'.

could not range further north than the entrance to Trondheim fjord. In 1943, there were no fighters available with sufficient range to escort the attacking Beaufighters to Norway, so that the twin-engined aircraft had to operate without protection from the Me 109s and FW 190s of Luftflotte 5, the German air fleet formed in 1940 and based on the aerodromes of Norway and Denmark.

One of the squadrons that specialized in flying over the North Sea and the Norwegian coastline was 404 (Royal Canadian Air Force) Squadron – the Buffaloes. Originally formed in May 1941, the squadron was stationed for most of the time in north-east Scotland. Its first aircraft were Blenheim IVs, but the Beaufighters arrived in September 1942. The Canadians flew armed reconnaissances and roving patrols. Sometimes they escorted the Hamdens and then the Torbeaus of 144 Squadron, and RAF squadron that frequently shared the same aerodromes as the Canadians. During the first half of 1943, these two squadrons had become accustomed to working in concert with each other but it was not until November of that year that they were to follow the example of the North Coates Wing and to combine into a single unit – the Wick Wing. Meanwhile the squadrons operating over this area continued their independent roles.

Flying Officer Sydney S. Shulemson of 404 Squadron reached up with his right hand and flipped over his Mark II reflector sight, locking it in position in front of his forehead. It was the standard gunsight used in fighter aircraft in 1943, adapted for use in the Beaufighters of Coastal Command. There were two movable rings around the base. On one of these the pilot set the range for opening fire; on the other he set the wing span of the enemy aircraft. A horizontal bar of orange light then left a gap into which the pilot tried to fit the enemy aircraft, manoeuvring so as to attack on its tail; his tracer should then converge to a series of hits. It was a good gunsight but dangerously placed in a Beaufighter, since during a belly landing the pilot usually smashed his forehead against it. He was supposed to unlock the gunsight and throw it over his shoulder before such an emergency, but since he usually needed both hands on the controls this was often impossible. Some of the Beaufighter pilots bore healed scars on their foreheads as souvenirs of this gunsight. Squadron Leader A.K. 'Ken' Gatward, one of Shulemson's Flight Commanders, sported one of these marks. They were common enough for airmen to refer to one as a 'Beaufighter scar'; even

today these men can sometimes pick out a former Beaufighter pilot
by the distinctive mark on his forehead.

It was 28 July 1943, the date of Shulemson's first operational
flight. He had set off forty minutes before, at 08.25 hours, from
Sumburgh in the Shetlands, flying a Beaufighter XIC. A small
detachment of 404 Squardon had been sent to this northerly aerodrome from their base in Wick, to work with six aircraft of 235
Squadron, another Beaufighter squadron, forming a tiny anti-
shipping force. This was not a fully-fledged Strike Wing but represented an experiment in that direction. The Canadians had
removed their machine guns and were armed only with cannon,
whilst 235 Squadron had already added the rocket projectile to the
cannon as part of its normal armoury. Accompanying the two
detachments were a couple of Mosquito IIs of 333 Squadron, a
Norwegian unit that specialized in reconnaissance and attacks over
the coast of their homeland. The small combined force had had
one success on 17 July, when they sank the submarine-chaser *UJ
1705* of 548 tons in an attack on a convoy off south-west
Norway.

Shulemson's first sortie was intended to be no more than a gentle
introduction for him. The Canadians had lost several new crews on
their first operational flights, but this was to be a peaceful occasion,
pairs of Beaufighters acting as screens for a naval task force. The
Allies had invaded Sicily earlier in the month, and the Home Fleet
was busy making diversionary sorties into the North and Norwegian Seas. Aircraft carriers, cruisers and destroyers, were 'trailing
their coats' not far from the Norwegian coast. Hitler was always
worried about an Allied invasion of Norway, and here was a move
to play on his nerves; perhaps it would induce him to move some of
his forces northwards, away from the main battle zone in the
Mediterranean.

Piloting the second Beaufighter was another Flight Commander
of 404 Squadron, Squadron Leader Al De la Haye. There had been
a close shave on take-off from Sumburgh. Shulemson had mis-
understood a hand signal from De la Haye whilst taxiing and had
taken off from the short runway; this was only 600 yards long, and
the wheels of the Beaufighter had lifted off only a few feet before the
sea appeared beneath them. The two Beaufighters had then flown
north-east, keeping strict R/T silence as instructed. It was a surprise
when this R/T silence was broken as soon as they approached their
objective, the cruiser *Belfast* and four escorting destroyers:

'SNO to aircraft screen. Bogey bearing 100 degrees. Pursue and attack.'

The Senior Naval Officer was reporting a probable enemy aircraft which had been on the radar, shadowing the warships.

'D-Dog to P-Peter. Did you hear that?' asked Shulemson, after he had turned, for De la Haye was not following. There was something wrong with De la Haye's R/T, for he could hear Shulemson but not the *Belfast*, and he turned late to the attack. In the leading aircraft, Shulemson put his throttles 'through the gate' and soon saw a Ju 88, climbing rapidly. He gained on the German aircraft but was still outside effective range, 2,000 yards away, when the Junkers reached the cloud base at 6,000 feet and disappeared. Baulked of his prey, Shulemson turned back. Almost immediately, another call came from the *Belfast*.

'SNO to aircraft screen. Another bogey bearing 285 degrees.'

Shulemson realized immediately that the second enemy aircraft must be between himself and the warships. He dived on the reciprocal course, pushing his Beaufighter to its maximum speed. In front and below, he saw an enemy aircraft that few Allied airmen had encountered. It was a massive flying boat, a tri-motored BV 138. This aircraft carried a crew of five, or sometimes six. Its defensive armament consisted of a 20 mm cannon mounted in a bow turret and another in the tail of the main hull, with a machine gun in a dorsal position behind the central engine. The Blohm and Voss flying boat was used for long-range maritime reconnaissance. It was a very strong and dependable machine, capable of floating in rough seas for such long periods that it often operated in concert with U-boats far from its base. The Germans called the BV 138 the 'flying clog', from its appearance. The wing span was just over 88 feet whilst the length was 65 feet.

At the rear of this monster, De la Haye was peeling away, followed by a long line of tracer. The flying boat was at 500 feet. Shulemson continued his dive down to sea level and then roared up again for a tail attack. The BV 138 was squarely in his reflector sight when he opened up with his four cannon, watching the shells explode along the hull to the central engine. There was a burst of return fire, but the German gunner was too late. A huge trail of black smoke poured from the doomed flying boat as it dived down to the sea. Shulemson broke away to port whilst his navigator, Sergeant Al Glasgow from Alberta, took a remarkable series of photographs. As he did so, there was a loud metallic bang underneath the Beaufighter. The flying boat glided down and settled in the sea, whilst Glasgow continued to take his pictures. A survivor scrambled out of the top hatch. Shulemson compassionately informed the *Belfast* over the R/T. It was to be half an hour before the cruiser could send a destroyer, the *Orwell*, to pick up the man but by this time the flying boat and the entire crew had disappeared.

'What was that noise?' Shulemson asked Glasgow.

'A panel's blown out of the floor,' replied the navigator. 'It's a bit draughty, but I guess I'll be able to take a drift without using the drift sight!' At this point the *Belfast* broke in again.

'SNO to aircraft screen. We've got another bogey for you, bearing 020 degrees.'

It was incredible. Yet another! Shulemson relayed the message to De la Haye. The two Beaufighters set off again, flying abreast. In a few minutes they identified the third 'bogey', another BV 138, flying a hundred feet above the sea.

'Let's take up positions above each quarter,' suggested Shulemson. 'Then whichever way he turns, one of us will be able to get on his tail.'

The German did not turn. He continued to fly straight ahead, going down to sea level. Signals began to arc upwards, five-star clusters of red.

'Does that mean that he wants to surrender?' asked De la Haye.

'Well, if he does, I can't circle him', replied Shulemson. 'I've used up too much juice on those other attacks, and I'm just about at my PLE*.'

'So am I,' said De la Haye. 'And if he lands, he can take off again. I'm going in.'

De la Haye dived down on the hapless flying boat. On his first burst, the BV 138 broke up and crashed in the sea. This time there was no hope of any survivors. Shulemson reported over the R/T to *Belfast* and in reply received the terse message that forms one of the highest compliments that a fighting unit can expect from the Royal Navy.

'Well done from the Commander-in-Chief of the Home Fleet.'

Shulemson had not exaggerated the problem with his fuel.

---

*   Prudent limit of endurance.

28 July 1943. The BV 138
attacked by Flying Officer
Sydney S. Shulemson
goes down in flames.

28 July 1943. The BV 138
in the sea before sinking.
One crew member got out,
but could not be rescued.

The Canadians of 404
Squadron study flak
damage in the wing of one
of their Beaufighters.

When the two Beaufighters reached Sumburgh, he had to ask Control for permission to forego the usual preliminary circuit. He went straight in to land, being careful to use the long runway on this occasion. His fuel gauges showed 'empty' as he taxied to dispersal.

Fifteen minutes after the first pair of Beaufighters left the naval force, another Beaufighter arrived, flown by Squadron Leader A. K. Gatward. He was joined half an hour later by another, flown by Sergeant J.J. Beaudet. The two pilots could see another naval force in the distance, which proved to be the aircraft carrier *Illustrious* and a destroyer escort. There was no incident with enemy aircraft. The two Beaufighters finished their patrol after two hours and then returned to Sumburgh.

There was then a delay of nearly three hours before the third and final pair of Beaufighters reached the naval task force, at 17.54 hours. These were led by a very experienced pilot, Flight Sergeant Ken S. Miller. The other pilot was a newcomer, Flying Officer E.J. Keefe. By then, the two naval forces had linked together.

'You're too late!' came the R/T message from the *Belfast*. 'We've shot down another BV 138!' Over an hour before, four Grumman Martlets had taken off from the deck of the *Illustrious*, and the Fleet Air Arm pilots had destroyed another of the shadowing flying boats.

Almost immediately after his arrival, Keefe, who was also on his first operational flight, saw a strange aircraft disappearing into a cloud bank. He turned to investigate, losing touch with his companion. At this point, the Senior Naval Officer must have thought that the presence of the two Beaufighters was unnecessary, for he ordered them to return to base. Miller complied and arrived safely, but there was no sign of Keefe in the other Beaufighter.

At first, gloom pervaded the little gathering of Canadian flyers at Sumburgh, for it seemed that yet another of the squadron's new crews had been lost on a first operational flight. As Ken Miller was being de-briefed, however, an urgent message was relayed to the operations room. Jimmy Keefe was still flying, coming in on one engine, and he asked over the R/T for immediate airfield clearance. The little band of Canadians trooped outside to cheer him in. The crippled Beaufighter came over the low hill at the end of the runway and overshot slightly. Keefe would have crashed off the end of the runway, but he quickly pulled up his undercarriage and the Beaufighter skidded to a halt on its belly. The pilot and his navigator, Sergeant B.G. Stead, walked away unhurt and made their way to the operations room, where they related what seemed to be an unlikely story.

Keefe said that he had heard the re-call instructions but had been busy chasing not just one, but two, BV 138s. He had made an attack on the stern of one and had sent it into the sea with the port engine and hull in flames. He had also attacked the other BV 138, scoring several hits, but his Beaufighter had then been hit by return fire. Nevertheless, he was circling for another attack when his navigator called to say that two FW 190s were diving on his tail. Keefe had turned and headed for Sumburgh. One engine had failed, and he had only just managed to nurse his Beaufighter home on the other.

The Canadians looked at Keefe in amazement. They might have swallowed the unsubstantiated story of the two BV 138s, but did Keefe really expect them to believe that there were FW 190s out there near the Shetlands? He had either gone crazy or was inventing the whole story! Shulemson strolled outside to take another look at the crashed Beaufighter.

'Hey, look at this! There's a bullet hole in the engine cowling! Jimmy can't have invented that!'

It took a few days to clear up the mystery of the two FW 190s. They were Martlets from the *Illustrious*. They had dived down on what they thought was a reconnoitring Ju 88, but had peeled away when they realized their mistake, before opening fire. So that left the two BV 138s. Did they exist and, if so, what happened to them? Ten days later, an even more improbable tale was told to the Canadians, but it is a story that can now be substantiated by piecing together British, Canadian and German records.

The flying boats came from Trondheim fjord. Their unit was called SAGr 130, the initials standing for 'Seeaufklärungsgruppe', a long-range sea reconnaissance group. It was a black day in the history of this unit, for they did indeed lose five of their BV 138s near the Shetlands. One of these must be credited to Shulemson, one to De la Haye, one to the Martlets, and the remaining two to Keefe. Of the five German crews, four perished in their entirety on that day. The body of one man, Oberleutnant Sebastian von Pander, drifted all the way to the Norwegian coast, borne in its life-jacket by the Gulf Stream. He was probably the man who had clambered out of the BV 138 that Shulemson had destroyed. He was the *Beobachter*, or observer; in these German aircraft the observer was the captain, and he was often an experienced pilot, whilst a more junior pilot sat at the controls. In one of the BV 138s, however, three of the five crewmen survived; it is the story of what happened to them that was told to the Canadians and is one of the most unusual in the history of the air war.

A week after the BV 138s were shot down, on 4 August, a Short Sunderland of 423(RCAF) Squadron based at Lough Erne in Northern Ireland, was on patrol 210 sea miles west of the Faeroes when it spotted a large U-boat on the surface. This was *U-489*, a type XIV tanker supply boat on her first war cruise. She had left Kiel on 22 July, commanded by Leutnant zur See Adalbert Schmandt, and was headed into the North Atlantic. The U-boat had been slightly damaged the previous day by a Hudson of 269 Squadron based at Reykjavik. Although the U-boat was capable of diving, Schmandt decided to stay on the surface and fight it out, these being the German tactics in the summer of 1943.

The Sunderland was flown by Flying Officer Albert A. Bishop. He went in with machine guns and depth charges, seriously damaging *U-489* but receiving such well-aimed flak that his aircraft crashed nearby. Six RCAF men got into the sea, but the remaining five of the crew were killed. Bishop supported a wounded man in the water, an action for which he was later to receive a DFC. Meanwhile, *U-489* was so badly damaged that Schmandt was forced to abandon her, leaving scuttling charges behind. The U-boat crew got into their life-rafts, making no attempt to help the RCAF men swimming nearby. Shortly afterwards, three British destroyers arrived on the scene, the *Castleton*, the *Orwell* and the *Orbit*, all part of a special anti-submarine force. They picked up the RCAF men and the entire crew of the U-boat. One of the U-boat men died but the remainder were taken to Reykjavik in Iceland.

After their rescue, the U-boat men were allowed to write home. One very indiscreet lad informed his parents that, a week before, his U-boat had rescued three survivors of a BV 138, number K6+BK, a *Leutnant* and two *Unteroffiziere*, but that these three men had been killed in the U-boat. Needless to say, the contents of this letter were examined by British censors and the truth came out. The three men were not killed in the U-boat, and they were soon identified before being sent to a POW camp. Their names were Leutnant Hans Knittel, the 22-year-old captain; Unteroffizier Werner Mohlau, the 23-year-old gunner; and Unteroffizier Heinrich Hengst, the wireless operator, who had experienced a memorable twenty-fourth birthday when the U-boat was sunk. These men must have been part of the crew of the BV 138 crippled by Jimmy Keefe, but Keefe received no recognition for shooting down either flying boat; he was killed in a Beaufighter crash some months later.

After the men of 404 Squadron had been told in broad outline what had happened, they received a visit from the Marshal of the Royal Air Force, Lord Trenchard, and Shulemson discussed these events with him. The Canadian recommended that the three Germans be repatriated to their own country without delay so that they could relate their experiences as a warning to their fellow-countrymen. Trenchard was amused by this novel suggestion but he did not act on it.

Sydney Shulemson was twenty-seven years old at the time of his eventful first sortie, slightly older than the average in his squadron. He came from Montreal and had had experience with the Royal Canadian Artillery before the War. After volunteering for the RCAF in 1941, he trained on Harvards and then took a General Reconniassance course on Ansons at Prince Edward Island. Posted to England, he converted to Beaufighters preparatory to flying one of these aircraft out to Burma, but was found to have a cyst on his spine and missed this posting whilst undergoing surgical treatment. On his recovery he was posted to 404 Squadron at Wick, where Al Glasgow was appointed as his navigator. Most wartime flyers acquired nicknames and the sibilant nature of Shulemson's initials gave him the squadron name of 'Slippery'; this was perhaps inappropriate, for he was a conscientious man, hard-working and rather studious.

The Canadian squadron formed part of 18 Group. Its area of operations covered the coast of Norway, usually from the Skaggerrak northwards to the limit of their range. In the month of August, 404 Squadron was withdrawn for re-equipping with the Beaufighter TFX and then for training with rocket projectiles. Meanwhile, 235 Squadron was sent down to Cornwall for operations over the Bay of Biscay. Their training finished, the Canadians were successful with one of their first rocket attacks. On 30 September, six Beaufighters found an unescorted Norwegian merchant vessel, the *Sanet Svithun* of 1,376 tons, and delivered such a careful attack with 60 lb high-explosive warheads that they set her ablaze. She later sank off Stadlandet.

During October, Shulemson was assigned an English navigator, a 22-year-old ex-bank clerk from Surrey, Flying Officer Peter R. Bassett. Although it was the policy of the RCAF to appoint their own nationals to their squadrons, there was a shortage of Canadian navigators who were also trained wireless operators. By rights, Bassett should not have been flying at all, for his eyesight was below the high standard required by the RAF. He had joined the RAF in January 1941 and had trained as a ground wireless operator at Blackpool and Yatesbury, but in the Spring of 1942 he tried again to remuster as aircrew. In the course of his medical examination, the optician was called out of the room, perhaps rather conveniently. Bassett leapt to his feet and memorised the second and third lines from the bottom of the chart. He passed, and was posted to Canada, where he took his air navigator's course at Port Albert in Ontario and his general reconnaissance course at Prince Edward Island. On his return home he was posted to 404 Squadron.

A month after Bassett's arrival, the Wick Strike Wing was formed. This consisted of 404 Squadron, commanded by Wing Commander C.A. 'Chuck' Willis, and 144 Squadron, commanded by Wing Commander David O.F. Lumsden. 144 Squadron was primarily a Torbeau squadron and had spent a couple of months in that role during the summer in the Mediterranean; prior to that, during the summer of 1942, a large detachment had operated from northern Russia in torpedo-carrying Hampdens.

The operational circumstances for the Wick Wing were in many ways different from those of the North Coates Wing. Although there were fewer enemy fighters defending the Norwegian coast than the Dutch, there was no chance of RAF single-engined fighters accompanying the Wick Wing on its far longer sorties. The only fighter capable of doing so was the Mustang, but there was not a single squadron of these long-range aircraft available in north-east Scotland at that stage. Another major problem was the difficulty of dropping torpedoes in the confined spaces of the fjords and most of the Leads. The Wick Wing was forced to seek its own solutions to these problems.

Fighter escort was usually flown by the cannon-firing Beaufighters of 404 Squadron, although sometimes the aircraft of 144 Squadron were employed in that capacity; the pilots were compelled to tackle the German single-engined fighters if need be. Maximum use was made of cloud cover, whilst R/T silence was essential on the way out. The pilots tried to deliver their attacks whilst flying away from the nearest enemy aerodrome, in the hope that the Me 109s and the

FW 190s would not be alerted quickly enough to catch them. Where torpedoes could not be used, rockets were employed. 144 Squadron was not fitted with rocket rails, but the pilots of 404 Squadron seem to have been the first to appreciate fully the lethal properties of the solid-shot 25 lb warhead and to use it primarily to *sink* enemy merchant vessels and their escorts, rather than merely damage superstructure with 60 lb high-explosive warheads.

The first attack by the Wick Wing was successful. On 22 November six Torbeaus of 144 Squadron escorted by eight cannon-firing Beaufighters of 404 Squadron attacked a convoy off Stadlandet. They sank the Norwegian merchant vessel *Arcturus* of 1,651 tons and badly damaged two others, the *Gol* of 985 tons and the *Kari Louise* of 800 tons. No aircraft was shot down, although a Torbeau was forced to ditch with engine trouble on the way back.

One of Bassett's introductions to operational flying was hair-raising. On 30 November, Shulemson was piloting one of five aircraft from his squadron which were attacking a convoy off Sogne fjord with 25 lb rockets when his Beaufighter was hit in the starboard wing and fuselage by 20 mm shells fired by an M-class minesweeper. Shulemson had trimmed his aircraft nose-heavy for the attack and one of the shells severed the control wire. He could not pull his aircraft out of the dive until Bassett rushed forward and helped him to heave back the control column. They flew back to Wick with some difficulty. The same shell killed their homing pigeon, rather unpleasantly, a bird that Basset liked and had dubbed 'Binder'. These pigeons had been known to save the lives of downed airmen, and the Canadians awarded poor Binder a mock DFC in a mock ceremony that evening.

In addition to their new function as a Strike Wing, the crews of the two squadrons were still required to fly on reconnaissances and as escorts for naval vessels. Some of the operations that the Beaufighters protected were those carried out by the motor-torpedo boats of the Royal Navy and the Royal Norwegian Navy. These long-range MTBs, called Fairmile Ds, would lie in wait in rocky inlets along the Norwegian coast, cleverly camouflaged with nets simulating rocks or snow, and pounce on unsuspecting enemy vessels with their torpedoes and six-pounder guns. There were thirty men in a crew serving anti-aircraft weapons which included pompoms, Oerlikons and machine-guns. On 10 December, the Beaufighters of 404 Squadron were detailed to escort *MTB 684* of the Norwegian Navy on its return trip from near Sogne fjord to the

Shetlands. The first pair of Beaufighters, flown by Shulemson and Warrant Officer V.P. McCallan, took off from Wick at around 09.35 hours, heading for a point about fifty miles west of the entrance to the fjord.

Bassett navigated the two Beaufighters plumb on to the little ninety ton vessel and the pilots began circling at 500 feet, with 15° of flaps and at their lowest economical cruising speed.

'That's funny,' said Bassett, after a while. 'McCallan seems to be coming up on our tail.'

Shulemson jumped, for he could see McCallan ahead. There must be something else on their tail. He immediately brought his Beaufighter around in an Immelmann stall turn, brought up his flaps, rammed his throttles forward, gave his propellers full fine pitch, and swung his gunsight into position. It was certainly a twin-engined aircraft in front of Shulemson, but it was a Ju 88 and not a Beaufighter. Evidently the captain of the Junkers preferred not to be at the business end of a Beaufighter; he must have realized that his adversary was able to outfly him, for he corkscrewed violently to escape, with Shulemson doing his best to bring his gunsight to bear on him. At one stage, the Junkers passed underneath the Beaufighter, flying to port.

'Take a shot at him, Peter!' called Shulemson.

Bassett opened fire enthusiastically from the navigator's cupola. He was armed with a .303 belt-fed Browning, a gun that was not altogether suitable as a free-handling weapon, for the movement could cause the belt of cartridges to jam in the breech. Moreover, Bassett had had no training whatsoever as an air gunner; it is unlikely that his tracer did more than startle the enemy. Eventually, Shulemson was able to manoeuvre his Beaufighter on to the tail of the Junkers and pressed his firing button. He could see his cannon shells striking home. The rear gunner, who was probably hit, did not reply. Nevertheless, the German was lucky, for he reached cloud at 1,000 feet and disappeared. Shulemson was tempted to hunt further and finish him off, but he knew that his first duty lay with the motor-torpedo boat; he returned to the little vessel and resumed circling. Bassett flashed a message to the Norwegians with his Aldis lamp, and a lamp flickered in reply. The Beaufighter men were congratulated and were invited to join the crew for drinks in Lerwick, an invitation that Shulemson was able to accept two days later.

Bassett enjoyed the companionship of the informal but determined Canadians. Like many other wartime RAF men, he now looks back at the unselfish atmosphere of those days with nostalgia. He had to endure some good-humoured leg-pulling, and one of his responses was to tell Shulemson that he had decided to levy a charge for every navigational course that he calculated. Both men had had some background in book-keeping. As the account built up, Shulemson would sometimes refuse to alter course immediately, saying that he could not afford to do so. Later in 1944, however, Bassett was to work out a course that would have led the Wing into the balloon barrage at Plymouth; Shulemson imposed a fine which he multiplied by the number of aircraft that he was leading, thus wiping the slate clean.

December 1943 was not a particularly successful month for Wing strikes, the most notable being on the 22nd when nine Beaufighters came across a destroyer escorting a U-boat off Egersund and went in to attack. Two Beaufighters were shot down but *U-1062*, a type VIIF U-boat of 1,084 tons, was damaged.

By the beginning of 1944, the Wick Wing was operating as a well-drilled entity. The first attack of the year was on 14 January, when eight Torbeaus of 144 Squadron with nine rocket-firing Beaufighters of 404 Squadron attacked a string of two convoys off Lister. They sank two large German merchant vessels, the *Wittekind* of 4,029 tons and the *Entrerios* of 5,179 tons, and seriously damaged the Norwegian *Maurita* of 1,569 tons. The two sunken vessels took 69 men and 15,600 tons of iron ore to the bottom of the sea. Me 109s harried the attackers and three Beaufighters were lost.

The second attack was on 20 January, an occasion on which there were no Torbeaus. Six cannon-firing Beaufighters of 144 Squadron escorted six of 404 Squadron armed with 60 lb rockets to an attack on a convoy off Stadlandet. They hit the German merchant vessel *Emsland* of 5,170 tons and set her on fire. She was beached and broke up soon afterwards; 60 lb rockets seldom caused a vessel to sink immediately but could cause complete destruction if the fire in the upperworks could not be controlled. There was no loss to the attackers.

The Germans now had cause for alarm with the additional threat to their coastal traffic from the Wick Wing. There is evidence that the Reichskommissar for Schifffahrt, Karl Kaufmann*, was coming under severe strain. There was a limit to the improvements and

---

* See Chapter I, p. 25.

rationalization of the German merchant fleet that Kaufmann could effect. He began to fall from grace with Hitler. Under the Reichskommissar, Rudolf Blohm had been responsible for a new ship-building programme. During 1943, work had begun on twenty-four ships of the 3,000 ton class. By December, only three of these vessels had been completed, although four more were being fitted out. The programme could not keep pace with the rate of sinkings. The unfortunate Blohm thought that the task was beyond him and resigned his position. From this time to the end of the War, the number of merchant vessels available to the Germans shrank steadily, until it almost reached vanishing point.

On 26 January, Shulemson took off on a flight that was to establish him as one of the most notable Canadians to fly in the Second World War. At about 09.15 hours, twelve Beaufighters took off from Wick to attack a convoy off Stadlandet, a favourite point for the Beaufighters since along this stretch of coast the convoys did not have the protection of the numerous outer islands of the Skerries. There were six aircraft of 144 Squadron armed with cannon, acting as anti-flak escort, together with six of 404 Squadron armed with both cannon and 60 lb rockets. The formation comprised two sub-sections, named Red and Green, each section containing both anti-flak and rocket-firing Beaufighters. The Green leader was the Strike leader, chosen irrespective of rank as the most experienced for the task ahead. On this occasion, Shulemson led, even though Wing Commander Lumsden was flying in a Beaufighter of 144 Squadron; Lumsden was an experienced torpedo pilot rather than an anti-flak or rocket projectile leader at this stage in his operational career.

The Beaufighters headed north-west to their target, skimming just above the sea in a large vic, the formation most favoured by the Wick Wing for only twelve aircraft. Bassett was navigating the Wing to Storholmen on the Norwegian coast, about ninety minutes away. The days were short in mid-winter, with few daylight hours available over the target area. Half-way across, a Beaufighter began to climb rapidly on the port side, turning back to the Scottish coast. Then morse from the aircraft began to chatter over the W/T. Shulemson had difficulty in restraining his fury. Maybe the pilot did have engine trouble, but the Germans had built radar installations high on the Norwegian hills, capable of picking up signals of all aircraft save those flying at sea level. Now the German fighters would probably be alerted. There would be a reckoning with that stupid and irresponsible pilot, if they got back to Wick.

The remaining eleven Beaufighters made landfall at Storholmen and turned south-east, hunting down the Norwegian coast. Shulemson first saw the German convoy when they were flying at 500 feet off Stadlandet. At 11.32 hours, he gave the order to attack.

The convoy was a small one, headed north-east. There were three merchant vessels: the Norwegian *Finse* of 1,618 tons, the German *Orland* of 1,289 tons, and the Norwegian *Klöveren* of 428 tons. Guarding them on the seaward side were three escort vessels: the submarine-chaser *UJ 1702* in the lead, followed by the mine-sweeper *M.154*, with the flak-ship *Vp 5908* in the rear. All these escort vessels were heavily armed, but this was the first time that the Wick Wing had encountered the *Drahtseilrakete*, or cable-carrying rocket. *UJ 1702* fired off five of these rockets at the diving Beaufighters. The aircraft split either side of these strange objects, the crews watching the yellow parachutes descending slowly, with the yellow mines dangling from the cables. The crews of the convoy pumped their flak into the sky. They later claimed that they saw two Beaufighters crash in flames, but only one was slightly hit, flown by Flying Officer Jimmy Keefe. The escort ships suffered badly.

By now, the pilots of the Wick Wing knew their business. Their reflector sights were adapted so that the range bars could be set to the estimated length of a ship. At 265 knots in a twelve degree dive, the pilots opened fire at 1,000 yards, their cannon being harmonized so that if they aimed at the ship's bridge their murderous fire would spread along the decks. At 400 yards, they released their 60 lb high-explosive rockets in salvo. *UJ 1702* was the first to be hit, her superstructure being peppered with cannon shells whilst two of her crew were wounded. *M.154* received the same treatment, although her war diary has been lost, so that there is no record of the damage. *Vp 5908* suffered the worst; her ready-to-use locker containing 88 mm ammunition was hit by cannon fire and exploded, putting the gun out of action; then two rockets penetrated her engine room and exploded; finally a Beaufighter machine-gunned her bridge whilst two more rockets failed to explode and bounced off her side into the sea. Two of her crew were killed and eleven wounded. She went out of control, on fire and making water.

UJ 1702 went to the assistance of the stricken flak-ship whilst

M.154 continued with the convoy, but it was to be three days before a salvage vessel could tow *Vp 5908* into the port of Aalesund. There is no record of damage to the merchant vessels, although several of the Beaufighter crews reported hits on them.

The attack took place from the sea, the Beaufighters then turning at mast height northwards well out of range. Cannon-firing upset aircraft compasses, so the pilots normally turned north for a few seconds and fired another short burst to correct the compass error before heading back to base. However, Shulemson turned south instead of north, for he had another plan. He knew that the *Emsland* was beached and broken in two a few miles south. He had taken part in the attack six days earlier, and his Beaufighter had been hit by flak. Now he wanted to inspect and photograph the wreck, bringing the evidence back with him.

As the ten Beaufighters streaked over the sea away from the shore, four Me 109s pounced on them. Their first victim was a Beaufighter of 404 Squadron flown by Flying Officer John A.C. Dixon of Alberta, which was sent crashing into the sea, killing both the pilot and his navigator, Sergeant Eric Pearce. Meanwhile, as Shulemson was flying over the wreck of the *Emsland*, shore-based batteries opened up on him. His Beaufighter received a few shrapnel holes, which were fortunately not serious. Shulemson turned and flew after the remainder of the formation, converging on them from the east but unaware of the air battle in progress.

'What on earth's that on our port?' Shulemson suddenly asked Bassett as he spotted aircraft milling about some four miles away.

'Goddamn it! 109s!' he shouted a few moments later, after he had turned towards the aicraft. Two Me 109s had fastened on to a Beaufighter of 144 Squadron, flown by Flying Officer B.A. Sansom; they were ripping holes in the fuselage and wings with their machine guns and cannon. As Shulemson approached, one of the Messerschmitts turned back to Norway, but the other persisted in his attack. Shulemson did not hesitate; he was the Wing Leader, and the aircraft were his responsibility. He closed in and at 600 yards fired a burst to attract the attention of the German pilot, who immediately turned towards the impudent 'Tommi'.

Then began a grim and unequal duel. Shulemson flew in as tight a circle as possible, with the Messerschmitt trying to turn inside him and close on the tail of the Beaufighter. Each time the German lined up for the attack, Bassett shouted a warning and Shulemson flipped

Rockets fitted on the rails of a Beaufighter of 404 Squadron, slightly angled to give a spread when firing in salvo. This Beaufighter is painted with the black and white stripes of the Allied Expeditionary Force.

Flying Officer Sydney S. Shulemson (left) and Flying Officer Peter R. Bassett (right), photographed soon after Shulemson was awarded a DSO in February 1944.

his Beaufighter around, so that the circling began in the other direction. At one point, Bassett was able to fire a short burst from his .303 Browning, without apparent effect. He could see the yellow nose and the black crosses on the Messerschmitt; it was an Me 109G – called the 'Gustav' by the Luftwaffe pilots. There was heavy cloud at 4,000 feet. Shulemson managed to climb and enter a rain cloud, but when he flew out again the Me 109 was still there. The duel began again.

Shulemson had applied himself attentively on an air firing course only eleven days before, brushing up the skill acquired on his previous training. This was called a 'Fighter Affiliation' course, during which the Beaufighter pilots fired at drogues towed by single-engined fighters, simulating aerial combat. Once he had hit the wire of the drogue, snapping it. Now his knowledge and skill paid off. During the encounter, he was able to evade the Messerschmitt continually, although the German managed to fire six bursts at the Beaufighter, hitting the tail wheel and the rear fuselage. Some bullets slammed into the armoured doors behind Bassett. Eventually, the German pilot must have used up his fuel or his ammunition, for he turned back to Norway.

Bassett split open two tins of orange juice with the aircraft axe, handing one to Shulemson, together with a ration of sandwiches. The navigator had a reputation for being permanently hungry. Shulemson never had to call out to him, 'Waiter, where's my snack?' in the manner of other Canadian pilots after combat. They came in gingerly to the approach and landing at Wick, not knowing quite what to expect from the damage that they had received. All was well apart from the bumpy effect from the damaged tail wheel. They were the last to land. The other aircrew, who had been eating their eggs and bacon, hurried out to the runway to greet them. Men who had saved the lives of their comrades deserved honour and respect.

Back in Montreal, Shulemson's parents heard that their son had been awarded a decoration, but Rebecca Shulemson was far from pleased.

'How is it that our son has only got this Distinguished Service Order?' she demanded of her husband Saul. 'Some of the other boys are getting the Distinguished Flying Cross. This is discrimination by the 'Goyim' against a Jewish boy!'

Patiently, Saul explained that not only was the DSO a higher award than the DFC, but it was rarely given to such junior officers. But Rebecca need not have worried in any event. Before the war was over, Sydney Shulemson would pin up the ribbon of the DFC behind his DSO, just as Peter Bassett would pin up the DFC in front of his Mention in Despatches.

CHAPTER FIVE

Blockade Runner

He wants worth that dare not praise a foe.
John Dryden (1631–1700)

'*Auf wiedersehen!*' The three German destroyers signalled to the *Pietro Orseolo*, before turning and sailing back to the Gironde. The blockade runner was left without escorts, heading for her second war cruise to the Far East. She was an astonishingly lucky vessel, having made a successful eighty-four day run from Kobe in Japan to Bordeaux in the Gironde; this was from 2 December 1941, during the period when the war spread in a blaze across the Pacific. On 2 October 1942, a day after leaving Bordeaux, she was now headed once more for Japan, ready to sail half-way round the world and back again, evading the vigilance of the Allied navies and air forces.

The *Pietro Orseolo*, an Italian freighter of 6,344 tons named after a former Doge of Venice, had been built in 1939 by Cantieri dell' Adriatico of Monfalcone. She was 470 feet in length and had recently been equipped with radar, smoke-making apparatus, a 105 mm gun, two 20 mm cannon, and two machine guns. Her captain was a civilian master called Tarchioni who had been given the rank of Tenente di Vascello (Lieutenant) in the Regia Navale (Italian Royal Navy). He was a skilful, wily and courageous seaman. He commanded a crew of 67, 42 of whom were Italian sailors. The remainder were 21 Italian soldiers and 4 German sailors, trained to serve the ship's specialized equipment and armament. The vessel had been rigged with an extensive telephone system for the lookouts, and special blasting charges for rapid scuttling in an emergency. She was carrying armament for re-stocking U-boats, but her most valuable cargo was destined for Japan and consisted of machinery, aircraft in crates, mercury in cylinders, and sacks of potassium nitrate; this amounted to 3,000 tons in all.

The Japanese occupation of Malaysia, Singapore and the Dutch East Indies had brought a new dimension to Germany's part in the global war. Japan needed some of Germany's products, but Germany was desperate for something that the Japanese could now supply – natural rubber. Since before the First World War, Germany had made great efforts to produce a synthetic general-purpose rubber. Some years before 1939, her scientists had evolved a substitute which they called 'Buna S', the 'Bu' standing for the gas butadiene and the 'Na' for natrium, or sodium, the catalyst used in the process of polymerization. However, the result was not a particularly successful substitute and required blending with a certain amount of natural rubber for use as tyres in the German war machine. Thus, natural rubber was described by the Germans as 'worth its weight in gold'. The *Pietro Orseolo* was one of the vessels ordered to supply this vital product.

Tarchioni set course for the central Atlantic. He passed north of the Azores before turning south-east for a position over 500 miles south of the Cape of Good Hope. The seas were almost empty, apart from Allied vessels sailing in convoy. An occasional blip showed up on the radar screen and Tarchioni altered course adroitly, just enough to pass out of sight but not so abruptly as to arouse suspicion. On 25 October, the *Pietro Orseolo* entered the Indian Ocean and, buffeted by westerly gales, turned east-north-east for Indonesia. She was a fairly fast vessel, able to cruise at about twelve knots. Thirteen days later, the captain turned north for the narrow and dangerous Straits of Sunda, between Sumatra and Java, where US submarines were known to lie in wait. On 10 November, with the crew on full alert, the blockade runner passed through these Straits, leaving the volcanic island of Krakatoa on her starboard. Two days later, the crew recorded that they could smell the spices and fragrances of Indonesia and watch the wheeling of petrels, when they docked outside Djakarta.

At Djakarta, the Japanese requested Tarchioni to sail to Singapore – or Shonanko, as they had renamed it after their occupation – and the *Pietro Orseolo* arrived there five days later. The blockade runners sometimes operated commercially in the Far East, earning Japanese yen to help pay for the rubber. The *Pietro Orseolo* loaded an additional cargo of scrap iron, naphtha, and bales of wool. On 22 November, she set off for Japan. In the South China seas, on the night of 26 November, she narrowly escaped disaster when she almost collided with an American submarine on the surface, but she managed to elude her adversary in the darkness. She arrived in Kobe five days after this incident and off-loaded her cargo.

In Kobe, the *Pietro Orseolo* was modified to take on board ninety extra passengers, mainly German military personnel who were being repatriated. This work lasted for nearly seven weeks; it was not until 25 January 1943 that the Italian ship left Japan for the reverse course of her outward voyage. Four days later, she sighted a submarine on the surface not far from her encounter two months previously, but Tarchioni avoided the danger by steaming away at full speed. By 3 February, the blockade runner had arrived in Singapore, where she loaded 5,500 tons of natural rubber. The enormous value of this cargo may be assessed by comparing it with the quantity of Buna S which Germany had produced in 1939 – 25,000 tons. Now she had to return safely with the precious contents of her holds.

The next part of the reverse course was back to Djakarta to replenish her fuel and water tanks. On 16 February the *Pietro Orseolo* left this Indonesian port for the long and lonely journey home. Passing once more through the Straits of Sunda, she headed south but, after several days sailing, was forced to alter course to avoid a large convoy headed for Australia. Then she navigated the southern reaches of the Indian Ocean, passed the meridian of the Cape of Good Hope, and entered the southern Atlantic. The horizons were bare of shipping as she headed north-west and finally turned eastwards to her home port of Bordeaux.

On 30 March she was met by the German U-boat *U-161*. The *Pietro Orseolo* was not the only blockade runner to be making this journey and the Kriegsmarine had prepared a sea operation to receive and protect them, under the code-name of Arno. Another U-boat, *U-147*, was to meet the *Karin* and the *Irene*, both headed for Bordeaux from Japan, whilst other blockade runners were headed direct for Germany via a northern route and the Denmark Straits. The purpose of the meetings was to supply the returning vessels with new radar equipment called *Metox*, a device which had recently been installed in U-boats and gave warning of the approach of Allied aircraft by picking up their radar transmissions. This equipment would not prevent an attack but would alert the defences so that the gunners would be ready, almost in ambush.

The following day, the *Pietro Orseolo* was met off Cape Finisterre by four German destroyers of the 8th Zerstörer-Flotille based in the Gironde, commanded by Kapitän zur See Erdenger. These were Z23, Z24, Z32 and Z37, and they had reached a point so far from the French coast that at first Tarchioni thought they must be British.

With these powerful escorts, the *Pietro Orseolo* began the last lap of her journey, at full speed.

At 03.42 hours the following morning, a lookout on the blockade runner spotted the wakes of three torpedoes running towards her starboard beam. Although it was only just first light, the sea was so fluorescent that the wakes could be seen. The vigilant Tarchioni steered hard to port and two of the torpedoes passed by the vessel, but the third struck the starboard beam at an acute angle. There was a colossal explosion and a plume of water rose to 300 feet.

It was an American submarine that had finally caught the Italian blockade runner, only seventy sea miles from her destination. The USS *Shad*, cruising near the Spanish coast on her third war patrol, had decoded a message three and a half hours previously. An aircraft had spotted the German flotilla steaming eastwards at about seventeen knots, and the *Shad* had been ordered to intercept. The captain, Lieutenant-Commander E.J. MacGregor, surfaced his submarine and steered northwards, also at seventeen knots, to reach his target before the vessels reached shallow waters. He picked up five blips on his radar at 02.00 hours and manoeuvred at full speed, about nineteen knots, to find a favourable position for the attack. The night was very dark, without a horizon, and he was operating entirely by radar. He could pick out the larger blip of the merchant vessel, but was worried about his highly fluorescent bow wave, which might have been seen by the enemy. The nearest destroyer was only 2,000 yards range when he fired all six bow tubes. A minute later, there were two terrific explosions, followed by three more soon afterwards. The *Shad* then fired two more torpedoes from her after tubes, and a further succession of explosions was heard. There was now only one destroyer moving on the radar screen. MacGregor concluded that he must have hit or sunk four vessels, but he was now near dangerously shallow water and was forced to turn away.

Although MacGregor had made a skilful attack, for which he was awarded a British DSC, the results fell short of his hopes. The American torpedoes were armed with magnetic pistols which were apt to explode prematurely. The only vessel hit was the *Pietro Orseolo*, and she did not sink. A great hole was blown in Number 2 hold and bales of rubber began to float out of the aperture into the sea. However, the watertight compartments held, and before long Tarchioni was able to resume his journey at almost the same speed.

The destroyers stopped to pick up the precious bales of rubber, but the five vessels set course again for the Gironde, their track marked by further bales of rubber bobbing in the waves. At 11.45 hours on the same day, the *Pietro Orseolo* entered the port of Le Verdon, the first haven in the Gironde.

Eleven thousand bales of rubber, amounting to 1,500 tons, were lost from the side of the blockade runner. The next day notices appeared in the local newspapers, and posters were pasted up by the Feldgendarmerie. These offered substantial rewards for the recovery of the bales, and before long eager French citizens were making small fortunes. Most of the lost bales were recovered, some by these treasure-seekers and some by the Kriegsmarine, so that finally 5,100 tons of natural rubber went into the German war industry. However, both the *Karin* and the *Irene* were sunk, scuttled on interception by Allied warships. So far in 1943, nine blockade runners had attempted the passage from Japan; four of these had turned back, four had been sunk, and only the damaged *Pietro Orseolo* had reached her destination. One has to admire the ingenuity and courage of the Italian master and his crew, but the Allies knew that this loophole would have to be closed. The *Pietro Orseolo* could be repaired. When the blockade-running season began in the long nights of the next winter, she would be ready to go again.

Admiral Theodor Krancke, the officer commanding Marinegruppenkommando West (Naval Group West), was a man beset with many problems in November 1943. His area of command stretched along the Belgian and French coastlines as far as Bayonne on the Spanish border. The heady days of victory and exultation were over. U-boats operating from western France were being sunk with grim regularity. The ports from which they operated were being hammered almost nightly by the RAF and USAAF; although their bombs could not penetrate the roofs of the colossal concrete shelters built for U-boats, vast tracts of the dock areas of Brest, Lorient, St Nazaire and La Pallice lay in ruins.

Now Krancke had to organize another season of blockade running. The Führer expected the results to be a great deal better than those of the previous winter, but the enemy seemed to be fully aware of the German intentions. So far, the blockade runners had always used the Gironde estuary as their haven, loading and unloading at Bordeaux. In the Atlantic, the navies of the 'Tommis' and the 'Amis'* lay in wait, ready to pounce on the almost defence-less merchantmen. It was time to re-think his tactics and to try to foil the vigilance of this powerful enemy. Perhaps the best plan would be to disperse the blockade runners along the French coast and risk the danger of air attack. In the areas to the north-east of his command, along the Dutch and Norwegian coast-lines, special squadrons of Beaufighters were taking a fearful toll of German-controlled shipping and their Kriegsmarine escorts, but fortunately these Strike Wings had not been seen in Krancke's western area. The high level bombers over the French ports rarely hit merchant vessels. Dispersal was the best plan.

Surprisingly, there were few deep-water ports in western France capable of accommodating deep-draught vessels. Apart from Bordeaux, only Brest and La Pallice were suitable. Brest was too near the English aerodromes, whilst it could be dangerous to crowd many of the blockade runners into La Pallice. Deep-water anchorages were the only answer, outside the main ports. Krancke selected two; the first in the roads of Concarneau, to the south of the peninsula of Brittany that jutted out into the Atlantic; the other off the Ile de Groix, about six miles from the port of Lorient.

Italy had surrendered to the Allies on 7 September 1943. Tenente di Vascello Tarchioni, the skilful master of the *Pietro Orseolo*, had been ousted from his position by the Germans, for Italians were no longer to be trusted; he might even steer his precious vessel and cargo straight into the arms of the Allies. The Italian vessel had been taken over by Hansa and her crew replaced with German sailors. After loading her cargo at Bordeaux she was ordered to anchor in deep water off Port-Tudy, a small tunny-fishing port on the wild and indented north-west coast of the Ile de Groix. She was given the code-name of Eifel.

Krancke's planning was to no avail. The French Atlantic ports and coastline had been kept under constant surveillance by PRU during the summer and autumn of 1943. By November, air reconnaissance and the French Resistance confirmed that eight blockade runners were preparing to leave for the Far East. Moreover, five other vessels were known to be ready to make the homeward run. Under the naval Commander-in-Chief at Plymouth, Allied naval and air forces were detailed to find and destroy these important vessels during the forthcoming season of blockade-running.

---

*   British and Americans.

On 26 November, a PRU Spitfire spotted the *Pietro Orseolo* in her new anchorage. German destroyers were also seen in the nearby port of Concarneau on the mainland. For the next few days bad weather prevented further reconnaissance, but on 29 November the *Pietro Orseolo* was seen to be in the same position, although the destroyers had gone. The Italian vessel was designated a 'Class I' target by the Admiralty and arrangements were made to attack her as soon as the weather permitted. The task of bombing the ship was given to the only squadron immediately available; this was 487 (RNZAF) Squadron, part of the Second Tactical Air Force, equipped with Mosquito VIs and based at Sculthorpe in Norfolk. Three Mosquitoes flew down to Predannack on 30 November, to link up with eight Typhoon IBs of 266 (Rhodesia) Squadron and four Typhoon IBs of 193 Squadron. The fighters were based at Harrowbeer and were part of 10 Group, Air Defence Great Britain.

The attack was made the following day. Only one of the Mosquitoes, flown by Squadron Leader A.S. Cussens, managed to take off on time; it was armed with four 500 lb general-purpose bombs fitted with eleven-second delay fuses. Escorted by the twelve Typhoons, Cussens flew just above sea level round the peninsula of Brittany to the target; the four aircraft of 193 Squadron were in the lead whilst those of 266 Squadron guarded the flanks. As they neared the Ile de Groix, the Typhoon pilots spotted a *Mausiflugzeug*, a Ju 88 fitted with a large mine-exploding ring, flying at 300 feet; three Rhodesians broke away to attack, shooting the unlucky German aircraft down into the sea. Cussens made a low-level attack on the *Pietro Orseolo* but his bombs fell short. Tracer arced up from several M-class minesweepers as well as the blockade runner; the Mosquito was hit and crashed into the sea. Meanwhile the Typhoon pilots also attacked, each with four 20 mm cannon, raking the Italian vessel and one of the minesweepers. On their way back, the fighters found and destroyed a Ju 88, but one Typhoon was lost and another pilot was rescued after baling out near the English coast.

The *Pietro Orseolo* suffered superficial damage, over sixty cannon shells having hit her bridge and deck, killing one sailor. In a further attempt to conceal her departure, Krancke ordered the vessel to move to the alternative anchorage off Concarneau, where on 11 December she joined another blockade runner called the *Ida*, a vessel of 6,131 tons. The two merchant vessels were protected by the fire power of six M-class minesweepers of the 24th Flotilla, but there were no torpedo nets available nor were there sufficient gun platforms to strengthen the shore defences. In the continued bad weather, the move of the *Pietro Orseolo* was not detected by PRU.

Wing Commander F.E. 'Monty' Burton, the commanding officer of 248 Squadron, was not altogether happy with the tasks on which his Beaufighter TFXs were employed. For nearly a year, his aircraft had operated from Predannack, on fighter patrols over the Bay of Biscay. Usually they carried long-range tanks, hunting for Ju 88s and Focke-Wulf Kondors. They were not fitted with machine guns, bomb racks or rocket rails, but relied solely on their four cannon. There was plenty of wearisome flying but rarely any action, although the pilots had bagged a few Ju 88s in the course of the year. There was more boredom than fighting. Burton, who looked with envy on his counterparts in the North Coates and Wick Strike Wings, was delighted when he learned that his squadron was scheduled to attack the *Pietro Orseolo*. He was fascinated to hear that a detachment of Torbeaus from 254 Squadron from North Coates would join his squadron in the strike against the Italian vessel. For a few weeks at least, there would be some excitement with the formation of a temporary Strike Wing at Predannack.

Burton's career in the RAF had been remarkably adventurous. He was aged twenty-six years and had entered the RAF with a short-service commission in January 1936. On the outbreak of war, he was flying Hudsons in 224 Squadron, based at Leuchars. He had shared with two other Hudsons in the destruction of a Do 18 flying boat on 8 October 1939, the first German aircraft shot down by the RAF during the war.* Awarded a DFC, he had been posted to Number Two Camouflage Unit at Heston in March 1940. Then he had flown a Lockheed 14 to Habbaniya in Iraq and from there had carried out two momentous flights, photographing the Russian oilfields and refineries at Baku and Batum in the Caucasus. Stemming from these flights, the British and French had prepared plans to bomb the installations. These plans were captured by the Germans after the fall of France; they can still cause embarrassment, even though the Russians were supplying Germany at the time. Burton was a man who fretted when life was too quiet.

---

* A Do 18 had been shot down earlier, on 26 September 1939, by Lt B.S. McEwan of 803 (FAA) Squadron, flying a Skua from the *Ark Royal*.

Had they been aware of Burton's enthusiasm for the forth-coming strike, few of the crews of 254 Squadron would have shared in his pleasure. It was not the prospect of danger that worried the men, for they were not aware of the purpose of their move to Pre-dannack; most of them had been on detachment so many times that they often referred to their squadron as the 254th Light Foot. What the men disliked was the fact that they had to leave North Coates. Flying from the aerodrome was dangerous, but in many ways it was one of the happiest stations in the RAF. The close co-operation of the squadrons of the Strike Wing created an atmosphere of unselfishness that those who survived would be unlikely to encoun-ter in peace time. The men were proud of their part in the RAF, even though the convoys along the Dutch coast were less in evidence since the summer. One of the squadrons had been posted away; in August, 143 Squadron had gone to Cornwall where it was engaged on fighter patrols over the Bay of Biscay. But 236 and 254 Squadrons continued to roam the Dutch coast in search of targets. Often the Torbeaus patrolled singly at night, for convoys had become a rarity during the day. The numbers of sinkings had declined, but the Strike Wing was sill making life very difficult for German sailors.

In particular, it was the possibility of being away from North Coates over Christmas that bothered the aircrews, especially the NCOs. Some of the men even took the view that it would be sport-ing to suspend the war for a day or two during the festive season. The food in their messes was excellent by wartime standards, and they were looking forward to their turkey dinner and Christmas pudding. There were also the attractions of the friendly pubs of Grimsby as well as dance halls where local girls were by no means averse to the sight of men in RAF uniform. This was the mood of the men of the Torbeaus who arrived at Predannack on 13 December 1943, led by their CO, Wing Commander A.W. Darley Miller, a pre-war officer with a permanent commission. Miller and Burton, who knew each other, discussed the proposed strike in detail, for they had been ordered to take off the following day. At this stage, it was thought that the blockade runner was still lying off the Ile de Groix. Enthusiastic as he was, Burton realized that he and his squadron were not trained as part of a Strike Wing. He suggested that Miller should lead the anti-flak section, leaving Squadron Leader F. T. Gardiner to lead the Torbeaus. There would be four cannon-firing Beaufighters escorting four Torbeaus, but no single-engined fighters were available. They would have to take advantage of the low cloud and bad weather to make a surprise attack. Burton would fly as Number Two.

The next day, the formation of eight Beaufighters took off on time, flying around the peninsula to the Ile de Groix. As they neared the target, the weather changed abruptly and they flew into winter sunshine. Reluctantly, Miller obeyed orders and turned the formation back to Predannack; it would have been folly to have continued, for the Beaufighters were within easy reach of the German fighter bases on the mainland. Three days later, the two squadrons tried again, mustering fourteen Beaufighters on this occasion; precisely the same weather conditions were encountered, so that once again the frustrated pilots were forced to return to Predannack.

It was evident to Miller that in the prevailing weather conditions his small Strike Wing must have fighter cover. But then the *Pietro Orseolo* was located off Concarneau by PRU. Events began to move quickly. A strike was ordered for the following day, 18 December. It was decided that this time the Wing must attack irrespective of weather conditions. A squadron of fighter escorts was alerted.

Some of the Typhoon pilots of 183 Squadron, also based at Predannack, had no doubts about the best choice of route to the target. The sea route to Concarneau and back could exhaust their fuel, expecially if they were involved in lengthy dog-fights with German fighters. It would be far preferable, they considered, if the formation flew straight across the peninsula of Brittany. This would have the added advantage of enticing the German fighters to come up and attack, thus giving the Typhoon pilots a chance to demonstrate to the Beaufighter boys that they could shoot down the enemy. Patiently, the Torbeau pilots explained that, much as they admired the aggressive behaviour of fighter pilots, the Strike Wing tactics were to attempt to execute a surprise attack rather than to fly deliberately into a hornet's nest. The crews were briefed to fly around the peninsula and to attack from the south-west, Squadron Leader Dring, the CO of 183 Squadron, would lead an escort of eight Typhoons.

One of the most experienced crews in 254 Squadron consisted of two flight sergeants, Thomas A. Cochrane and Frederick L. Hinks. Tom Cochrane, a 23-year-old Lancastrian, had joined the RAF as a trainee pilot in 1940. He had trained in Southern Rhodesia and South Africa, including a course at the School of General Reconnaissance at George in Cape Province. During September 1942 he had crewed up with Fred Hinks at the Beaufighter OTU at Crosby-on-Eden, near Carlisle. Fred Hinks, a Warwickshire man, was a few days short of his twenty-second birthday. He had joined the RAF as an air observer, but had first trained as a wireless operator at Cranwell. This was followed by courses on navigation, bombing and gunnery at Staverton near Cheltenham and at Stormy Down in South Wales. Then came the School of General Reconnaissance at Squires Gate and the OTU. The two men had joined 254 Squadron at North Coates in December 1942, but had next been sent on torpedo courses at Gosport and at Tain. By the time of the attack on the blockade runner, they were both highly trained and operationally experienced.

The Wing assembled at Predannack and took off at around 11.00 hours. There were six Torbeaus and six anti-flak Beaufighters, with the eight Typhoon escorts. The weather was typical of the Atlantic in winter. Low grey clouds scudded just above the surface of the sea. There was a heavy swell, with spume streaking in a strong wind from the tops of the white caps. The formation flew at about thirty feet, and the pilots were compelled to spread out loosely, with the Typhoons guarding the flanks and rear. Monty Burton kept in sight of Darley Miller, looking forward to using his cannon on this occasion. Tom Cochrane looked out of the side window at the Typhoons as they flew in and out of fragmented cloud and rain squalls. He admired the Typhoon pilots, flying all that way without navigational aids, guided solely by the Beaufighters; they had only a single engine apiece, and one piece of German metal in the coolant system would bring the pilot down into the bitterly cold ocean. As usual, Fred Hinks said little, listening to his wireless receiver and trying to follow the courses flown by Miller.

The formation flew in a series of short dog-legs around the French coast, as close as possible to conserve the fuel of the Typhoons but far enough away to keep beneath the German radar screen. The visibility worsened, making flying difficult even in this loose gaggle. Then they flew over a small fishing fleet, roaring just above the red sails of the tunny-boats. The experienced Torbeau men felt qualms of apprehension, for these little vessels could carry wireless sets and German guards. But the Wing left the French boats alone and turned north-east towards Concarneau.

As the aircraft approached the target area, they suddenly flew

new Torbeau, equipped
th a Mark XV torpedo,
ur cannon and eight
cket rails. This is a
eaufighter TFX.

Mark XV torpedo being
aded on a Torbeau.

Torbeau showing the
ve brakes in operation.
e tactics of diving from
gh level, then flattening
ut and making a torpedo
tack were not used by
e Strike Wings. Dive
akes were not normally
sed in the Beaufighters
the Strike Wings.

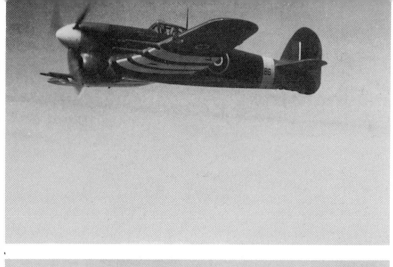

The Hawker Typhoon w
sometimes used as a
fighter escort for the St
Wing Beaufighters on
short-range attacks. Th
Typhoon carries the bla
and white stripes of the
Allied Expeditionary Air
Force, and is thus post
June 1944.

A Beaufighter Mark IC
248 Squadron. At the ti
of the attack on the *Pie*
Orseolo, the squadron
was equipped with the
Beaufighter TFX.

A French tunny boat in
Bay of Biscay. The aircr
flying over the boat is a
Bristol Beaufort I.

through the edge of the cloud bank, a dead straight line at right angles to their line of flight. Through a slight haze they could see the French coast ahead. The six anti-flak Beaufighters climbed to 1,500 feet, with the Typhoons buzzing around them. The navigation had been absolutely precise. The largest of the black dots ahead broadened into the shape of a motionless merchantman. There was another merchant vessel, slightly smaller, nearer the shore, with several minesweepers or flak-ships in attendance.

'Here we go again', thought Cochrane as he watched the familiar series of flashes that preceded the bursting of the heavier calibre flak fired by the minesweepers. He knew that the Jerries took about fifteen seconds to re-load and re-lay those guns. After the first salvo, a canny pilot could sometimes fly straight and level for a few seconds, then make a slow weave and watch the second salvo explode where the gunners thought that the Beaufighter would be. But little evasive action was possible in making a torpedo run. One just had to keep one's nerve and turn into the streams of light tracer that were beginning to hose-pipe towards them. The next series of lightning events would seem to happen in slow motion to an experienced operational pilot.

The Wing flew on until it was alongside the *Pietro Orseolo*, the anti-flak Beaufighters and the Torbeaus now strung out in two straight lines. Flak continued to burst around them.

'Attack attack attack!', said Miller. He turned and dived, followed by the delighted Burton. The Torbeaus wheeled and formed into three groups of the units known as 'fluid pairs'. When Cochrane had trained on torpedo work, the tactics had been different. The Torbeaus would fly at several thousand feet, manoeuvring ahead of the path of their target. Then they would dive down, a section for each bow and another from straight ahead, flatten out, fly straight and level, and try to release their torpedoes simultaneously so that the enemy vessel could not 'comb their tracks' The Beaufighters had been fitted with dive brakes, gadgets like inverted bellows in the wings, so that they could descend smoothly and gently. It was an excellent method – for the enemy gunners, who could pick them off, almost at their leisure. Now they operated in these pairs, hoping that the enemy gunners would be ducking away from the cannon fire of the anti-flak Beaufighters, at the precise time that they were lining up on their targets at close quarters.

The anti-flak Beaufighters swept over the *Pietro Orseolo* in a single ferocious pass. There were insufficient aircraft to tackle all the minesweepers, but some of the Typhoon pilots, who failed to find any German fighters, could not restrain themselves and joined in the attack. For the first time in his eventful career, Burton had an enemy vessel in his reflector sight. He pressed the cannon-firing button, ignoring the return fire, watching his shells dance along the superstructure of the blockade runner. A fire broke out on the bridge, as though he had hit some ammunition. He thought it was one of the greatest experiences of his life.

Cochrane could see no balloons, those additional occupational hazards for the crews of the Strike Wings. He watched the myriads of sparkles on the decks of the enemy vessels and the tracer that curved up slowly from them. Setting his controls to their maximum cruising mixture, he flew at 2,400 rpm straight for the target. The Torbeau was at 150 feet, flying at 180 knots. At least there was no problem with sighting this time, normally one of the greatest difficulties in the delicate art of dropping torpedoes. On the left of the instrument panel in front of Cochrane was a manual control for the torpedo sight. This was a dial giving the ship's speed graduated up to thirty knots, divided into two parts according to whether the pilot was attacking on the port or starboard bow. When the pilot set a pointer on the dial to the estimated speed of the ship, a brilliant pinpoint of light moved along a curved and mirrored bar set in front of his forehead, giving him the 'aim-off angle'. Provided the Beaufighter was flying at the correct height and speed, and the pilot closed to 1,000 yards from the target, this device solved the trigonometrical problem of the relative speeds and angles of the torpedo and the ship in the water.

However, some of the Torbeau pilots never used this sight. They preferred to use their own judgement, for a convoy usually sailed at the slow speed of only eight knots and there were other factors that could affect the path of a torpedo, such as a cross-wind. But this time Cochrane's target was stationary, so that he could ignore the torpedo sight and simply use his gunsight. He aimed carefully, without skid or yaw. At 1,000 yards from the *Pietro Orseolo*, he pressed the release button on the grip by the throttles. There was a reassuring slap as the torpedo fell away and the steel retaining wire, caught momentarily in the slipstream, smacked back underneath the fuselage. Cochrane opened up the controls fully. He flew directly over the *Pietro Orseolo*, then began to skid and twist at maximum speed just above sea level. Flak was still coming from the minesweepers and from the shore. Hinks looked back through his cupola, cranking his camera and photographing the scene.

For the first time in his career, Burton saw the explosion of a torpedo. He banked to port and, looking through his side window, saw a gout of water shoot up from the starboard side of the vessel, followed by a stream of black smoke. A torpedo had hit her amidships, in the engine room. A few seconds later, there was another violent explosion, which the German crew thought was caused by a bomb striking number three hatch but must have been caused by another torpedo. Immediately, the vessel began to list to starboard. On her bridge, the captain and five of her crew lay seriously wounded, with another five injured; they had all been hit by splinters from cannon fire. One of the minesweepers, *M.432*, had also been hit by cannon shells, wounding two of her crew.

The Germans thought that the Beaufighters were Whirlwinds, although they identified the Typhoons correctly. The minesweepers recorded that they fired eight rounds of 105 mm, 42 of 37 mm and 118 of 20 mm, quite light by Strike Wing standards. The two merchant vessels and the shore batteries also joined in, however, but there is no record of their expenditure of ammunition. The Germans claimed that three twin-engined aircraft were shot down, one by the *Pietro Orseolo* alone and two by combined fire. They reported that they saw one of the attackers crash into the sea. As usual, these claims were incorrect.

The Typhoons closed protectively around the Beaufighters, harrying them into some sort of order. The formation flew out to sea again, re-entered the cloud and headed for home. In one of the Torbeaus, Sergeant N. Yates nursed an aircraft with holes in the main keel, stern frame and tailplane. The Torbeau of Sergeant T. Neilson was also damaged but less seriously. One of the Typhoons made a belly landing at Predannack, with severed hydraulics. No aircraft was lost and no one was injured.

Amazingly, the two torpedo hits did not sink the *Pietro Orseolo*. Her engine room was flooded, but once again her watertight compartments held. All her crew were taken off and she lay at anchor for two days whilst a storm from the south-west raged about her. Then a tug came out and towed her to a nearby sandbank, where she was beached as a temporary measure. The following morning, 21 December, she was being towed off again when a bulkhead in her afterpart collapsed. Sea water rushed in and she began to settle by the stern. Suddenly there was an internal explosion, from some unknown cause, and she sank quickly in 72 feet of water. Her floating

18 December 1943. Two views of the *Pietro Orseolo* smoking after being hit by two torpedoes. Weather conditions were poor and the photographs are rather muzzy.

(*Left*)· F.E. 'Monty' Burton, photographed as a Flying Officer in 1940. (*Right*): Tom Cochrane, shortly after receiving his commission.

Fred Hinks, now commissioned, makes a spirited attempt to conduct an RAF band as a party progresses in the officers' mess at North Coates.

cargo, including all the torpedoes, was recovered.

Monty Burton and his squadron returned to the less exciting routine of their normal operational flying. The crews of 254 Squadron flew back to North Coates, thinking with pleasure of their Christmas dinner. Then fate dealt them a cruel blow, for on 24 December they were all sent back to Predannack once more. On Christmas day itself, the two squadrons had to fly into the Bay, looking for another blockade runner. It was the price of success, but in the event they accomplished nothing. In clear sunshine, the formation flew almost to the Spanish coast but returned with a nil report. The crews sat down to a miserably inadequate Christmas dinner; most of them pushed their plates on one side in disgust and stumped off to bed. They returned to North Coates to hear glowing accounts of the feast that they had missed.

The vessel that the Strike Wing had hunted was the inward-bound *Orsono*, escorted by German destroyers. She reached France safely but struck a wreck in the mouth of the Gironde and had to be beached, although most of her cargo of raw rubber was saved. All the remaining four blockade runners returning from the Far East were sunk, however, by aircraft or warships, as well as one German destroyer and two torpedo boats. On 17 January 1944, Gross-admiral Dönitz was forced to recommend to the Führer the cancellation of the whole blockade-running programme. Hitler had no option but to agree. Henceforth, no blockade runners sailed again, other than U-boats with their inadequate carrying capacity.

In 1951, efforts were made to salvage the *Pietro Orseolo*, probably by Sorimo, an Italian salvage company that has long ceased to exist. There is no record of the result, or of the cargo that was in her holds.

CHAPTER SIX

D-Day Destroyers

> The eyes of the world are upon you. The hopes and
> prayers of liberty-loving people everywhere march
> with you.
> *General Dwight Eisenhower (1890–1969)*, as the invasion
> began, 6 June 1944.

In December 1943, Germany had lost the battleship *Scharnhorst* in a
grim sea battle off the North Cape of Norway. Only one operational
battleship remained, the *Tirpitz*, tucked away in a Norwegian fjord.
All her other major units, two pocket battleships, seven cruisers and
two obsolete battleships, were used for training purposes in the
Baltic. Her major offensive weapon at sea was the U-boat, a fleet
consisting of 419 boats in December 1943, of which 161 were
operational.

It was clear to Grossadmiral Dönitz that his fleet could not
oppose effectively the combined might of the Allied fleets in the
forthcoming invasion of Europe. Other defensive measures had to
be found. He favoured the use of midget submarines, the
strengthening of coastal artillery, and the scattering of RMK mines,
a cheaply made concrete device with a contact fuse. E-boats, destroyers and U-boats could also attack the flanks of the invasion
force at sea.

On 6 June 1944, Marinegruppekommando West (Naval Group
West)* comprised a personnel strength of 30,940 men with 463
miscellaneous vessels, including flak-ships, minesweepers, R-
boats, *Sperrbrecher*, gunboats, etc. In addition, there were ten destroyers, one torpedo boat and thirty-four E-boats. These vessels
were disposed at harbours along the length of the Belgian and
French coasts. German Intelligence had no accurate knowledge of
where the first blow might fall. There was even a special force of U-
boats standing by in the Bay of Biscay – Group Landwirt – in case
the Allies tried to invade the west coast of France.

The role of the Strike Wings in this immense project was to help

---

* See Chapter Five, page 100.

protect the flanks of the Allied sea forces. On the left or eastern flank, two Wings were ordered to operate north-east of a line from Dover to Calais. The first of these was the North Coates Wing, consisting of 236 and 254 Squadrons, rejoined by 143 Squadron from its operational work in Cornwall. The second was a new ANZAC Wing based at Langham in Norfolk, comprising two squadrons, 455(RAAF) and 489(RNZAF); this Wing had been formed at Leuchars during the previous March.

The Australian squadron had been the first from that Dominion to form as a bomber squadron in Britain, when it was equipped with Hampdens in June 1941. In April 1942, it was transferred to Coastal Command and the crews were trained in torpedo-dropping from their Hampdens before operating off the Norwegian coast. In September 1942 a large detachment was sent to Vaenga in northern Russia; after some operational work in that rather unappreciative country, the crews left their aircraft behind and returned to the UK in a British warship. Back at Leuchars, the squadron began to operate with their New Zealand partners, but not as an integrated Strike Wing. In December 1943, the squadron was equipped with the Beaufighter TFX and the crews worked up to proficiency by specializing in the anti-flak role.

The New Zealand squadron was formed at Leuchars in August 1941, originally as a torpedo-carrying Beaufort squadron, but their aircraft were taken away from them for urgent requirements in the Middle East and replaced with Blenheim IVs. Two months later, the squadron was re-equipped with torpedo-carrying Hampdens; it then moved around the coasts of the British Isles, operating from St Eval in Cornwall, Thorney Island in West Sussex, and Skitten and Wick in north-east Scotland. The New Zealanders somehow contrived to achieve many successes in their lumbering and unescorted Hampdens off the Norwegian coast, although their crews suffered many casualties. The squadron converted to the Beaufighter TFX at the end of 1943, the crews still specializing in torpedo-dropping although they were also proficient in the anti-flak role.

On this eastern flank, the primary task of both the Langham and the North Coates Strike Wings was to knock out any E-boats or midget submarines that would attempt to attack the invasion forces. The aircraft operated from their own aerodromes but also used forward bases such as Manston in Kent. The code-name for the operations against the E-boats were Conebo, a name that might not have fooled a German with an elementary knowledge of English and Latin.

On the right or western flank, Coastal Command was ordered to operate west of a line across the Channel from Weymouth to St Mâlo, crossing over the island of Jersey. The hard-hitting Wick Wing, still consisting of 404(RCAF) and 144 Squadrons, was brought down from Scotland on 11 May to cover this area. Since February, the Wick Wing had found fewer targets to attack, for the Germans had begun to move their convoys at night along the Norwegian coast, in the same manner as along the Dutch coast. Nevertheless, the two squadrons of the Wing were operationally experienced and at a peak of efficiency; they were a formidable fighting force, of a kind that had not been required in Cornwall since the days of the German blockade runners.

Operational flying in the wartime RAF was almost wholly dependent upon weather conditions. One of the worst hazards that the airman faced was fog. In the eastern counties of England, the radiation fog that forms when the earth cools at night under a cloudless sky in conditions of high humidity, was greatly intensified by impurities in the air from industrial pollution in the Midlands and London. At times, particularly during autumn and winter, a woolly blanket lay across the land for days, thickening at night and in the early morning. The crews of returning aircraft, equipped with only primitive blind-landing instruments, faced a nightmare in such conditions unless they could find an aerodrome fitted with Fido, a system of petrol burners either side of a runway that burnt away the fog.

In south-west England, the crews encountered fog of a different kind. In spring and summer, warm air travelling from the west over the Atlantic met the cooler waters off the north Cornish coast and often condensed into a great bank of sea fog, rolling over the coastal aerodromes. Meteorological staff in the main Coastal Command base of St Eval, near Newquay in Cornwall, were unable to forecast these sea fogs with consistent accuracy, so that many accidents were caused and many flying days lost from the hazard. In an attempt to locate an aerodrome freer from these adverse weather conditions, the RAF built Davidstow Moor, 970 feet high on the north of Bodmin Moor. History must record, however, that flying was no easier from this new aerodrome. Although the sea fog seldom rolled up on the moor, the locality was covered with low cloud for much of the time, a form of stratus like wet fog. This cloud hid the nearby danger of Brown Willy, a peak some 400 feet higher than the aerodrome that claimed many aircraft and the lives of their crews. Some airmen estimated that in 1943 there were only 65 days fit for flying from Davidstow Moor.

The Beaufighters of 144 and 404 Squadrons touched down on the runway at Davidstow Moor on 11 May 1944. This aerodrome already housed 524 Squadron, equipped with Wellington XIIIs and employed on anti-submarine patrols and bombing E-boats off the French coast, as well as the air-sea rescue Warwicks of 282 Squadron. There had been no time to prepare the site allocated to the newcomers, however. Events were moving so quickly that there were no administrative staff and no proper messing facilities; WAAF drivers improvised meals in a single mess for all ranks until more normal arrangements were made.

The Canadians of 404 Squadron were now commanded by an Englishman, Wing Commander A.K. 'Ken' Gatward. Their partner in the Strike Wing, 144 Squadron, was commanded by a Scot, Wing Commander David O.F. Lumsden. Both men were highly experienced airmen and operational fliers.

Lumsden was aged twenty-nine and had graduated at Cranwell in 1935. His first experience had been flying Handley-Page Heyfords in 10 Squadron, the last heavy bomber bi-plane in service in the RAF. This was followed by a Fleet Air Arm conversion course and a tour flying the Swordfish torpedo bombers of 813 Squadron from HMS *Eagle*, which was in the China Station at the time; it was a not unpleasant experience for a young officer to cruise around the Far East, even though the Sino-Japanese war was raging on the mainland. The outbreak of war with Germany found Lumsden as a specialist armaments officer and instructor at Brize Norton. This was followed by a long stint at the Ministry of Aircraft Production; it was not until April 1943 that Lumsden escaped to a refresher flying course before taking over 144 Squadron the following September, shortly before the new Wick Strike Wing was formed.

For several days, the activities of the Strike Wing were hampered by the bad weather that preceded the invasion of Europe. Some training and practice took place, but there were several accidents in the low cloud that covered their hilly aerodrome. Several aircraft were damaged in the boggy ground off the runway. Wet cement at the end of the runway caused one Beaufighter to skid and to suffer serious damage.

The first strike was on 19 May. A sighting had been made of 'two destroyers and four escorts' rounding the tip of the Brest peninsula in a northerly direction. Gatward led ten aircraft from 404 and twelve from 144 on a sweep, taking off at 19.30 hours. One aircraft of 404 turned back with engine trouble, but the remainder continued, with a powerful escort of twenty-eight Spitfires. The Canadian squadron was armed with 60 lb rockets and cannon. 144 Squadron was acting as anti-flak escort, armed with cannon only, led by one of their Flight Commanders, Squadron Leader Peter W. Dunn.

The warships that the Strike Wing was hunting were not destroyers but torpedo-boats. These were, however, as large and as powerful as many British destroyers. Before the war, most torpedo-boats carried a torpedo armament and little else, but *T-24*, a vessel of 1,294 tons, had been completed after hostilities broke out and was thus equipped for modern conditions; her flak armament consisted of no less than four 37 mm, seven 20 mm and two 15 mm guns, as well as her four 105 mm large guns. Her companion was the *Jaguar*, 1,320 tons, built in 1924; she was armed with three 105 mm, three 37 mm and an unrecorded number of 20 mm guns. These two torpedo-boats had been stationed at Brest, but the Germans had received reports of extensive mining off the coast of north-west Brittany and had decided to transfer them to Cherbourg, where they would be better placed to help repel any Allied invasion force. They sailed from Brest at 17.30 hours on 19 May, hoping to escape attack before darkness would allow them to reach Cherbourg unscathed.

On the first part of their journey, the torpedo-boats were escorted by the minesweepers *M.4044* and *M.4014*, but they parted company at 19.14 hours. Ahead were four more minesweepers, *M.422*, *M.442*, *M.343*, *M.452* and *M.432*, from the 24th Flotilla stationed at Brest. At 20.28 hours, before reaching this protection, *T-24* suffered a stroke of bad luck. She ran over a ground mine, a magnetic mine resting on the sea bed. This exploded, causing damage to her hull and putting some of her armament out of action, but the torpedo-boat was able to continue at reduced speed under her own power. Fifteen minutes later, the two torpedo-boats were passing through the Fromveur channel, between the island of Ushant and the mainland, closing with the minesweepers, when they sighted the Strike Wing.

The Beaufighters of 144 Squadron dived down on the torpedo-boats and the minesweepers. Their cannon fire made no impression on the torpedo-boats but one seaman in a minesweeper was killed and several were injured. The leading Beaufighter flown by Squadron Leader Dunn burst into flames and exploded on impact with the sea. Pilot Officer Reid, flying another Beaufighter, was hit in the left forearm by a cannon shell but returned to make a belly-landing at Harrowbeer. 404 Squadron followed close behind the anti-flak section, firing their 60 lb rockets. Although the pilots claimed afterwards that hits were scored on every vessel, the German records show that all the rockets missed. Almost certainly, the inadequacies of the heavier 60 lb high-explosive warhead, including its curved trajectory, against this type of vessel were responsible for the failure of the squadron on this occasion. The return fire from the flotilla was so tremendous that it must have put many pilots off their aim. Some of the aircrews saw parachute rockets fired from the minesweepers as well as strange bursts of black smoke which, unknown to them, must have come from flame-throwers. Several aircraft were hit, and one was forced to land at Predannack with a damaged wing.

In spite of their success in repelling the air attack, the Germans did not continue their journey for long. At 21.40 hours they turned back for Brest, mainly in order to repair the mine damage to *T-24*. *Jaguar* was later to reach her new port, but *T-24* remained behind to suffer more air attacks; her ultimate fate will be related in a subsequent chapter.

By D-Day, 6 June, the vessels of Marinegruppenkommando West stationed on the west coast of France were:

Destroyers	5	warships
Torpedo boat	1	warship
Fast escort	1	warship
Sperrbrecher of various types	22	ships
Minesweepers of various types	110	boats
Flak-ships of various types	34	boats
Small flak-ships of various types	16	boats

The main concentration of this force was in the Gironde estuary, at the ports of Royan, Pauillac, Blaye and Bordeaux. There were other concentrations at Brest, Lorient, Concarneau and San Nazaire, with scatterings at six other ports. The majority of these vessels fulfilled a defensive function, clearing floating or ground sea mines, and acting as flak platforms against aircraft. Of the offensive vessels available to the Kriegsmarine in France, many U-boats operated from concrete shelters in the western ports; the E-boats which continued to harry Allied shipping were stationed on the north coast of France, as well as the coasts of Belgium and Holland; the destroyers and the torpedo-boat constituted the remaining danger to the western flank of the invasion forces.

On the historic day of the invasion, three destroyers were spotted moving north from the mouth of the Gironde estuary. They were *Z-32* commanded by Fregattenkapitän von Berger, *Z-24* under Korvettenkapitän Heinz Birnbacher and *ZH-1* under Korvettenkapitän Klaus Barckow. These destroyers formed part of the 8th Zerstörer-Flotille. They had left Royan at 12.30 hours, heading for Brest before setting out to attack the western flank of the Allied sea forces. The Senior Officer of the Flotilla, Kapitän zur See Graf (Count) von Bechtelsheim sailed in *Z-32*. The men of the Kriegsmarine must have known that they were heading into a hornet's nest.

The Beaufighters of the Strike Wing at Davidstow Moor now looked like hornets, with the distinctive black and white bands of the Allied Expeditionary force painted on their wings and fuselages; identification rather than camouflage was considered more important now that the Allies had achieved such air superiority. The Beaufighters of 144 Squadron were still equipped only with cannon, for their pilots had not been trained in rocket-firing, but the 60 lb rocket warheads of 404 Squadron had been replaced with the more deadly anti-shipping 25 lb warheads.

The crews of the Strike Wing now faced opponents who were far more formidable than most had experienced in their operational flying. *Z-32* and *Z-24* were modern destroyers of a type which the Germans called the *Narvik* class to commemmorate the battles of 1940 in Norwegian waters. Both were very large by British standards, each being 2,603 tons and about 400 feet in length. *Z-32* had been launched in 1941 and *Z-24* in 1942, sufficiently late in the war for them to be built to repel air attacks; each was armed with five 105 mm and six 37 mm guns, as well as eight 20 mm cannon, the flak armament having been increased following the removal of one of the heavy guns. This class of destroyer carried a complement of 321 seamen. *ZH-1* was a smaller vessel of 1,204 tons. This destroyer had been scuttled whilst under construction by the Royal Netherlands Navy, but raised and completed by the Germans; she was powerfully armed with four 120 mm and four 37 mm guns, together with four 20 mm cannon, and carried a crew of 236. The crews of all three destroyers included many professional seamen, including gunnery experts.

The Wing was led by Wing Commander David Lumsden. There were sixteen cannon-firing Beaufighters from 144 Squadron, whilst Flying Officer Sydney Shulemson led fourteen of the rocket and cannon-firing Beaufighters of 404 Squadron. The crews of both squadrons, already keyed up for the previous few weeks whilst awaiting the launching of the invasion, had been on tenterhooks all day with orders to fly being issued and then cancelled. At last, they began taking off at 18.30 hours. Twenty minutes later, they headed towards Land's End. There, they met the fighter escorts, eight Mosquito VIs of 248 Squadron, which by then had moved its base from Predannack to Portreath. At 19.12 hours, the entire formation of thirty-eight aircraft left the Cornish coast behind, heading for the island of Ushant. All the crews knew what to expect when they reached the target near Belle Ile. It would have been an unusual airman who did not feel his stomach muscles tighten at the prospect of the flak barrage. It is probably true to say, however, that not one man would have wished to be left out of that historic day.

The flight out was packed with incidents. Some fifteen miles south of Ushant, the formation flew near six M-class minesweepers heading north-east, with a large aircraft circling overhead. The minesweepers opened fire, quite accurately. The Wing could probably have sunk them all, but the aircrews knew that they had to conserve their ammunition for the destroyers. Lumsden led the formation away from the temptation, to the south-east. Twelve minutes later, they passed three more minesweepers, but again maintained their course.

Navigating the Wing in Lumsden's Beaufighter was Flight Lieutenant E.H. 'Tommy' Thomas, a young but operationally experienced Welshman. Thomas spoke little to his Commanding Officer, concentrating on navigating carefully to the point of interception. At 20.15 hours, a U-boat was spotted near Belle-Ile. This was a target which had to be attacked under all circumstances. Four Beaufighters of 144 Squadron and four Mosquitoes of 248 Squadron peeled off towards it, but the U-boat submerged before they could attack. The Wing continued on its way to the south-east. At 20.27 hours, Lumsden saw the three destroyers in the distance, sailing north-west. Two of them were in line ahead, with the third on the starboard quarter.

Lumsden continued on his course for a few minutes, watching the destroyers carefully, bringing the Wing to the west of the target so that the attack could be made out of the low evening sun.

Shulemson ordered the fourteen rocket-firing Beaufighters of 404 Squadron into three sections, five under him to attack the centre destroyer, four under Flight Lieutenant A.H. Hodson on his port side to attack the leading vessel, and four under Flying Officer P. Dwornik to take the rear vessel. The formation was flying at 1,000 feet, with the eight Mosquitoes circling protectively, when Lumsden gave the order to attack. The Wing turned to port. It was exactly 20.30 hours.

The Beaufighter crews thought that they had taken the Germans by surprise, but the war diaries of the destroyers verify that the sailors spotted the attackers a minute before they dived. The Germans thought that all the aircraft were Mosquitoes and that there were sixty of them. They recorded that the attackers fired 'machine guns and 88 mm', references to the 20 mm cannon and the warhead of the 25 lb rocket, which was about 88 mm at its maximum diameter. They stated that 'accurate flak' put the aircraft off their aim, but the results show that this is not correct. Certainly, the three destroyers put up a tremendous barrage, but the gunners must have been confused by the unexpected experience of a simultaneous attack by sixteen aircraft, with another wave of fourteen close behind, all diving out of a setting sun.

The leading destroyer, *Z-32*, was hit by several rockets just above the waterline. Sea-water began to gush in. One warhead passed clean through her forward magazine, damaging thirty time fuses in its path, ending up in the hydrophone office; the Germans thought that this was a dud – obviously they were unaware of the purpose of solid-shot warheads. In her forward W/T office, all the wireless equipment was destroyed, save one short-wave receiver. Several rockets holed the oil bunkers on her port side. The rudder room on her port side was flooded, although she was still able to steer. Several small fires were started. The casualties amongst her crew are not recorded.

The next destroyer in line, *Z-24*, was also peppered with cannon and rocket hits, even more seriously. One barrel of her starboard 37 mm gun was blown away. Her aerial was put out of action. The bunkers on her port side were also holed, leaking oil into the sea. Two men were killed and thirteen wounded. Fires broke out in several places, accompanied by dense black smoke. Her engine revolutions dropped and she began to fall back.

The rear destroyer *ZH-1*, was not damaged at all. As the attack developed, she steamed closer to the starboard side of *Z-24*, so that she was screened from the attackers. Thus, both Shulemson's and Dwornik's sections concentrated on *Z-24*. Only one Beaufighter of 404 Squadron attacked the former Dutch destroyer; this was flown by Flying Officer J.D. Taylor, who was squeezed out of the combined attack on the centre destroyer and turned in frustration to *ZH-1*, firing rockets that missed.

The Beaufighters escaped surprisingly lightly. The Germans did not claim any aircraft shot down, and they were correct. All the Beaufighters set off for base three minutes after the attack. In the leading aircraft, Lumsden was lucky to receive no more than a shrapnel gouge in the windscreen. A 20 mm shell exploded in the fuselage of the Beaufighter flown by Pilot Officer J.H. Barnett of 144 Squadron, injuring his navigator, Flight Sergeant R.F. Chapman in the right leg. Barnett landed at Predannack on his return, the nearest aerodrome that could give medical attention. Flight Lieutenant J.M. Talman of 144 Squadron made a successful belly-landing at Davidstow Moor, with hydraulics failure. None of the aircraft of 404 Squadron was damaged.

The aircraft most seriously hit was flown by Flight Sergeant P.E.C. Morton of 144 Squadron, who was forced to ditch on the way back. The pilot and the navigator, Flight Sergeant D.C. Mascall, got into their dinghy unharmed. Fortunately for them, they were escorted by Flying Officer H.L. Wainman of 404 Squadron, who watched them ditch. Wainman approached a nearby Liberator for help, calling on the R/T and waggling his wings, but was met with a burst of tracer. However, the Canadian crew reported an accurate ditching position on their return to Davidstow Moor, so that the following day a Warwick of 282 Squadron was able to drop an airborne lifeboat near the dinghy. The two men got into the lifeboat, started the engine and began to chug back towards safety; two days later, they were picked up by a Canadian destroyer.

The Mosquitoes of 248 Squadron found a lone Ju 188 near the destroyers. Two aircraft attacked and sent it crashing into the sea.* The Wing crossed over the three minesweepers again on the way back, but were without ammunition and could not attack.

The battered German destroyer flotilla headed towards Brest, shielded by the protection of nightfall. However, they were not allowed to escape further attentions from the Davidstow Moor Strike Wing. Half an hour after midnight, six Beaufighters of 404

---

*   The relevant records of the Luftwaffe for the day do not exist.

Squadron, armed with rockets, and six of 144 Squadron, took off to hunt singly for them. The Beaufighters of 144 Squadron were armed with two 500 lb and two 250 lb medium-capacity bombs on this occasion; the pilots had been practising dive-bombing for this eventuality, prior to flying down to Cornwall. At different times, three rocket-firing and two bomb-carrying Beaufighters found what appeared to be three destroyers, with smoke coming from the centre vessel, near the entrance to Brest estuary. These five aircraft made night attacks and reported explosions, but there is no record of further damage to the destroyers, which moored in the harbour at Brest at 05.00 hours.

In Brest, the killed and wounded sailors were taken ashore. The Germans must have worked like the furies to repair the two damaged destroyers. The scars and holes in the upperworks did not matter, provided any smashed equipment or armament was replaced, but the holes at the waterlines were more serious. Fortunately for the ship repairers, the holes made by 25 lb warheads were so small that plates could be easily welded over them if the vessel reached port. In the event, the destroyer flotilla was delayed for only about thirty-six hours, but even this short period was critical in the securing of the Normandy beach-heads. Nevertheless, the three destroyers did sail again, and the courage of their crews must be applauded. Their orders were to round the Brest peninsula, sail up the Channel as far as Cherbourg, and attack the overwhelmingly superior Allied navies. They obeyed unquestioningly. Late in the evening of 8 June, they slipped out of Brest, in company with *T-24*, the large torpedo-boat that the Davidstow Moor Strike Wing had attacked on 19 May.

The result was almost a foregone conclusion. The Germans were sighted off Ushant at 22.27 hours by a Liberator of 547 Squadron based at St Eval. Three hours later, they were brought into action by eight destroyers of the 10th Destroyer Flotilla, some thirty miles north-west of the Ile de Batz on the north coast of France. A bitter sea action followed, lasting several hours. The German vessels fired torpedoes, which the Allied destroyers avoided. There was then an exchange of gunfire. *T-24* was badly damaged, but managed to escape to the south-west, together with Z-24, and regain Brest. *Z-32* inflicted damage on the British destroyer *Tartar* but this vessel, in company with the *Ashanti*, found *ZH-1* and sank her. The Canadian destroyers *Haidi* and *Huron* then found and engaged *Z-32*, setting her on fire; the German crew beached the destroyer on the Ile de

Batz and abandoned her.

The Strike Wing at Davidstow was detailed to 'finish off' the grounded destroyer. Twelve aircraft of 404 Squadron, armed with 60 lb rockets for maximum fragmentation effect on the upperworks, and twelve aircraft of 144 Squadron, each carrying two 250 lb bombs, took off at 20.30 hours on 9 June. Gatward and Lumsden* led their respective squadrons. They were escorted by twenty-four Spitfires. Originally, the Wing intended to make a combined attack, for the crews did not realize that the warship had been abandoned. When they met no opposition, however, the strike developed into a practice rocket and dive-bombing attack. Many of the Beaufighters went in singly, the crews not only feeling relieved but actually enjoying themselves. Someone fired a machine gun from the island, without effect. It was a fine and clear summer evening and the Allies were winning the war. This was the way it ought to be, all the time.

Incredibly, *T-24* made one more attempt to reach Cherbourg during that night, but failed to penetrate the surface patrols and was forced to return once more to Brest. Together with *Z-24*, she then retired to the Gironde, further away from the danger of air attacks. There we must leave the two warships for the present, and return to North Coates.

---

*   Lumsden was awarded a DFC for his leadership on 6 June.

CHAPTER SEVEN

Combined Attack

God is usually on the side of the big squadrons and
against the little ones.
Roger de Bussey-Rabutin (1618–1693)

Whilst the air and naval forces of the Allies were obliterating the
Western Command of the Kriegsmarine along the French coast, the
two Strike Wings based in eastern England continued to hunt for
German convoys in the North Sea. In the officers' and sergeants'
messes at both North Coates and Langham, morale was at its
highest. The aircrews at North Coates numbered about 120, whilst
there were about 80 in the ANZAC Wing at Langham. At both stations, the officer aircrews out-numbered the NCOs in the ratio of
about two to one, but distinctions between ranks had become
somewhat less marked at this stage in the war. There was an
atmosphere of easy informality in the messes, espcially amongst the
men from the Dominions. The numbers were small enough for
most aircrews to know each other. There was plenty of evidence of
courage under wings and brevets, in the diagonal violet and white
stripes of DFCs and DFMs, with the occasional red and blue bands
of a DSO. Nor was enthusiasm lacking amongst the hundreds of
ground personnel who kept these squadrons in the air – riggers, fitters, armourers, electricians, drivers, instrument mechanics, radio
operators, medical staff, cipher clerks, photographers, fire tender
crews, operations room staff; these men and women represented
the most advanced and efficient technology of the times.

Some of those who contributed most to the high morale of the
aircrews were the young women of the WAAF. A few of these girls
worked as fitters and riggers on the Beaufighters; they looked
almost dumpy when swathed with several layers of clothing
covered by grease-stained overalls, each topped with a battered hat,
usually with a screwdriver stuck in the belt and a piece of dirty rag
hanging out of the pocket. Others cooked the 'flying meals' for the
aircrews before take off, often in the early hours of the morning.
The last face that a flier would see before take off was usually that of

a young girl who drove him in a truck to the dispersal pen; the first welcome on his return was from a smiling young girl who drove him back to the Operations Room, bantering cheerfully as she shared in the mood of intense relief and elation.

It was these girls who often took the edge off the private fears of some of the fliers. On one occasion at North Coates, a young pilot could not accept the appalling news that his twin brother had been lost on a sortie from the same station. For two days he sat in a vigil in the Operations Room until he was at last convinced that the nightmare was a reality. During those two days of bleak despair he was never without the company of a WAAF officer, one of six who voluntarily gave up their spare time to take turns in sitting with him and sharing his grief.

On 14 June 1944, a Jim Crow Mustang brought back the information that a major enemy convoy had set off northwards from Rotterdam. This information was expected at the Tracking Room in the Citadel, for it verified information already gathered, including messages radioed at great risk by a small cell of the Dutch Resistance. Over two years before, the framework of the Dutch Resistance had been penetrated and smashed by the Gestapo, but a few courageous men and women continued their dangerous task. Two important vessels had left Rotterdam, both newly completed. The larger was an old enemy of the North Coates Wing, none other than the *Versuchsschiff* or experimental ship of 7,900 tons down as the *Schiff 49* or the *Coburg* by the Germans, originally laid down as the *Amerskerk* by the Dutch. She was the incomplete vessel that the North Coates Wing had attacked unsuccessfully and at such cost when she was under tow on 20 November 1942. She had been fitted out at Rotterdam; the Beaufighter crews had an old score to settle with her. The other vessel was 3,500 tons, also newly completed. She was the *Gustav Nachtigall* – the nightingale. Both ships were destined for the port of Gdynia in Poland, where the *Amerskerk* was to serve as a large flak-ship and the *Nachtigall* as an E-boat depot ship. Moving in stages up the coast, the first call was at Den Helder.

It was too late to mount an attack on 14 June, and the operation was scheduled for early the following morning. For the first time, two Wings were briefed to attack simultaneously. North Coates could muster ten Torbeaus, led by their CO, Wing Commander R.E. 'Paddy' Burns, and four anti-flak Beaufighters, all from 254 Squadron. Only five Beaufighters from 236 Squadron were available, armed with 25 lb rockets and led by a New Zealander in the RAF, Squadron Leader E.W. 'Bill' Tacon. 143 Squadron was at Manston, hunting E-boats. The force from Langham consisted of twelve cannon-firing Beaufighters of 455 Squadron, the Australians being led by Squadron Leader Colin G. Milson, whilst 489 Squadron provided eleven cannon-firing Beaufighters, the leader of the New Zealanders being an Englishman, Squadron Leader Peter A. Hughes. This powerful force of forty-two Beaufighters was scheduled to be protected by ten Mustangs of 316 (Polish) Squadron, led by Squadron Leader P. Niemiec. These Allied squadrons and crews formed the largest anti-shipping strike force gathered together by Coastal Command at that stage in the war.

The officer detailed to lead the attack was a tall, 27-year-old Englishman, Wing Commander Anthony Gadd. He had joined the RAF in 1935 and, after training, had flown with the Aircraft Torpedo Development Unit at Gosport. During four years at the ATDU* he had dropped the astonishing total of over 1,000 torpedoes in trials, an experience that was to stand him in good stead when he was posted to 22 Squadron at North Coates in 1940, where he survived an operational tour on torpedo-carrying Beauforts. After a spell in Australia with the RAAF and a period commanding the RAF station at Tain, near Inverness, he had pressed to return to operational work. At the Beaufighter OTU at East Fortune, near Edinburgh, he had crewed up with a navigator, Flying Officer Duncan Marrow.

Like many other Beaufighter navigators, Marrow had joined the RAFVR as a wireless operator and had then taken a navigator's course. He was also an experienced operational man, having already completed a tour on Beaufighters, partly in 235 Squadron at Chivenor and partly in 248 Squadron at Talbenny in South Wales, flying over the Bay of Biscay. Together, Gadd and Marrow formed one of Coastal Command's most experienced crews on strike aircraft; by 14 June, the two men had flown together on fourteen operational flights. Gadd's function at North Coates was that of Wing Commander Flying. For the strike on the next day, Burns lent Gadd one of his Beaufighters, letter 'C', serial NT924.

The CO of the Torbeau squadron, Wing Commander Paddy Burns, was a 32-year-old officer of Northern Irish parentage. He was an unusual commanding officer, for he was a civil engineer

---

*   See Chapter One, page 24.

with the qualification of BSc(Eng) from London University. After joining the RAF in 1934, he trained in Egypt and then joined 6 Squadron at Ramleh in Palestine, where he flew Hawker Harts in the nasty little conflict called the Arab Revolt of 1936. Most unusually, he had been awarded a DFC, a decoration that was so rare between the wars that senior officers sometimes told him to remove the ribbon in the belief that he was wearing it by mistake. In spite of this decoration, the RAF seemed intent on preventing Burns from flying operationally. At the outbreak of war, he was the officer commanding the Torpedo Support Unit to 22 Squadron at North Coates, and was under pressure to join the newly-formed Technical Branch. He was determined, however, to remain on flying duties, and his wish was realized when, in 1940, he became the Squadron Leader Development at the ATDU, and later commanded the unit. Although these duties involved a considerable amount of flying, he longed to join an operational squadron; in January 1944 he was given 254 Squadron, taking over from Wing Commander Darley Miller.

Burns' navigator was also rather older than the average, thirty-two years of age. He was Flying Officer G.W.E. 'Frank' Woolley, a man who had joined the RAF in 1933 and served as a wireless operator in Iraq. After taking an air observer's course, he was posted to Malaya in 1939, with the rank of sergeant. He managed to escape from Singapore just before it was occupied by the Japanese in February 1942. Afterwards, he flew operationally in Hudsons from India, receiving his commission. After a spell as an instructor in Northern Ireland, he had joined 254 Squadron. Together, Burns and Woolley formed an experienced crew of older and perhaps wiser men. ·

North Coates and Langham were barely fifteen minutes' flying time apart, but the problem of forming up such a large strike force could be solved only by precise timing and careful flying, for the Beaufighters had to take off at night to make their interception. The first step was to link up the two Wings. The nineteen Beaufighters at North Coates took off at 04.10 hours Double British Summer Time (two hours ahead of Greenwich Main Time) on 15 June and set course for Langham. It was still dark, but Marrow and the navigators of the other section leaders fired their Very pistols and signalled with their Aldis lamps, guiding the pilots of the two squadrons to their formation lights. The night was starlit but the sky was paling as they flew south-east over the Wash. They swept round the aerodrome at Langham from which the twenty-three Beaufighters of the ANZAC Wing had already taken off in quick succession. Soon there were forty-two Beaufighters in the air, heading for the coastal town of Cromer, the roar of their engines disturbing the sleep of the residents in the flat East Anglian countryside a thousand feet below. Near Cromer, they were joined by ten Mustang IIIs of 316 Squadron from Coltishall, flown by eager Poles.

Duncan Marrow gave Tony Gadd the course for Ameland in the Dutch Frisian islands, 155 sea miles away, and fired a green Very light as his pilot turned on a course slightly north of east. One of the Australians turned back with engine trouble. Gadd's leading section consisted of nine anti-flak Beaufighters from North Coates, five with rockets and cannon, four with cannon only. He was Outgrow leader, whilst Niemiec in the Mustangs was Peafowl leader. The eleven Beaufighters of the New Zealand squadron, code-named Barnhut, kept a close station to port. The eleven aircraft of the Australian squadron flew slightly further away, to starboard; their code-name was Bowsaw. Burns tucked his ten Torbeaus behind the gap between the leading section and the Australians; he was Volga leader. The ten Mustangs weaved protectively above and behind the Beaufighters.

Soon after leaving the coast of Norfolk, Gadd brought the combined force down, almost to sea level, below the German radar screen. There were masses of bluey-black clouds ahead, a layer of strato-cumulus with the sky lightening above it, the undersurface tinged with red. A misty horizon gradually appeared in the east. A great wake in the sea, formed by the propellers, stretched back towards the English coast. All the pilots kept R/T silence, although some spoke to their navigators over the intercoms. Everything was going to plan. It was the sort of occasion when the experienced airman would be suspicious and extra-vigilant.

Convoy Nachtigall had sailed from Den Helder at 21.55 hours the previous evening, headed for the next halt at Borkum. Three minesweepers of the 7th Flotilla led the convoy, in vic formation; they were *M.201*, *M.82* and *M.131*. Behind them sailed the *Nachtigall*, heavily armed with two 105 mm and two 37 mm guns, as well as ten 20 mm cannon, eight of the latter being fitted as quad guns. In the wake of the *Nachtigall* sailed the *Amerskerk*,* armed with

---

* The Germans reverted to the original Dutch name in their later records.

eight 20 mm cannon, six of which were in twin mountings. On the flanks of the two large ships were four more minesweepers of the 7th Flotilla, *M.33*, *M.23*, *M.103* and *M.104*. Each minesweeper carried two 105 mm guns and six cannon, whilst most were also armed with machine guns. There were also a number of R-boats in the convoy, but these are not recorded. By dawn on 15 June, the convoy was making good time and nearing the Dutch Frisian island of Schiermonnikoog. There was a westerly wind of about 15 mph, a moderate sea swell, and good visibility under an almost cloudless sky.

In the leading aircraft, Duncan Marrow busied himself with the drift sight in the floor of his navigator's compartment. The target was under an hour's flying from the English coast. By early 1944, Gee radar sets had been installed in most Beaufighter TFXs, but these did not work at low level; Marrow would have to wait until they climbed above the radar horizon before he could obtain a Gee fix. His job was to navigate the entire combined Wing, whilst other navigators had been detailed to concentrate on their wireless sets, the 1155 receiver and 1154 transmitter, listening for any signals from base. Looking out of his cupola, around the awkwardly placed Browning, he could see the remainder of the formation, on either side and behind. It was a grand sight, a demonstration of the growing power of the Allied air forces. He rarely spoke to his pilot. Tony Gadd had enough to do, concentrating on his formation and running over the plan of attack in his mind. The reconnaissance had given him an idea of the disposition of the convoy and he hoped to achieve a single synchronized sweep over the vessels and to leave a shattered ruin behind them.

Paddy Burns and Frank Woolley were more talkative. Woolley was working on his Mercator chart pinned to the narrow table folded down into position. He had inadvertently left his intercom switch on, and was humming a bouncy and nonsensical tune of the times.

'Mares eat oats and does eat oats and little lambs eat ivy . . .'

'For God's sake, shut up, Frank!' snapped Burns, who wondered if Woolley knew any other tunes. He always sang that bloody silly song.

'Sorry, skipper,' replied Woolley, cheerfully, flicking down the switch on his mouthpiece. 'A kid 'll eat ivy too, wouldn't you . . .'

His CO had a quick and fiery temper, but he wouldn't swap him with any other pilot. In spite of the difference in their ranks, the two men were friends. Woolley stood up to look out of his cupola at the other sections, banged his head on the butt of his machine gun for the hundredth time, and cursed.*

Burns did not like the look of the weather. The formation was passing in and out of low cloud, and the horizon was getting mistier. Still, perhaps it wouldn't get worse. Meanwhile, perhaps he had better be cheerful with his navigator.

'Don't eat all the rations, Frank', he instructed. 'And don't try to pinch all the chocolate this time!'

'Wouldn't dream of it, skipper! You'll get your share!' replied Woolley, grinning broadly. In fact, neither man ate his 'flying ration' of chocolate, for it was too precious. They were both married men, and they took the chocolate bars home to their children.

'Thirty-five minutes to target, skipper,' saw Marrow.

'OK, Duncan', replied Gadd. The cloud and the sea mist were getting worse. If need be, he'd climb above it. That would alert the German radar, but he wasn't going to scrub a strike like this if he could help it. It was daylight now, and that convoy would be safely tucked away in a German port if they didn't attack in the next hour or two.

The whole formation flew into thick fog and cloud. Each section lost sight of the others. It was a dangerous moment, but there was a contingency plan to cater for it. Gadd's leading section maintained its course but began to climb. On either side, the Australian and New Zealand sections opened out, each by ten degrees, and also began to climb. No one used the R/T, for the pilots knew what had to be done. After five minutes, they would resume their original course. When they broke above cloud, they would look for each other.

Burns did not fancy leading his Torbeau section blindly into the gap between the Australians and Gadd's section. They had closed up a few moments before, when the visibility worsened, so that the Torbeaus were in their slipstream. They might open up again, but on the other hand they might not. He reduced speed slightly, climbed cautiously to 600 feet, saw nothing except cloud and

---

*   These actions and conversations are not imaginary. They are based on the recollections of the aircrews.

his own section, and decided to risk his R/T.

'Volga leader to Outgrow leader. On instruments. Still in cloud. Sticking to six hundred feet.'

Switching his R/T to 'receive', all Burns could hear was a yowling note in his earphones. Some aircrews thought that such noises were indications that the German radar had bearings on them, but it was probably a faulty valve in the set.

'Frank, the bloody R/T's not working. Can you see anything?'

'Don't worry, skipper', replied Woolley. 'The boys are still tucked in behind us.'

With the remainder of the Torbeaus following, Burns led his section gently back down to 100 feet. Below, the sea was smooth and glassy, with no horizon and sea mist ahead. Still with the maddening howl in his ears, Burns climbed back to 600 feet. If he maintained the same course and speed, perhaps he would be able to join up with the others nearer the target.

After about half an hour, the weather began to clear. The cloud and sea mist thinned, and the horizon began to reappear. Suddenly, the Torbeaus flew out into brilliant morning sunshine. Burns could see the Dutch and German Frisian islands ahead, stretched out in a string, with flat sandy beaches and dunes looking like a holiday-maker's paradise. The men in the Torbeaus felt exposed and alone. Burns wondered if he should turn. They were supposed to be making for a point ahead of the convoy, before turning to intercept it. They had reached that point, and there was no sign of the ships. The convoy was either too late or early. Burns' instinct told him to carry on for a while. He slipped down to 200 feet and flew straight ahead, gazing at the pencil line of the horizon. A series of tiny dots, black and barely visible, appeared on his windscreen. That must be the convoy, ahead of its estimated position. He turned slightly to port, to run along the seaward side of the convoy, the direction from which the attack should be made. That screech was still in his earphones and there was not a sign of the anti-flak Beaufighters or the Mustangs. Had they turned back?

'What the hell are we supposed to do?' he thought. 'Win the bloody war on our own?'

'Volga leader to Outgrow leader! Enemy convoy ahead! Where the hell are you, for God's sake?'

No reply. Well, this was why he'd joined the RAF, and why he'd moved heaven and earth to command an operational squadron. He could count about seventeen escorts around those two

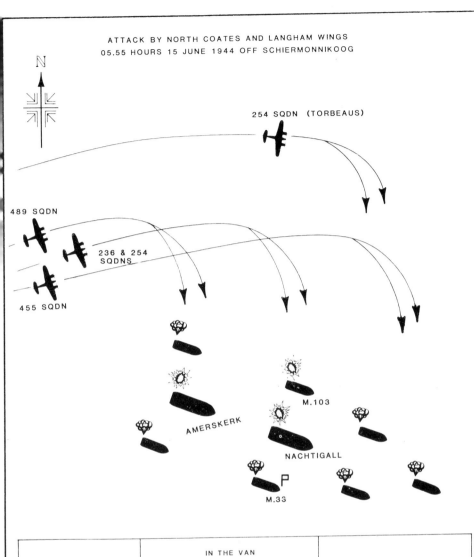

ATTACK BY NORTH COATES AND LANGHAM WINGS
05.55 HOURS 15 JUNE 1944 OFF SCHIERMONNIKOOG

N

254 SQDN (TORBEAUS)

489 SQDN

236 & 254
SQDNS

455 SQDN

M.103

AMERSKERK

NACHTIGALL

M.33

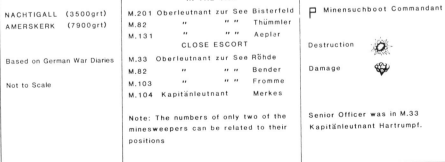

	IN THE VAN		
NACHTIGALL (3500grt)	M.201 Oberleutnant zur See Bisterfeld		⊓ Minensuchboot Commandant
AMERSKERK (7900grt)	M.82 " " " Thümmler		
	M.131 " " " Aepler		
	CLOSE ESCORT		
Based on German War Diaries	M.33 Oberleutnant zur See Röhde		Destruction
	M.82 " " " Bender		
Not to Scale	M.103 " " " Fromme		Damage
	M.104 Kapitänleutnant Merkes		

Note: The numbers of only two of the minesweepers can be related to their positions

Senior Officer was in M.33 Kapitänleutnant Hartrumpf.

merchant vessels, and the flak from that lot could blast every Torbeau out of the sky. Nevertheless, he would have to attack.

'Aircraft four o'clock high!' called Woolley. 'They're Beaus!'

'What are they doing?' asked Burns, his heart jumping with relief.

'They seem to be doing a split-arse turn to port!' replied Woolley.

The anti-flak Beaufighters had not climbed high enough for Duncan Marrow to obtain a Gee fix, and he was still working on dead reckoning.

'Twenty minutes to Position A*, skipper. The cloud seems to be thinning out a bit.'

'OK, Duncan', replied Gadd. 'Keep a look-out for the Torbeaus.'

Gadd's section and the Mustangs had closed up again, flying at 2,300 feet. In the Australian section to starboard, Flight Sergeant Payne drew up alongside Squadron Leader Colin Milson and waggled his wings, before turning back with a faulty engine. Gadd had experienced no trouble with this R/T. He could hear Burns and had replied, but he could not see the Torbeaus. Then his formation flew out of the cloud into clear air, and he saw the convoy ahead, off the island of Schiermonnikoog, further away than expected. He could also see the Torbeaus, low down and ahead to port. He would have to put the anti-flak sections in position for the attack, somehow synchronizing their dives with the Torbeaus.

'Outgrow leader to all aircraft', he called over the R/T. 'Am turning to port. My section will take the centre of the convoy. Barnhut will drop back and take the rear. Bowsaw will go ahead and take the front. Take up your positions. Watch those balloons.'

Twenty-eight Beaufighters wheeled to port in response to their leader's directions, far more gently than the impression given to Frank Woolley. The crews looked down at the convoy, the two large ships with seven minesweepers and a flotilla of about ten R-boats. They knew what to expect. A few of them would probably be shot down into the sea in the next few minutes and their petrol tanks would explode. Most of them had seen it all before, the funeral pyres of their comrades amidst the chaos of gunfire and burning ships. Well, at least there didn't seem to be any Jerry fighters about; the Polish boys would go at them like demons if they appeared, anyway.

---

*   The point ahead of the estimated position of the convoy. Once reached, the Wing would turn and hunt down the convoy's track.

Then flak began to burst around them, the heavy shells of the 105 mm guns of the minesweepers and the medium 37 mm guns of the *Nachtigall*.*

Burns R/T still yowled at him, but he could see that the anti-flak sections were trying to manoeuvre into attacking position. His Torbeaus were now in line astern, ready to turn to starboard and attack the two large merchant vessels on their bows and beams. He ignored the flak-bursts pockmarking the sky and looked closely at the wakes of the two targets. They were far ahead of their estimated position and must be moving quickly. Then he made a decision that was to ensure the success of the mission.

'Volga leader to all Volga aircraft. Convoy speed fifteen knots. Faster than standard eight knots. Acknowledge.'

'Blue two. Understood. Acknowledged.'

'Blue three. Understood. OK.'

One by one, the pilots in the Blue, Green and Red sections of the Torbeaus replied in sequence over the R/T. But Burns knew that he was still in danger of attacking too early.

'Volga leader to Outgrow leader', he called. 'Suggest you attack from rear.'

Suddenly the noise in Burns' earphones cleared. Possibly one of his Torbeau pilots had left his microphone on but had switched it to the 'off' position after the acknowledgements. At last, Burns could hear Gadd's voice.

'Attack attack attack!'

Burns turned to starboard with his ten Torbeaus, now in 'fluid pairs'. In the back of Burns' aircraft, Woolley had cocked the four cannon and was looking forward through the cupola, holding his camera. He hoped that there was no *Sperrbrecher* amongst that lot, and that there was no flak-controller clever enough to recognize the torpedo bombers and concentrate the fire against them. Once again, he thought how graceful the tracer looked as it curved up towards them. Burns concentrated on the first large vessel, the *Gustav Nachtigall*.

'How beautiful it looks, with those clean lines', he thought briefly. 'It seems to be painted white. What a shame to have to sink a ship like that!'

The professional airman took over. Burns had dropped hundreds of torpedoes in trials as well as some in action. He did not use

---

*   Many escort vessels had been equipped with heavy 105 mm guns, replacing medium 88 mm and 37 mm guns.

the 'Travelling Lamp' torpedo sight, for this instrument was accurate only if the pilot flew at a fixed height and speed and dropped from a set distance away. There were so many other factors that affected the path of a torpedo, especially in action, that he preferred to rely on his experience and the ring of his reflector sight to estimate the 'aim-off angle'; this would have to be wider than the usual fifty yards, since the ship was travelling so fast – about twice the length of the ship in front of its bow. He jinked and skidded his Torbeau to avoid some persistent tracer that was following him, then brought his aircraft back to straight and level flight.

'Wait until you can see the line of rivets along the hull', was his dictum, for he knew that this would give him a range of about 1,000 yards. Many pilots dropped too far away in action, and that was why they missed. He switched on his torpedo master switch and his two camera switches – the F24 and the torpedo assessment camera. God, that tracer was bloody close! It would get him in a moment. Most of it was coming from a minesweeper he could see out of the corner of his eye.

Suddenly, the minesweeper stopped firing and blew up. There is a strange trick in the sensory perceptions when flying in action. Events that are flashing past seem to happen in slow motion. So it was when the aircrews saw the minesweeper *M.103*. She seemed to expand slowly and then burst as bits of her superstructure flew into the air and great jets of steam shot out. Rockets, fired by Bill Tacon's section and led by Tony Gadd, stuck her in the bows and above and below the waterline. Cannon shells raked her. Both boilers, her main engine and her steering gear were put out of action. Three men were killed and twenty-two wounded. She stopped and began to sink.

The manoeuvring of the attackers had enabled the Germans to prepare their defences, against what they thought were forty Beaufighters and twenty Mustangs. They opened fire with their heavy flak when the attackers were over 8,000 yards away, later recording that the Beaufighters flew determinedly through the barrage. They thought that as many as fifteen torpedoes were dropped against each of the two large vessels, although the Torbeaus dropped only ten torpedoes in all. The *Amerskerk*, which was first holed by rockets below the waterline on her port side, was struck by a torpedo in Number Four hold. She began to settle rapidly, stern first. Six men were wounded. One life-boat was damaged by cannon fire, but the crew hurriedly lowered the remaining three and abandoned the vessel. They were picked up by minesweepers after the *Amerskerk* sank.

The *Nachtigall* suffered a more protracted ending. Her crew thought that they could see ten torpedo tracks running towards them. They tried evasive action, but at least one torpedo hit the vessel in her after-part. The stern section broke away, like a hinge, and was dragged along the sea bed in about fifty feet of water. Two men were killed and seven wounded, whilst another man was missing. In spite of being split, almost in two, she did not sink immediately. Four tugs came out in an attempt to tow her to shallower water, aided by a pump steamer, but she continued to settle slowly. Over ten hours later, the last of her crew abandoned her. She heeled over to port and sank.

All the minesweepers were damaged, two only lightly, but the others seriously. *M.23* was particularly badly holed; with three compartments flooded, one of her crew dead and twenty wounded, it was a hard struggle to save her from sinking. Meanwhile, the crew of the badly-hit *M.103* was working desperately against time, aided by some sailors from *M.104* and *M.82*. They succeeded in repairing the engines and one of the boilers, but they could not stem the inrush of water; an hour later, she capsized and sank.

Apart from the records of *M.103*, which went down with her, the convoy recorded that the vessels fired a total of 206 shells of 105 mm, 35 of 37 mm and 5,044 of 20 mm against the attackers; in addition they fired 856 rounds of 15 mm and 1,120 of 8 mm. In total, the convoy suffered losses of nine dead, one missing and seventy wounded. The sailors claimed that they had shot down at least fifteen aircraft, but higher authority revised this figure to ten, which they distributed amongst all the vessels in the convoy.

The Beaufighters swept round to port after the attack, heading back out to sea. The Mustangs closed round them like sheepdogs, chivvying them into some sort of formation. An excited chatter broke out over the R/T, incomprehensible to the English-speaking pilots.

'Look out, all aircraft!' called Paddy Burns, urgently. 'There must be Jerries about. Watch your tails!'

'No, no! Not Jerries! I am saying good show, Beaufighters!' It was Squadron Leader Niemiec, the Polish leader of the fighter escort.

'Thank you, Mustangs. Good show to you, too. Sorry there were no bogeys for you!'

15 June 1944. The *Nachtigall*, gleaming in the early morning sun, preceded by three minesweepers with sweeps out. In the background, the Dutch Frisian island of Schiermonnikoog.

15 June 1944. The *Amerskerk*, hit by a torpedo. In the background, two minesweeper escorts. All vessels are flying balloons.

15 June 1944. The *Nachtigall* under cannon fire.

15 June 1944. The *Nachtigall*, flying a balloon, hit by a torpedo. In the background, a minesweeper escort under cannon fire.

Flying Officer Duncan Marrow (left) and Wing Commander Tony Gadd (right).

Flying Officer Frank Woolley (left) and Wing Commander Paddy Burns (right) at a wedding presentation for one of their WAAF drivers. These girls also helped cook the 'flying meals' for the aircrews at North Coates, at all times of the day.

In the Officers' Mess at North Coates. Left to right, Group Captain 'Joss' Braithwaite, Air Vice Marshal 'Hoppy' Hopps, Wing Commander 'Paddy' Burns, Flight Lieutenant 'George' Fern, Wing Commander Engineering (name unknown).
'George' Fern is looking a little puzzled, for the senior officers are playing practical jokes. Every time he reaches for his glass of beer it is in a different position.

The Polish pilots had been frustrated since the German fighters had failed to appear. Some had given vent to their feelings by joining the anti-flak sections, diving down and using their cannon on the R-boats and minesweepers. Frank Woolley had seen some German sailors dive over the side rather than face the withering fire.

Burns drew up alongside Torbeau 'B' of his squadron, flown by a Canadian, Flying Officer J.A. Biehler. The aircraft looked as though it had been operated on by a gigantic tin-opener.

'Hallo, Johnny! What's happened to you?' asked Burns.

'Some bastard's been throwing rocks', growled the Canadian.

Gadd nursed a Beaufighter with a cannon shell rip in the fin and rudder. In Beaufighter 'O' of 455 Squadron, the Australian pilot, Flying Officer E.W. Watson, could see holes in his port wing and engine nacelle. In 'X' of the same squadron, Flying Officer N.R. Smith, could feel the holes torn by flak in the collar of his Mae West; with his hydraulics severed and the fuselage like a sieve, he returned to make a belly-landing at Langham. Several other Beaufighters were damaged, but not a single aircraft was lost on the operation. Had the German authority – the *Befehlshaber der Sicherung der Nordsee* – known the truth of its assessment of ten aircraft destroyed, there might have been fewer iron crosses to distribute amongst the survivors of the shattered convoy.

Reconnaissance later in the day was able to report that balloons were still flying above the sunken vessels. Both the North Coates and Langham Wings received congratulations from the AOC of Coastal Command and the C-in-C of Nore Command. The attack was assessed as the most devastating delivered so far by the Strike Wings. Tony Gadd received a DFC, whilst Paddy Burns was awarded a bar to his DFC. Both Duncan Marrow and Frank Woolley received their DFCs later in the year. For once, Coastal Command were granted a little publicity; Tony Gadd and Duncan Marrow actually spoke on the nine o'clock news of the BBC.

CHAPTER EIGHT

Second Squirt

Propaganda is a soft weapon: hold it in your hands too
long and it will move about like a snake and strike the
other way.

Jean Anouilh, born 1910

'Never go back for a second squirt!' This was the advice that the
pilots of the Strike Wings gave each other, again and again. Being
human, most airmen felt fear before taking off. Some also felt fear
on their return, once the mood of elation had worn off. The attack
itself was a different matter, however. The sense of power when diving, the thudding of the four cannon, the smell of cordite, the lines
of tracer or the jets of rockets converging on the ship, even the
return fire – these were exhilarating beyond belief. The attack was
supposed to be a single synchronized sweep, then down to wave-
top level at full boost and head for home – but the temptation to go
in again was strong. Some of the ships seemed undamaged – why
not give them another dose? There were unexpected cannon shells
left in the ammunition boxes – why not make good use of them? Yet
the second squirt didn't work out. Paddy Burns tried it once and
ended up with a sliver of shrapnel in his leg and a Beaufighter
damaged beyond repair. Peter Hughes tried it once and ended up
with a lifetime of regrets and the marks of the Gestapo on his
face.

By August 1944, the successes of the three Strike Wings were
undeniable. Moving from aerodrome to aerodrome around the
coasts of England and Scotland, the North Coates Wing and the
Wings originally formed at Wick and at Leuchars had left a trail of
sunken freighters, *Sperrbrecher*, flak-ships, E-boats and R-boats,
from Kristiansand in Norway to Bordeaux in France. Yet the public
knew little about the activities of these Wings. Splashed across the
newspapers were accounts of the massive attacks by the RAF and
the USAAF on the heartland of Germany and of the great land battles
in Europe. Few people were even aware of the existence of the strike

aircraft of Coastal Command, for their sorties merited only a few lines in the newspapers or a brief mention on the BBC news. Very few of the vivid photographs of their daylight attacks were shown in the daily papers, although some appeared in the Sunday papers that specialized in pictures accompanied by stories written in a lighter vein. The British public did not identify itself with the men of Coastal in the same way as those of Fighter or Bomber Commands. It was time that Coastal had a publicity boost, the public relations people of the Air Ministry decided.

The Ministry of Information made the arrangements. Two Dakota loads of newspaper reporters and photographers, about forty men, were to be flown from London to North Coates during the afternoon of 7 August 1944. The Station Commander and the COs of the squadrons had been notified of the date of this visit. They were asked to provide a large-scale strike within the twenty-four hours of the arrival of the representatives of the Press. The intention was that the eager newsmen would be able to examine the preliminary photographs of an enemy convoy taken by reconnaissance aircraft, witness the crews being briefed and watch them take off. The finale would come when the crews returned with reports and photographs of their success, their aircraft perhaps bearing some flak damage as dramatic evidence of their encounter. It was hoped that the story would be acclaimed in many countries, for Australian, Canadian and New Zealand crews would be involved, as well as other nationals serving in the RAF. To cap everything, long-range Mustangs of the 4th Fighter Group of the USAAF, based at Debden in Essex, were expected to escort the Beaufighters. An international scoop was in the making!

There was, however, a snag bedevilling these careful preparations. Coastal Command's targets were seldom static and there was no method of arranging for the Germans to provide a suitable convoy to coincide with the day allotted for the visit of the newspaper men. The Germans seemed to be unaware of the part they were expected to play in the short period that the reporters could spare from their busy schedules. Reconnaissance aircraft found that the shipping lanes along the Dutch and German coasts were empty of convoys. A few isolated and tiny vessels could be seen, but nothing to match the grand occasion. Higher authority began to worry.

However, later in the morning of the 7th a few freighters were spotted in parts of the Norwegian Leads and it was hoped that these would combine to form a sizeable convoy. Then the weather began to behave in an awkward fashion. A slow-moving depression with low cloud and rain was reported to be approaching Norway, sufficiently troublesome to throw doubt on the possibility of operational flying in that area. The weather deteriorated between London and North Coates, preventing the Dakotas from taking off on the 7th. The visit was deferred to the early morning of the following day, but the newspaper men were adamant in their insistence that they had to be flown back to London in the evening of the same day.

By now, everything seemed to be falling apart. The time available for arranging a strike had contracted to just a few hours. The officer ordered to lead the whole formation was Wing Commander Paddy Burns. As yet, he had no definite target, but he was certainly having a harassing time on the ground. During the night of the 7th, he was called repeatedly into the Operations Room at North Coates to reassess the situation. At one time, it was suggested to him that sections of the Beaufighters at Langham and North Coates should attack a single *Artillerieträger*, or naval gun barge, which had been spotted off the coast of Denmark. Burns struggled to control his amazement and annoyance; he pointed out that a shallow-draught vessel of about 300 tons was a most unsuitable target for Torbeaus, whilst about thirty anti-flak Beaufighters would get in the way of each other's fire when jockeying for position. This idea was abandoned.

Burns recommended that they should risk the weather, take off at night and arrive at daybreak at a point north of Stavanger, where the vessels were forced out to sea without the protection of the Leads or shore batteries. Group Headquarters demurred; the senior officers said that the Press might not have arrived by this time and that the depression might not have moved away. Burns pointed out that if the strike were deferred to later in the day, any southbound convoy would have reached a position close to shore batteries and the fighter aerodrome at Sola. Group Headquarters then produced a trump card. The fighter escort would amount to no less than forty-eight P-51s of the USAAF; there need be no fear of enemy fighters with such a force. Take-off was deferred to midday.

During the morning of the 8th, the posse of Press men arrived from London. They seemed suitably impressed with the preparations for the attack. Thirty-nine Beaufighters were detailed for the Reconnaissance in Force as it was called, for no one was sure if there really was a convoy off the Norwegian coast. There were twelve Torbeaus of 254 Squadron, armed with cannon and with Mark XV torpedoes set to run at a depth of ten feet; three more Beaufighters armed with cannon only, including Burns' aircraft; fifteen Beaufighters of 489 (RNZAF) Squadron, armed with cannon only; and nine from 455 (RAAF) Squadron, all armed with cannon although four were carrying rockets as well. The Australian and New Zealand sections had flown up from Langham during the previous afternoon so that the Press could see the whole formation taking off together from North Coates.

The Beaufighters took off at 12.30 hours. They were met over Spurn Head by their powerful P-51 Mustang escort, the 4th Fighter Group of the USAAF, based at Debden. This unit was the oldest and probably the most renowned of all the American Fighter Group in the European theatre, having been formed when the three American Eagle squadrons of the RAF were transferred to the USAAF in September 1942.

The commander of the Group was Colonel D.J.M. Blakeslee, a 26-year-old American from Fairport Harbor in Ohio. Blakeslee had joined the RCAF in July 1940 and had first flown operationally in 401 (RCAF) Squadron, which was then equipped with Spitfires. His present unit, known by the Americans as the 'Blakesleewaffe', was renowned for its dash and aggression, being considered the highest-scoring US Fighter Group in Europe; by August 1944, it claimed that it had destroyed or damaged 996 enemy aircraft. Among its exploits, the Group had formed part of the escort of some 800 B-17 Fortresses and B-24 Liberators of the USAAF in the massive daylight raid on Berlin on 6 March 1944. To escort the Beaufighters, forty-seven P-51s took off, but eight were compelled to turn back with engine trouble; a fighter pilot dare not set off across the North Sea to Norway unless his single engine was running smoothly. Blakeslee had taken off with the P-51s; he was Mascot leader, whilst Burns was Cafel leader.

Burns was not in his sunniest mood. He had managed only a few snatches of sleep the night before and was still feeling frustrated from the verbal exchanges with his senior officers. He was a professional airman who would always obey orders, but he also conceived it his duty to ensure that his squadron fought in the most effective way possible. The North Coates and the Langham Wings contained skilled and dedicated airmen; their lives should not be squandered by misguided attempts to provide an exhibition for the benefit of the Press. A plan of attack should follow proper reconnaissance, be carefully thought out, and then executed with maximum courage and efficiency. Burns felt in his bones that there was something wrong with this Reconnaissance in Force; nevertheless he was prepared to use every ounce of his ability to ensure its success.

Leading the New Zealanders of 489 Squadron was Squadron Leader Peter A. Hughes, a 25-year-old Englishmen in the RAF who had graduated from Cranwell two months before the outbreak of war. In October 1939 he had begun a long tour of operations in the Avro Ansons of 217 Squadron, flying from St Eval in Cornwall. After a period as an instructor on Beauforts, he had joined the New Zealanders whilst they were still operating in Hampdens off the Norwegian coast. When 489 Squadron converted to Beaufighters in October 1943, Hughes' New Zealand crew had been replaced by Freddie E. Spink, a young Yorkshireman who was an ex-art student and had trained as a navigator in Canada. Both men had been awarded their DFCs; Hughes in May 1944 and Spink two months later.

The New Zealand section flew on the left wing of the Beaufighter formation. Hughes was relieved to find that his port engine was now running smoothly, for it had misfired alarmingly on take-off. He had wondered if he would be forced to land, but had decided to continue since he was leading the section; after banging and spitting, the engine of his aircraft, letter 'E' and serial NE741, had settled down to a steady roar. Like the crews of 254 Squadron, the New Zealanders normally operated in the torpedo rather than the anti-flak role. On this occasion they would have to rely solely on their cannon to suppress the enemy gunners, for their Beaufighters were not fitted with rocket rails.

In the leading aircraft, Frank Woolley gave Paddy Burns a course for Stavanger in south-east Norway. One Beaufighter of 455 Squadron turned back with engine trouble. The formation flew low over the sea, as usual, with the USAAF Mustangs slightly above. There was no sign of the expected weather front as they flew north-east. If anything, the weather was becoming clearer than at North Coates.

The Americans had no respect for the careful R/T discipline of the Beaufighter pilots. One Mustang pilot began to chatter to his friends and several more joined in. Burns began to fidget.

'Cafel leader to Mascot leader. Please observe R/T silence!'

snapped Burns. There was a pause, but the American voices began again. A Beaufighter pilot broke in with an effective obscenity.

'What's wrong with you guys?' came an aggrieved American voice. 'Don't you want the Krauts to come up and fight us?'

A hurt silence followed this somewhat surprising question. The last thing that the Beaufighter crews wanted was to let the Germans know that they were on their way. If the convoy expected them, the ships would be huddled together, perhaps with their bows pointed to shore and their sterns presenting tiny and uninviting targets for torpedoes, protected by shore batteries. Moreover, they did not want a swarm of Me 109s and FW 190s around their ears, but this was exactly what the Americans hoped would happen. Their standing orders were to entice the German fighters into the sky and to shoot down as many as possible. The US higher authorities had calculated, quite correctly, that the number of experienced fighter pilots in the Luftwaffe had thinned out considerably by the second half of 1944. Moreover, there was insufficient aviation fuel available to the German squadrons. In a war of attrition, the Allies must win. The 4th Fighter Group of the 8th USAAF remained silent for the rest of the outward flight, the pilots probably contemplating the ingratitude and over-cautious attitude of the pig-headed Limeys.

A German convoy of four merchant vessels had sailed from Kristiansand South at 05.00 hours, whilst Paddy Burns was discussing the plan of attack and its timing with his superiors. There was a German tanker of 1,836 tons, the *Inga Essberger*, whilst the other three were freighters. The German *Carsten Russ* of 994 tons carried a cargo of sea mines and military supplies. The Norwegian *Dione* of 1,620 tons was loaded with saltpetre, whilst the Norwegian *Vim* of 1,221 tons carried wheat. All these merchant vessels were armed with cannon and machine guns. There were eight escort vessels. Kapitän-leutnant Bilger was the senior officer in *K.2*, an ex-Dutch gunboat of 1,290 tons heavily armed with four 120 mm and two 37 mm guns as well as twelve 20 mm cannon. There were two minesweepers, *M.5207* and *M.5210*. There were five submarine-chasers equipped as escort vessels, *UJ.1707*, *UJ.1711*, *UJ.1103*, *UJ.1113* and *UJ.1105*. These minesweepers and submarine-hunters carried 88 mm and 37 mm guns as well as rocket launchers and machine guns. The convoy was headed north, the next call being at Stavanger. At 14.40 hours, Bilger received a warning from the W/T station at Lister of the approach of a large formation of Allied aircraft. The crews were called to action stations. The guns were manned and ready. Two minutes later, the lookouts sighted the North Coates and Langham Wings, escorted by the Mustangs, over eight miles away on their port bow. After another two minutes, the convoy opened up on the Beaufighters with its long-range flak.

Fifteen miles off the coast of Norway, the Strike Wing had turned south-east, hunting down the coast for a suitable target. The P-51s were still thirty-nine in number; one of those who had long since turned back with engine trouble was Colonel Donald Blakeslee. The senior officer of the 4th Fighter Group was now Major Leon Blanding, from Sumter in South Carolina.

When Burns saw the enemy convoy, off the island of Eigerøy, his worst fears were confirmed. The merchant ships had closed up near the shore under the protection of shore batteries, forming a small target. The majority of the escorts were to seaward. He knew that the enemy must have been alerted, for not only had the R/T discipline been poor but the Wing had flown over a large fishing fleet which would certainly have had a German W/T monitoring service on board. These ships were so close together that some of the Beaufighters would be crowded out, but Burns had no time to attempt a complicated briefing of his pilots over the R/T. It would be foolhardy to fly over the shore batteries and attack towards the sea. He gave the order to attack, flying from the sea, selecting the nearest minesweeper, *M.5210*, as his own target.

Two Beaufighters were shot down early in the attack. In the New Zealand section on the left, an aircraft flown by Pilot Officer R.J.W. Hey and navigated by Flight Sergeant G.R. Clemens, dived uncontrollably into the sea near the seaward escort vessels. Alongside Burns, the anti-flak Beaufighter of 254 Squadron flown by Squadron Leader R.T.H. 'Jimmy' James burst into a sheet of flame and exploded in the sea. James had wanted desperately to join an operational squadron for a second tour and this was his first attack with 254 Squadron; he and his navigator, Warrant Officer B.A. Reynolds, lost their lives.

Then tracer poured up to meet the Beaufighters and the sky was full of yellow parachutes with mines dangling from them. About forty of these rockets were fired. Over 5,000 shells of 20 mm calibre were expended by the convoy. There were also about 200 bursts of

88 mm shells, about 600 of 37 mm and even 30 of the heavy 120 mm, quite apart from the flak put up by the shore batteries at Eigerøy and Egersund.

As Burns dived, opening fire with his cannon on the mine-sweeper, several other Beaufighters converged into his line of sight, so that he was forced to shift his attention to the *Vim* behind the minesweeper. Breaking away to port, he flew over land. Looking back, he was disappointed to see that, although the vessels had been covered with spray, there was not the usual evidence of exploding and burning ships. He saw one torpedo hit the rocky coastline. The sight of James's Beaufighter had sickened him, and he regretted having helped the pilot to join his squadron. Flak continued to follow him as he headed out to sea. Of all the attacks he had led, he thought that this was the least successful.

Peter Hughes led his section on the left wing into the attack. He also saw Jimmy James's Beaufighter burst into flames, but the flak seemed to be directed at the centre of the formation rather than towards himself. He opened fire with his cannon at the leading escort vessel, *UJ.1707*, cleared it at mast-top height and headed towards the land. The weather was so brilliantly clear that he could pick out a German camp on the headland as he turned out to sea once more. There were plenty of shells left in the ammunition boxes. He decided to go back for a 'second squirt'.

Once again, Hughes raked *UJ.1707* with his cannon, before streaking out to the west; so far as he could tell, it had been a successful second attack.

'Captain, there's smoke coming out of the port engine!' came the worried voice of Freddie Spink.

From where he sat, Hughes could not see the smoke at first. The Beaufighter seemed to be flying quite well. He carried on, climbing a little. Then he saw flames and smoke coming from underneath the engine cowling, and immediately put the fire precautions into effect. He closed the port throttle and turned off the fuel to the engine. The fire spread at once, presumably because the engine was no longer using fuel; it raced along the balance pipe, so that flames started to come into the cockpit between his legs. It was the sort of situation that all wartime pilots dreaded.

It is impossible to say what hit the Beaufighter. It may have been flak from the ships or from the shore. It may even have come from another Beaufighter attacking in the confined space of the ships huddled together; this was a danger that had to be borne by those in the Strike Wings.* Whatever it was, it had a catastrophic effect. Hughes feathered the engine and pressed the fire extinguisher button, but the fuel pipes underneath him were ablaze. It was evident to Hughes that he could not stay at the controls for more than a few seconds. He called urgently:

'Freddie! Bale out, Freddie! Bale out!'

There was no reply from Spink. Hughes pulled the Beaufighter up into a climb, for he was flying at only about 200 feet, too low for parachutes to open. He reached up and yanked at the lanyard that should have opened the pilot's escape hatch in the floor of the fuselage immediately behind him, preparatory to grabbing the handles above him and looping himself backwards over the seat and through the aperture. Nothing happened. Glancing back, he could see a sheet of flame by this escape hatch; evidently the release mechanism had burnt away.

There was another escape hatch on his right side; he pulled the lever and pushed the window clear, knowing that this was a very dangerous means of exit, for the pilot would probably hit the tail and injure himself. Nevertheless, it was all he could do. He was still trying to climb to parachute-dropping height. This was 500 feet at the very minimum, provided one pulled the ripcord immediately on jumping. The flames intensified, burning his hands and face, singeing away the eyebrows above his goggles. He leant away from the flames, towards the open window, with his hands on the control column. There was still no word from Spink. They were at about 300 feet and climbing a little. Suddenly, the slipstream sucked him through the window of the Beaufighter.

Some pilots of the low-flying aircraft of the Strike Wings thought that their parachutes were little more than encumbrances, for it was such a rarity for anyone to have the opportunity to jump out in an emergency. A few navigators did not even bother to carry their packs, but the pilot needed to take his parachute into the aircraft since it formed part of his seat in the cockpit. Ditching was an ever-present possibility, however, and the parachute dangling around the pilot's rear could snag in the narrow top escape hatch. For this reason, some pilots thought it advisable to unstrap their parachute harnesses as soon as they had settled into their seats, but Hughes

---

* Wing Commander Tony Gadd, who was Wing Commander Flying at North Coates at the time of this attack, estimates that his aircraft were hit by 'friendly' fire on no less than seven occasions during his numerous anti-shipping attacks, usually from ricochets off the sea hitting his leading Beaufighter.

never shared this view. He always kept his parachute harness strapped tightly to his body and also took the precaution of clipping on the lanyard of his 'K' type single dinghy pack. These actions saved his life on 8 August 1944.

Hughes found himself spinning around in the air. He was fortunate to miss the tailplane completely, and pulled the ripcord. The parachute opened at once, probably blown open by the slipstream of the Beaufighter. There was a slight jerk and Hughes found himself descending gently towards the sea. He was in the air for only a few seconds before plunging into the water.

We will never know exactly what happened to Freddie Spink. As soon as he heard the order to bale out, it would have been part of his escape drill to unstrap his seat belt, unplug his intercom and reach for his parachute pack. He would then have clipped the pack on to the front of his harness, within a couple of seconds of hearing Hughes' urgent words. Then he would have dived towards his escape hatch in the floor of his compartment and pulled the release lanyard. Provided the hatch opened – and it is probable that it did, for he could also push it manually – it would have swung forward on its hinges and the slipstream would have locked it in the down position. Then he would have looked at the sea, only about 300 feet below, and probably hesitated before jumping to his death, for the aircraft was still climbing. It would have been natural to wait for a few more seconds, unless the flames had already reached him. Then Hughes was sucked out. The Beaufighter was seen by other pilots to turn on its back and dive into the water. Somehow, Spink scrambled clear, but too late for his parachute to open sufficiently. A remarkable photograph taken by the navigator of another Beaufighter at that instant shows Hughes descending by parachute, the Beaufighter hitting the water, and a secondary splash which is probably Spink striking the sea with an incompletely opened parachute.

The remaining Beaufighters turned back to North Coates, some of them badly hit by flak. The Mustangs split into two formations, one to escort the Beaufighters and one to fly inland over Norway. Second-Lieutenant Thomas A. Underwood reported over the R/T that the engine of his Mustang was on fire and that he was having to bale out near the enemy convoy. Some of the Mustangs strafed the aerodrome at Sola, near Stavanger. Second-Lieutenant Robert G. Fischer was hit by flak and reported that he was making for Sweden.

Major Leon Blanding was injured on the side of his head when his canopy was hit by flak. Streaming blood, he tore off part of his trousers to bind up the wound. Semi-conscious at times but coaxed by his two wing-men, he flew back across the North Sea to land at Acklington in Northumberland, where he was found to have a fractured skull. Captain Frank C. Jones of Montclair in New Jersey went down in the sea on his return journey and did not leave his aircraft; it was to have been the last mission of his tour, for he was to have been married ten days later.

The attack on the German convoy was not as fruitless as Paddy Burns feared. Twelve torpedoes were dropped, but the small and agile freighters were able to avoid them with ease; the Germans reported that four torpedoes passed by the vessels and exploded on rocks near the shore. But the cannon and rocket fire was devastatingly effective. *M.5210*, the minesweeper attacked by Paddy Burns, was badly hit, as was *UJ.1707*, the submarine-chaser attacked twice by Peter Hughes. The merchant vessels *Vim* and *Carsten Russ* suffered serious damage to their upperworks. Three more submarine-chasers were badly damaged. In all, 15 seamen were killed, 37 badly wounded and 33 lightly wounded. No vessel was sunk but the shattered convoy was forced to turn into the harbour of Egersund, where two of the submarine-chasers were left behind for repair and the dead and wounded were taken ashore. It had been a bad day for the Germans in Norwegian waters.

One Beaufighter of 455 Squadron headed back to Langham. The Press men saw the remaining thirty-five land at North Coates. Some of them were damaged enough to cause excitement. Last to arrive was the Torbeau of 254 Squadron flown by Flying Officer E.R. Ridgeway, which came in on one engine and burst into flames after crash-landing, fortunately without injury to the crews but providing a spectacular finale. Paddy Burns answered the questions posed by the Press men with politeness; after all, what had happened was not their fault, and they could not be expected to realize that it was far more difficult to time an attack on a convoy by the Strike Wings than on a town somewhere in Germany.

But Burns had something else on his mind that he did not wish to discuss with the Press. On leaving the target area, he had spotted a small yellow dinghy with a man inside it, about ten miles from the Norwegian shore. He had thought hard before making up his mind. The airman might be injured; he was drifting in a frail rubber

8 August 1944. Views of an escort vessel under attack by rockets and cannon.

(*Top*):
The North American Mustang was the most effective fighter escort that accompanied the Strike Wings to Norway. This version is the P-51D, called the Mustang Mark IV in the RAF. It carried four .50 inch Browning machine guns. This photograph was taken in the USA in 1981.

(*Left*): Squadron Leader Peter A. Hughes. (*Right*): Flying Officer Freddie E. Spink.

8 August 1944. Beaufighter TFX, letter 'E' serial NE741, crashes near Eigerøy. Squadron Leader Peter Hughes descends by parachute. The small secondary splash, to the right of the major splash, is probably caused by Flying Officer Freddie Spink, whose parachute does not open in time.

dinghy some way off a dangerous coast; he could not hope to get back to the UK, although there was a possibility that he might be helped by the Norwegian resistance if he reached shore. On balance, Burns had thought that it was better to arrange a rescue service. He had instructed Woolley to send out an international distress signal on the W/T, giving the position of the dinghy; this would be picked up by the Germans.

There were two dinghies off the coast of Eigerøy that afternoon. Thomas Underwood of the USAAF was in one of them, but he was the second to come down. A few miles away, Peter Hughes was already in another dinghy. Hughes had released his parachute harness when his feet touched the water and had inflated his Mae West. Then he had taken the cover off his 'K' type dinghy and partly inflated it by turning the valve on the CO_2 bottle. He had slithered inside the dinghy and topped it up with the bellows. Positioning the wooden thwart across his legs, he had checked the equipment – waterproof apron, small mast and sail, paddle, signals, heliograph, compass and leak stoppers. So far, it had gone by the drill book. He was not at all cold, for there was no wind and the sun was beating down on a shiny and placid sea. He felt that the salt water was helping to cure his burns, which were not very painful, although he had lost a lot of hair.

A Mustang came over, the engine misfiring badly, and disappeared out of sight. Through a slight summer haze, Hughes could see the distant hills of Norway. He could also pick out the ships of the convoy, careering about in various directions, and it gave him some satisfaction to think that some of them must be in trouble. He looked out to sea in case Freddie Spink had somehow survived, but he knew in his heart that this was a vain hope. After about an hour, an He 111 flew directly overhead at about 1,000 feet, but Hughes made no move to attract attention. Eventually, the German flew off. Hughes also spotted some Norwegian fishing boats on the horizon and, when the German ships had disappeared, fired off one of his signals, but there was no response. He began to paddle towards the east.

Darkness gathered, and Hughes was still paddling towards shore. He was unable to tell the time, for his prized Rolex Oyster watch had let in water and stopped; the thread of the waterproof winder had stripped earlier, and he had been unable to have this repaired during wartime. At about midnight, he reached a rocky shore and climbed to dry land, taking the dinghy with him. He was on the island of Eigerøy.

Hughes spent the remainder of the short night on the shore. It was not cold and he did not feel hungry. His thoughts were centred on escape, and he wondered if he could cross Norway and reach the neutral country of Sweden. He took out his Norwegian money and hid it in his flying boots. At first light, he could tell that he was on an island and realized that he might have to hide during the day before paddling to the mainland the following night. Then he spotted a rowing boat with a man at the oars who appeared to be a Norwegian fisherman, and thought that this might be his salvation. He waved and shouted to the man, but to his acute disappointment the Norwegian indicated that the Germans were nearby and that Hughes should give himself up to them. Hughes refused and the man rowed away. He must have been a Quisling, or someone sent out by the Germans in response to the distress call over the W/T, for he returned in half an hour with German soldiers.

Hughes was marched into the German battery of Eigerøy, past groups of Norwegians who shook their heads sadly and made gestures of sympathy and friendliness. At least he was alive. He was taken next to Egersund, where he spotted two U-boats and wished that his 'second squirt' had been directed against these targets; every airman in Coastal Command wanted to sink a U-boat. From Egersund, he was taken by train to Oslo, in company with Second-Lieutenant Thomas Underwood, who had also been picked up. Underwood told him of his extraordinary experience: his engine had been misfiring so badly that he intended to bale out and had undone his straps; then the engine had cut completely and he had come down in the sea, being hurled through the open hood and landing unharmed in water.

At Oslo, patriotic Norwegians marched past their cells, bearing placards that bore the news of the invasion of southern France by Allied troops. After about a week, the two men were taken by train to Frederikstad on the border with Sweden and then by boat to Frederikshavn in Denmark. Once again, they were put on a train, trundling southwards. By Aarhus, the guards had gone to sleep and Hughes thought that here might be an opportunity to dive through the door and escape, but he could not get past Underwood before the guards woke up.

The next stop was at Hamburg, a scene of such complete devastation that even Hughes was astonished. The two men were marched, feeling somewhat vulnerable in their air force uniforms, to the Gestapo Headquarters. Here they were separated. Hughes was taken into a cell and stripped. After standing in the cold for some time, he was given back his clothes and marched through corridors in the mediaeval prison, past clanging steel doors, to another cell. Here, two Gestapo thugs entered and beat him up, leaving marks on his face with their fists. There was no apparent reason for this brutality. Indeed, it was unusual treatment for an Allied airman to receive – almost unknown amongst German fighting men, who normally behaved with correctness and even compassion towards RAF prisoners. The thugs were perhaps trying to demonstrate to themselves, unsuccessfully, that they were 'the master race'.

From Hamburg, the next move was to Dulag Luft, at Frankfurt, the interrogation centre for RAF prisoners. Hughes was impressed by the fact that the Germans had an accurate and complete history of his career in the RAF.* Then Hughes was sent to Stalag Luft III at Sagan. By Christmas 1944, the POWs were on the move, away from advancing Russian troops. Hughes experienced the notorious 'death marches' that many RAF prisoners had to make, during which his column was sometimes shot up by Allied fighters. He was liberated by tanks of the Cheshire Regiment near Lüneberg and flown back to Wing aerodrome in a Dakota.

There was a minor flurry of publicity following the visit of the Press men to North Coates on 8 August. Two national newspapers carried brief accounts of the attack, each of about 150 words, making somewhat exaggerated claims of the enemy losses. But the newspapers gave far more publicity to other happenings, such as the activities of British warships off the west coast of France on that day. Then Coastal Command slipped back into its usual state of near-oblivion with the news media.

---

*   Such histories of RAF officers could easily be compiled from an examination of London Gazettes and Air Force Lists for the period, freely available to all in public libraries.

CHAPTER NINE

Sailor's Grave

Auf einem Seemannsgrab da blühen keine Rosen. (On a
sailor's grave no roses bloom.)
*Part of refrain of song sung by the Kriegsmarine in wartime
Germany*

Air Chief Marshal Sir Philip de la Ferté Joubert, the Air Officer
Commanding-in-Chief of Coastal Command, looked speculatively
at the two airmen standing in front of him.

'You have been sent to me on the recommendation of your CO,
Wing Commander Wood', he said. 'I need a Beaufighter crew for a
dangerous special mission. The problem is that I can't tell you what
is involved unless you volunteer to go. How do you feel about
that?'

'I'll go, sir', said the pilot, Flight Lieutenant A.K. 'Ken' Gatward
of 236 Squadron.

'So will I, sir', said his navigator, Sergeant G.F. 'George' Fern.

'Good!' said Joubert. 'That's exactly what I thought you would
say. Now for the operation itself. It's over Paris, in daylight. Take a
look at this map. According to Intelligence, the occupying Germans
hold a parade every day along the Champs Elysées between 12.15
and 12.45 British Double Summer Time. We thought it would be a
good idea if a Beaufighter went over there and gave them a few
squirts of cannon fire. That would shake them up and also help the
morale of the Parisians. It ought to be a job for Fighter Command
really, but Paris is out of range of their Spits and all their Beaus are
filled with secret equipment. So it's come round to Coastal.

'If by chance the Germans don't turn up on time, there is a
secondary target. You can have a crack at this building here with
your cannon, on the north side of the Place de la Concorde. This
was the French Ministère de la Marine before the occupation but
now it's taken over by the Kriegsmarine Headquarters, so it's a very
suitable target for us in Coastal.

'Now, you are not to go unless there is complete cloud cover all
the way, because you can't be escorted. And one more thing. This

operation is entirely secret. You are not to mention it to anybody at all, including those on your squadron. The code-name is Operation Squabble. When you come back you will report to me and to no one else. Is that understood?'*

'Yes, sir!' The two airmen snapped to attention. They returned to their base at Wattisham in Suffolk, carrying a collection of maps, guide books and photographs to study. Shortly afterwards, they flew down to Thorney Island on the Sussex coast, nearer their target. It was May 1942. They were flying in Beaufighter letter C, serial F4800, a Mark IC version with the straight tailplane, more manoeuvrable but less stable than the Mark VIC which succeeded it; it was armed with four 20 mm cannon in the nose and six .303 machine guns in the wings, but there was no defensive machine gun in the navigator's cupola.

Ken Gatward was twenty-seven years of age and came from Hornsey in Essex. Pre-war, he had been the director of a small family business, but his heart was in flying. In 1937 he had joined the part-time RAFVR and had spent his weekends learning how to fly Tiger Moths and Hawker Harts at Hatfield in Hertfordshire. He entered the RAF with the rank of sergeant on the declaration of war, but was commissioned in August 1940, after conversion to twin-engines on Airspeed Oxfords. Then he had completed a tour of operations in Blenheims with 53 Squadron, based mainly at Detling in Kent, bombing the French ports. After a short period of rest, he joined 236 Squadron in November 1941, soon after the squadron converted from the Blenheim Mark IVC to the Beaufighter IC. Gatward's navigator, George Fern, was another RAFVR entrant, an ex-schoolmaster from the area of the Forest of Dean in Gloucestershire.

Whilst the two men were awaiting for suitable weather for their dangerous sortie, a very large tricolour flag was sent to them with instructions to drop it over the tomb of the French Unknown Warrior in the Arc de Triomphe. This caused some technical problems. They experimented with pushing the flag down the flare chute, but it was so large that they had to cut it across, horizontally. They then wrapped the two parts around metal bars so that they could be conveniently handled inside the Beaufighter.

On four occasions in early June 1942 they took off for their

---

*   This conversation cannot be quoted verbatim. It is based on the official record and the recollections of Group Captain Gatward, expressed in the phraseology of the wartime RAF.

target, but each time they neared the French coast the cloud cleared, so that Gatward had to obey instructions and return to base. Finally, he had had enough of turning back.

'George, we'll never get cloud cover all the way to Paris at this time of year. If that happens again, I'd like to press on, at deck level. I reckon we could get through OK if we stay just above nought feet. Are you game?'

'Suits me, sir', said the sanguine George Fern.

On 12 June, they took off for their fifth and final attempt, a sortie that was to prove a historic flight. At 11.31 hours, they set course from Thorney Island for Paris, 165 miles away, flying at wave-top height. There was continuous cloud at 2,000 feet above them, with a steady downpour of rain. Crossing the French coast a little east of Fécamp, Gatward brought his Beaufighter up to tree-top height and swung over his Mark II gunsight, locking it in front of him. Fern lifted his camera and stood in the navigator's cupola. They streaked over the French countryside, straight as a die for Paris.

Their course took them over the eastern outskirts of Rouen. By now, the cloud had cleared completely to yield brilliant sunshine. Even at thirty feet, Gatward could see the horizon ahead, fifteen miles away. It was an ideal day for photography as Fern clicked and wound his camera with steady precision. They passed slap over the Luftwaffe aerodrome at Rouen and were not challenged. Twice, Gatward lifted his Beaufighter to clear high-tension cables. There were horses in the fields, some rearing and galloping at the un-accustomed noise. The Beaufighter was a quiet aircraft, but the noise of piston engines can be heard from afar, the sound dying quickly as the aircraft whips past.*

Gatward looked at the oil temperature gauge of his starboard engine. It was far too high, justifying turning back, but he could not face cancelling the sortie at this late stage. Had he known, the trouble was caused by a large and unlucky crow that had smashed into the oil radiator in his wing. Way ahead, something like a matchstick stood up above the horizon.

'Look at that, George', Gatward said. 'It must be the Eiffel tower, and we're dead on track.'

Nearly 1,000 feet high, thirty miles away, the Eiffel tower seemed to beckon to the two men in the Beaufighter. They flew straight

---

* This phenomenon, known as the Doppler Effect, is the rapid lowering of the pitch of a note as it goes past. It was a factor that entered into the Theory of Relativity formulated by Albert Einstein.

towards it, over the suburbs of Paris. Amazed French people stared at this strange aircraft with the roundels on its wings and fuselage. '*C'est la RAF!*'

At exactly 12.27 hours, Gatward recognized the Arc de Triomphe, a few seconds away.

'Are you ready with the first flag, George?'

'Yes, but the slipstream is nearly breaking my arm!' replied the suffering navigator, who was hanging on to the end of the metal bar sticking through the flare chute.

'Now!' called Gatward. Fern thankfully released the tricolour. The RAF's tribute to the dead of France fluttered in the air above a people sunk in the misery and humiliation of the Nazi occupation. Gatward banked to port and headed down the broad avenue of the Champs Elysées, looking eagerly for the sight of those goose-stepping German soldiers. There was not a sign of them. There were a few vehicles, some people on bicycles and plenty of pedestrians, but the enemy soldiers failed to appear.*

The Beaufighter flew below roof-top height, roaring down the avenue whilst the airmen looked intently ahead to pick out their secondary target, the building of the Ministère de la Marine. Gatward spotted it within seconds and swept round to starboard, circling over the easily recognisable landmark of the Opéra before making a second run. He flew south over the Seine and headed north again. This time he had the tall building in his gunsight. There were pedestrians in the Place de la Concorde. Some threw themselves flat on their faces but others stood upright and waved joyously. It must have been a warm day in Paris, for many of the men were in shirt-sleeves. There were several army vehicles in front of the building, but pedestrians were mixed with the German soldiers. Fern was shouting:

'That's it! Dead ahead! I'm ready with the flag!'

'Mustn't hit any of those civilians', thought Gatward, easing up the nose slightly so that he was aiming at the second floor. At 500 yards, he pressed the cannon-firing button with his right thumb.

In the home of his parents near the Jardin de Luxembourg, about a mile away from the Place de la Concorde, a seventeen-year-old youth called Pierre Lorain was musing idly in the garden of his parent's house. Suddenly he heard a most peculiar and protracted

---

*   It was thought by British Intelligence that there must have been a breach of security, but a post-war enquiry revealed no evidence of this. It seems probable that the Germans were alerted by an alarm giving of the approaching Beaufighter.

12 June 1942. A view of
Paris seen by Flight
Lieutenant Ken Gatward
and Sergeant George
Fern.

12 June 1942. A corner of
the Grand Palais in Paris.
The Germans are advertis-
ing an exhibition of 'La Vie
Nouvelle', presumably
their 'New Order'.

12 June 1942. A view of
the river Seine.

thudding noise. He thought he was hearing a building crumbling and falling down, but the sound was that of Gatward's cannon fire. Immediately afterwards came the rattling of German light flak and the wailing of sirens. There was little petrol-driven traffic in the streets of wartime Paris, so that sounds carried well.

The 20 mm shells raked the Headquarters of the Kriegsmarine in France, smashing windows, bouncing and ricocheting off the stonework. Gatward pulled up the nose of his Beaufighter and cleared the top of the building by a few feet, banking to port. Fern had pushed out the second flag and was looking backwards through the cupola. To his delight, he saw a beefy German soldier emerge from his shelter behind an army truck and shake a fist furiously at them. A few streams of tracer followed the departing Beaufighter as the two men set off on their return journey.

The flight back was uneventful. As instructed, Gatward landed at Northholt, near London, and made his report to Joubert.

At dawn two days later, a shower of leaflets descended on Paris, proclaiming the success of the mission. After a further five days, on 17 June at 12.15 hours, the French people clustering around their clandestine radio sets heard the familiar opening notes of Beethoven's Fifth Symphony that signified a broadcast from the BBC, which began:

Vendredi dernier avant midi, les Parisiens reçurent une visite imprevue. Un avion anglais de la section côtière survola Paris à la hauteur des toits. Il monta et descendit les Champs Elysées. En hommage à la France, et à la mémoire glorieuse de ses fils tombés sur le champ d'honneur, l'avion laissa tomber un grand drapeau au dessus de l'Arc de Triomphe. Puis il fit demi-tour, vola entre les immeubles des Champs Elysées. Il passa devant le Ministère de la Marine, Place de la Concorde, maintenant occupé par les Nazis, et lâcha une salve d'obus qui s'ecrasèrent contre la façade et briserent les fenêtres. Le pilot de l'avion était le capitaine Gatward et l'observateur le sergent Fern . . . *

---

*   'Last Friday before mid-day, Parisians had an unexpected visitor. A British aircraft of Coastal Command flew over Paris at roof-top height. It flew up and down the Champs Elysées. In homage to France and the glorious memory of her sons fallen on the field of battle, the aircraft dropped a large tricolour flag over the Arc de Triomphe. Then it made a half-turn and flew between the buildings of the Champs Elysées. It arrived in front of the Ministry of Marine in the Place de la Concorde, now occupied by the Nazis, and fired a salvo of shells which burst against the facade and broke the windows. The pilot was Flight Lieutenant Gatward and the navigator Sergeant Fern . . ."

The sortie made by these two men did not destroy any part of the enemy's forces, but it was certainly of considerable military significance. Firstly, it humiliated the Germans and gave a message of hope to a proud people suffering brutality, forced-labour and privation under an evil dictatorship; in the words of Pierre Lorain, it was a *beau geste* which resounded throughout the French nation and stiffened the will of the Résistants. Secondly, it demonstrated the high degree of skill and courage that Coastal Command aircrew had attained, although this seemed to achieve public recognition only when directed against targets on land. Lastly, it showed the calibre of a man who was later to command a squadron of the Strike Wings which was to destroy many German vessels and their crews, including those commanded by the Kriegsmarine Headquarters which had come under his cannon fire.

Gatward and Fern completed their operation tour in 236 Squadron about six weeks after their dramatic flight to Paris. Gatward was awarded a DFC. Fern was awarded a DFM and also commissioned; he became the Station Navigation Officer at North Coates during 1944, with the rank of Flight Lieutenant. After leaving 236 Squadron, Gatward – who was by now a Squadron Leader – became aide-de-camp to the Governor of Gibraltar. By May 1943, however, he was back in the UK with a posting as a Flight Commander in 404(RCAF) Squadron. It was not normally part of RCAF policy to include British pilots in their squadrons but sometimes the presence of a few experienced men was desirable as a leavening for newly-trained Canadians. Gatward found that he mixed in well with the eager if boisterous Canadians – so well that when their Commanding Officer, Wing Commander C.A. 'Chuck' Willis, was shot down and taken prisoner in March 1944, he was invited to take command of the squadron, then part of the Wick Wing.

An Englishman commanding a large squadron of tough, forthcoming and rather unruly Canadians might find his appointment a mixed honour. Wing Commander Gatward experienced initial problems with discipline. The squadron was based at Wick when, in April 1944, the new CO led a detachment to Strubby in Lincolnshire on some operational work. On his return he found that some of his over-exuberant officers had taken too much alcohol and caused damage in their Mess; in the eyes of the Station Commander, they were uncontrollable hooligans. Something had to be done. Gatward gathered all his officers together, delivered his icy and contemptuous opinion of those responsible, confined them all to camp and forbade all alcoholic drinks. Surprisingly, the Canadians accepted their punishment with docility, sitting around the Mess and drinking milk until Gatward was ordered by a superior officer to end his ban. The fact was, of course, that the Canadians admired their leader, especially since he did not exclude himself from the prohibition. Gatward's reputation was such that they wanted to live up to his standards; if they had let off a little too much steam, it was not unfair to receive punishment.

By May 1944, the country was buzzing with rumours of the forthcoming Second Front. During this month, Gatward* took his squadron down to Davidstow Moor in Cornwall, accompanied by 144 Squadron under Wing Commander David Lumsden. Together they attacked the German destroyers and the torpedo boat, as related in Chapter Six. By now, the squadrons of the Strike Wings were constantly on the move. In July, the bases of both 144 and 404 were moved northwards to Strubby, but the Canadians left a large detachment behind to continue mauling the Kriegsmarine operating off the coasts of western France. On 6 August the Canadians were joined by a large detachment of 236 Squadron from North Coates, forming an unusual combination of elements of two different Wings operating together.

One of the Flight Commanders in the detachment from 236 Squadron was the lively 27-year-old New Zealander, Squadron Leader E.W. 'Bill' Tacon. Born in Napier in the North Island of New Zealand, Tacon originally joined the RNZAF in July 1938, but transferred to the RAF under an arrangement whereby New Zealand supplied six trained pilots each year to the UK. He arrived in England in May 1939 and then joined 233 Squadron at Leuchars, flying Ansons at first but converting to Hudsons on the outbreak of war. He completed an eventful tour of operations in Hudsons, a mixture of anti-submarine work, escorting naval vessels during the Norwegian campaign, and bombing airfields. He was intercepted by German fighters on no less than nine occasions but survived each encounter, shooting down two of his adversaries. He was awarded the DFC in May 1940 and completed his tour in January 1941.

After leaving 233 Squadron, Tacon was whisked from posting to posting. First he went to a North Atlantic Ferry Unit and flew a Flying

---

*   Gatward was awarded his DSO on 2 June 1944.

Fortress from Portland in Oregon to Prestwick in Scotland. Then he spent some months introducing the Hudson to the newly-formed 407(RCAF) Squadron at North Coates. Next, he was responsible for converting 59 Squadron at Thorney Island from Blenheims to Hudsons. This work brought him the additional award of the AFC.

Next, Tacon was sent to Nova Scotia to open up a new Operational Training Unit; then back to New Zealand for a while; then on to Fiji as Commanding Officer of 4 Squadron, equipped with Hudsons. Back in the UK, he converted to Beaufighters and joined 236 Squadron in May 1944, where he rapidly demonstrated his worth as a determined and skilful Commander. On 23 June he attacked four R-boats entering Boulogne harbour; his aircraft was badly hit and his navigator killed, but *R.79* was sunk. Tacon was seldom out of the air, participating in attack after attack. He was also one of the best-liked men in his squadron, with a recommendation for a bar to his DFC.* His prowess with his front guns and rocket-firing was such that he became known as 'Deadeye' Bill Tacon.

The Commanding Officer of 236 Squadron was Wing Commander P.D.F. Mitchell, but this officer was nearing the end of his operational tour and Tacon was scheduled to take over. In addition, Wing Commander Tony Gadd, the Wing Commander Flying at North Coates, arrived to join in the operations.

The detachments of 404 and 236 Squadrons at Davidstow Moor thus contained some very remarkable men. Their job was to help smash the remains of the Kriegsmarine vessels in the ports and along the coast of western France. Nevertheless, it might be argued that it was unnecessary to do this job. The Allied advance on land was cutting off the western French ports from the main German forces in Europe, although Hitler's 'fortresses' at Brest, St Nazaire and La Rochelle were to remain defended enclaves until almost the end of the war. Only the U-boats in these ports, fitted with the new *schnorkel* which enabled them to remain under water for long periods, were contriving to slip away and reach the comparative safety of Norway. The remaining German vessels, four destroyers, a torpedo boat, several *Sperrbrecher*, minesweepers, flak-ships and other craft, could not hope to make the passage around the British Isles to their home ports. The fate of many was to be scuttled rather than to be sunk or

---

*   This arrived the following September.

captured. However, the tradition of the Royal Navy was to attack on every possible occasion. The Admiralty had no intention of missing this opportunity, and strike aircraft of Coastal Command constituted the most effective means of assisting the Navy to obliterate the remains of Marinegruppekommando West. 236 Squadron wasted no time in attacking. Within hours of arrival at Davidstow Moor, Gadd led eleven aircraft of this squadron, including Tacon, on a sweep off the west coast of France. In the outer harbour of the fishing port and seaside resort of Les Sables d'Olonne, they found a worthy target. This was a fast escort ship, or *Geleitboot*, called the *Sans Pareil* by the French and the *Jupiter* by the Germans. Four of these vessels of the *Sans Souci* class had been under construction in France when they were captured by the Germans. Originally designed as seaplane tenders, they were adapted by the Kriegsmarine for convoy escort work. Each was of 1,372 tons, the size and appearance of a small destroyer, fitted with two 105 mm, four 40 mm and four 20 mm guns.

The *Jupiter* was to receive the full effect of an improved method of firing armour-piercing 25 lb rockets, largely devised by Tacon in collaboration with the armaments officer at North Coates. They had calculated that, in a dive of 25° from 1,500 feet at a speed of 230 knots, the pilot should always score hits if he closed to a distance of about 800 yards. First, the pilot flew straight and level at 1,500 feet towards the target until the ship disappeared under the nose of the Beaufighter. Then he opened up to full throttles and dived, keeping the centre of the ship – the engine room – squarely in his gunsight. At about 1,100 yards he began firing his four cannon, watching the shells 'walk' across the water to the ship as the range decreased. Just before the shells reached the ship, at 800 yards, he 'ripple-fired' his rockets in pairs at half-second intervals. Tests on the destroyer *Sherwood* moored near the end of the runway at North Coates had demonstrated that there would usually be four 'dry' hits above the waterline and four 'wet' hits below. The cannon were harmonized to 800 yards. The armaments officer had devised a method of increasing the initial velocity of the rocket; he wired up the release catch with copper wire so that pressure built up before it sheared and the rocket left the rail. This method of attacking might not have been popular with all aircrews, for it involved flying steadily at the target whilst ignoring the return fire, but it worked. The *Jupiter* disappeared under a hail of cannon fire and armour-piercing rockets. There were three huge explosions aft of the funnel; she caught fire and sank. There was no loss to the attackers, but a shell hit Gadd's Beaufighter in the port wing, blowing out the dinghy, which promptly inflated. Gadd had great difficulty with the controls until the retaining rope snapped.*

The second attack was equally spectacular and successful. Fifteen Beaufighters of 404 Squadron accompanied by nine of 236 Squadron set off on 8 August on another armed sweep. The Wing was led by Gatward, with Tacon leading the section from 236 Squadron. Coastal Command was working in concert with naval units on these attacks. A naval squadron called Force 26, consisting of the cruiser *Bellona* and four destroyers, was steaming down the Biscay coast, eagerly hunting vessels at sea. Two days before, Force 26 had wiped out a German convoy of small ships near St Nazaire.

The Beaufighter Wing swept down the coast from Lorient to Fromentine, where a causeway submerged at high tides connects the long and narrow Ile de Noirmoutier to the mainland, enclosing the shallow Bay of Bourgneuf. There, Gatward spotted four specks on the sea.

'I think we've got something to port', he called to the Wing. He led the formation over the mainland, passing near the pretty little fishing port of Pornic. Ahead lay the familiar shapes of four M-class minesweepers, the traditional enemies of the Strike Wings. These vessels, each of 637 tons were purpose-built for the Kriegsmarine. Each was 189 feet long, served by a crew of 76, and carried a single 105 mm gun with a single 37 mm and as many as seven 20 mm. Originally designed as oil-burning, the shortage of fuel had compelled the Germans to convert them to coal-firing. All four had steam up as Gatward gave the order to attack; they were *M.366*, *M.367*, *M.428* and *M.438*.

Flak poured up to meet the attackers, both from the minesweepers and from the mainland. Flying Officer Forestall of 404 Squadron dived steeply into the sea, engines smoking, and his Beaufighter exploded. Cannon fire and rockets streaked down to blast the four minesweepers. As the Beaufighters left the scene, all four vessels were burning and smoking; before long, they and many of their crews would lie beneath the waters of Bourgneuf Bay. On the way back, the Beaufighters flew over Force 26, south of Belle Ile.

---

*   It seems to the author that the retaining ropes of dinghies were too strong. They often tore holes in the dinghies instead of snapping.

(*Left*): 6 August 1944. A rather scratched photograph of the *Jupite* under attack by the Davidstow Moor Strike Wing off Les Sables d'Olonne. (*Above*): 8 August 1944. An M-clas minesweeper in Bourgneuf Bay. On the right, Flying Officer Fore stall of 404 Squadron, w both engines on fire, jus before crashing.

8 August 1944. The four M-class minesweepers under attack in Bourgne Bay.

8 August 1944. The four M-class minesweepers c fire after the attack.

'Hallo, Pimms', said a naval officer on the *Bellona*, using Gatward's R/T call-sign. 'Did you have any luck?'

'Yes, we found four M-class minesweepers in Bourgneuf Bay', replied Gatward. 'They were all on fire when we left.'

'I wish you chaps would leave some for us!' said the cheerful naval officer, somewhat jealously.

'They were too small for you', replied Gatward, eyeing the great bulk of the warship.

'*Nothing's* too small for us!' came the bloodthirsty reply.

So the attacks of annihilation continued, day after day. On 12 August, it was the turn of Wing Commander Peter Mitchell to lead the Wing, twelve of 236 and twelve of 404 Squadrons. They found the large *Sperrbrecher 7* – the German *Sauerland* of 7,087 tons – off Royan in the mouth of the Gironde, and left it in flames, with dense black smoke pouring out following an explosion amidships. One of the Beaufighters of 236 Squadron, flown by Flight Sergeant R.F. Hollands, was forced to ditch some distance away. Another pilot, keeping careful watch over his friend, directed a nearby naval squadron to the dinghy; this was Force 28, consisting of the cruiser *Diadem* and two destroyers. Hollands and his navigator were picked up unhurt and promptly reported the position of the stricken *Sperrbrecher*. The naval force sped to the scene and finished off the unfortunate vessel. No survivors were found.

The following day, Gadd led ten Beaufighters of 236 and eight of 404 Squadrons on another sweep. En route, the Wing was diverted to hunt three U-boats in the Bay of Biscay. These were not spotted but Duncan Marrow, who was still navigating for Tony Gadd, brought the Wing precisely into the mouth of the Gironde for a surprise attack on two large vessels. These were *Sperrbrecher 6* of 6,128 tons and *Sperrbrecher 5* of 5,339 tons, which were left enveloped in smoke, burning and sinking, for the loss of one aircraft and crew of 236 Squadron. Flak was intense from both the ships and the headlands, but some of the shore batteries were late in replying. As Gadd broke away, he could see the Wehrmacht crews scurrying to their gun pits, buckling on their gear and ramming their steel helmets on their heads. Some soldiers raised rifles and fired at him; back at Davidstow Moor, a flight engineer levered a rifle bullet from his starboard engine.

The last operational flight made by Gatward was in the early evening of the next day, 14 August. He led a small formation, only seven of 404 and seven of 236, sweeping southwards down the coast from the mouth of the Gironde. In the Bay of Arachon, they found a number of small craft scattering in all directions. As usual, they went into attack, experiencing intense return fire from the vessels and the shore. A tiny harbour defence vessel called *Le Leroux* was sunk. Gatward's Beaufighter was hit twice. First, his port wing and engine were damaged during the attack; then his starboard wing and aileron were hit as he was flying out over a lake called the Etang de Caraux. The fuselage was also holed, but neither Gatward nor his young Canadian navigator, Pilot Officer W.K. 'Red' McGrath from Bartonville in Ontario, were wounded. McGrath had a proven record for bravery. The previous December, he had been involved in a crash when his Beaufighter, flown by Flying Officer J.S. Cummins, had suffered an engine failure on take-off at Wick. McGrath had clambered through the burning fuselage to free his trapped and unconscious pilot, lifting his limp body through the top hatch and dragging him to safety. Both men were burnt slightly. McGrath was awarded the George Cross. Now he came forward to help Gatward, who was struggling with the controls of an aircraft flying round in circles.

'We need something to jam the control column grip!' shouted Gatward.

McGrath went back and wrenched the aircraft axe off its fittings. Gatward was having to use both hands to keep the spectacles of the column over to the left, to compensate for the smashed aileron. They jammed the head of the axe under the spectacle, so that Gatward could take off one hand to throttle back the port engine, which was still giving full power. The pilot eased the sluggish Beaufighter round on a northerly course, beginning the long haul back to Cornwall. Another Beaufighter nosed up alongside them. Inevitably it was Sydney Shulemson.

'Push off, Slippery', said Gatward, over the R/T. 'We'll be OK. You get back home.'

'I'm in no hurry,' said the laconic Canadian. 'I guess I'll stay with you as long as I can.'

And so Shulemson shepherded his Commanding Officer back towards the English shore as twilight deepened into summer night, whilst Peter Bassett took careful notes of their positions in case he needed to report a ditching. Gatward made a skilful landing at Davidstow Moor. It was his last operational flight; he had completed so many sorties that even Coastal Command, the hardest and most implacable of task-masters, decided that he had done enough. Later that month, Gatward handed over his squadron to Wing Commander E.W. Pierce.

Meanwhile, the Strike Wing continued to attack. Bad weather kept the aircraft on the ground for a few days, but they went out again on 20 August. This time, Gadd led ten Beaufighters of 236 and twelve of 404, hunting primarily for U-boats. None was found, but on the homeward run Gadd took the Wing back to Les Sables d'Olonne. Near the spot where the formation had sunk the *Jupiter* a fortnight before, they sank the flak-ship *Vp 409* of 401 tons and the minesweeper *M. 4214* of 156 tons. It was very nearly the last flight for Tony Gadd. On the way back, he instructed Duncan Marrow to send an attack report and began to fly visually up the coastline. Inadvertently, he flew between the Ile de Groix and the coast and had to run the gauntlet of heavy and light flak for a full five minutes. All aircraft returned from this attack, however.

By now, the work of the Strike Wings* in France was nearly over. Their attacks, combined with those of Bomber Command and the Navy, had almost wiped out the remains of Marinegruppekommando West. The surviving U-boats had departed for Norway. In their hopeless situation, the Germans were scuttling many of their damaged surface vessels, after removing their guns. Only two important warships were still afloat. These were the destroyer *Z.24* and the torpedo boat *T.24*, the two vessels that had survived when the Kriegsmarine had tried so courageously to attack the western flank of the Allied invasion forces. These two warships, still well-served and deadly, were thought to be in the port of Le Verdon on the southern tip of the mouth of the Gironde estuary. Yet another Allied naval squadron, called Force 27 and consisting of the cruiser *Mauritius* with two destroyers, had damaged *T-24* on 15 August in an engagement near La Pallice, but now the German warships were in the shelter of coastal batteries. The Allied warships positioned themselves ten miles off the mouth of the Gironde and waited for an air attack.

This was the last major effort required of the Davidstow Moor Strike Wing. Tacon was briefed to lead ten Beaufighters from 236 and ten from 404, all armed with cannon and 25 lb rockets. Take-off was late in the day, at 16.15 hours. The Wing was scheduled to

---

*   Two more squadrons of Coastal Command were beginning to form into a Strike Wing, operating over the Biscay area. See Chapter Eleven.

attack near the limit of its range, perhaps returning in darkness. Tacon's navigator, Flying Officer W. Brian Wardle, gave his pilot a course for a position a few miles north of Arachon Bay. En route, two Beaufighters of 404 Squadron turned back with mechanical trouble. The remaining eighteen aircraft made their landfall and turned north to the Gironde estuary. Tacon could see the two warships in the harbour of Le Verdon.

'Keep down low, everyone', he called. 'We'll head to the estuary first and fly along it for our climb. Then straight out to sea after the attack.'

Tacon hoped to take the enemy by surprise, but the two vessels had steam up by the time the Beaufighters dived. The flak was probably the most intense that the crews had ever experienced, streaming up from the warships and the harbour defences. Nevertheless, every Beaufighter followed Tacon's leadership in one of the most dangerous and determined attacks made by a Strike Wing. Records of the results of the attack from German sources are understandably fragmentary. It is known that several 25 lb warheads smashed into *T-24* below the waterline. These 'wet hits' must have caused an uncontrollable rush of sea-water into the hull, for she sank almost immediately. There is no record of the casualties amongst her complement of 198 or of the fate of her captain, Kapitänleutnant Meentzen; many must have been killed or wounded.

Z-24 lasted a little longer. She received numerous hits above and below the waterline. Her starboard engine was put out of action but she remained afloat. There was time to tow her the short distance to a quay at Le Verdon, where she was made fast alongside the harbour railway station. Frantic efforts to patch the underwater holes were to no avail, for at 23.55 hours the same night she capsized and sank. There are no records of the casualties or the fate of her captain, Korvettenkapitän Birnbacher, but it seems likely that they were less severe than in *T-24*. It is known that the Senior Officer of the 8th Zerstörer-Flotille survived, but the attack marked the end of Kapitän zur See von Bechtelsheim's command, which was now entirely obliterated.* Survivors of the two vessels claimed to have shot down Beaufighters but, once again, these claims were incorrect.

Although none of the Beaufighters was shot down, fifteen were

---

*   The last two destroyers in Western France were scuttled by the Germans after air attacks by Bomber Command. They were *T-23* at La Pallice and *Z-37* at Bordeaux.

damaged. They were a long way from home, with darkness ahead.

'Call in, anyone in trouble', said Tacon. There was plenty of response over the R/T.

'Can't maintain height, sir', said Flight Sergeant E.J. Prince of 236 Squadron.

'Call up the naval force and try to ditch near them', Tacon instructed. Prince turned towards the destroyers and ditched successfully, watched over by an aircraft of 404 Squadron, but it was to be ten hours before he and his navigator were picked up from their dinghy.

'One of my engines has packed up', said Flight Lieutenant G. Gregory, who was flying as Tacon's Number Two from 236 Squadron.

'Mine's the same', said Flight Sergeant T.G.F. Buffey, from the same squadron.

'So is mine', said Flight Lieutenant W.R. Christison, the leader of the section from 404 Squadron.

It was evident to Tacon that these three aircraft might not stay in the air all the way back to England. He had a short conversation with his navigator. Then he called back to the three crippled Beaufighters and to Flying Officer J.P. Allan of 236 Squadron, flying alongside him.

'We'll head for Vannes aerodrome, between St Nazaire and Lorient', he instructed. 'With any luck, the Germans won't be there. You land with me, Allan, and help pick up the crews.'

The aerodrome at Vannes appeared to be deserted as the five Beaufighters circled above. Christison and Gregory landed safely but Buffey overshot the runway and crashed. Tacon and Allan landed after them. Buffey was injured but his navigator was unhurt; after destroying their Beaufighters, the other crews had no alternative but to leave the two men there and hope that medical help would arrive before long. The other two crews were taken aboard the two serviceable Beaufighters within minutes, and the journey back to England was resumed.

After leaving France, the two Beaufighters climbed. Then Wardle brought forward some unwelcome news from his W/T. Davidstow Moor was closed in with bad weather, and the returning aircraft were advised to try Chivenor, Portreath or Exeter. The cloud base was at 200 feet, whilst dusk was approaching. The twelve Beaufighters landed at these alternative aerodromes, apart from

12 August 1944.
Sperrbrecher 7 – the
Sauerland – under attack
by the Davidstow Strike
Wing off Royan.

13 August 1944.
Sperrbrecher 6 – the
Magdeburg – under attac
by the Davidstow Strike
Wing in the Gironde.
These *Sperrbrecher* were
converted merchant
vessels used as mine de
tructor ships. They were
very heavily armed with
flak defences.

24 August 1944. The
destroyer *Z-24* and the
torpedo-boat *T-24* under
attack by the Davidstow
Moor Strike Wing off Le
Verdon.

(*Left*): December 1943. Warrant Officer W.K. McGrath (centre) looks down at the bandaged head of his pilot, Flying Officer J.S. Cummins. McGrath was awarded the George Cross after pulling Cummins out of a burning Beaufighter. (*Right*): 14 August 1944. Wing Commander Ken Gatward in the Operations Room at Davidstow Moor, immediately after bringing back a badly crippled Beaufighter on his last operational flight.

25 May 1944. Squadron Leader Bill Tacon talking to his English navigator, Flying Officer Reg West. West was killed in action when they were flying together over Boulogne on 23 June 1944.

one which had to put down at Perranporth. Their fuel was almost exhausted, and one Beaufighter of 404 Squadron actually landed just after both engines had cut. Tacon landed at Portreath, six hours after take-off.

The destruction of the two German warships caused a stir of excitement in the Admiralty. Some naval officers were incredulous, whilst others were dismayed. If powerful destroyers could be sunk by these tiny 25 lb warheads, what future was there for similar vessels in the Royal Navy?

Tacon assumed command of 236 Squadron the day after this attack, the detachment returning to North Coates almost immediately. He continued to fly with the same determination until his last operational flight on 12 September 1944. On this day, he led forty Beaufighters of the Wings of North Coates and Langham on a strike against a convoy assembling in Den Helder harbour. Diving down against a hail of fire from the ships and the harbour, his Beaufighter was badly hit in the wing. Fuel poured out. Tacon fired his rockets for the last time. Then his aircraft was hit in the fuselage. The ammunition in the cannon boxes caught fire and exploded. Wardle cried out and Tacon turned round to see him lying dead on the floor. He began to climb, tugging on the lanyard of his bottom escape hatch, but this remained closed. Flames were licking around him, burning his face and helmet. There seemed to be no way out.

Then his Beaufighter was hit for the third time. Tacon could see the gun post that was firing at him and decided to take the gunners with him. He rolled the Beaufighter on its back and dived straight at the gun post. His last recollection of the aircraft is that the airspeed indicator was showing 360 knots. Then there was a violent explosion and he floated through the air, pulling his ripcord just in time.

He landed on the island of Texel, so badly burned around the eyes that he could hardly see. There he was found by German soldiers, who bundled him roughly aboard a boat which took him to Den Helder. On arrival, he was surrounded by a group of sailors who had evidently suffered from the Beaufighter attack. He was punched and kicked violently before more soldiers intervened and marched him off to the local gaol. After medical treatment, he was taken to Dulag Luft, at Frankfurt, and then to Stalag Luft I near Barth on the Baltic coast. He was eventually released by the Russians and quietly made his way back to North Coates. In his absence, he had been awarded the DSO.

CHAPTER TEN

Crash Call

To endure the unendurable is true endurance.
Japanese proverb

The arrival of a telegram during wartime was dreaded by the parents or wives of men serving in dangerous branches of the armed services. The one opened on 3 October 1944 by the mother of Donald Kennedy of Southport brought an appalling shock:

DEEPLY REGRET TO INFORM YOU THAT YOUR SON FLIGHT SERGEANT DONALD MATHEW KENNEDY REPORTED MISSING FROM AIR OPERATIONS OF TUESDAY 3 OCTOBER LETTER FOLLOWS STOP ANY FURTHER INFORMATION RECEIVED WILL BE IMMEDIATELY COMMUNICATED TO YOU PENDING RECEIPT OF WRITTEN NOTIFICATION FROM THE AIR MINISTRY NO INFORMATION SHOULD BE GIVEN TO THE PRESS = OC SQUADRON AEROS LANGHAM

Some days later in Christchurch, New Zealand, the young wife of Warrant Officer Douglas Haig Mann was horrified when she read a similar telegram concerning her husband.

The families of these two men, the crew of a TFX Torbeau, letter 'E' and serial NT909 of 489 (RNZAF) Squadron, were to suffer several days of bitter distress before they learned the truth of what happened to the two men.

By August 1944, the Germans had been forced to cease sending convoys by day along the Dutch coast. The toll taken by the Allied air forces had become too heavy. The only possible tactic was to sail the convoys by night, in short hops from port to port, sheltering in heavily defended harbours during the long daylight hours. In response, Coastal Command tried to attack the convoys at night, employing the Torbeaus of the Strike Wings. These squadrons were joined by two bomb-carrying squadrons based at Bircham Newton in Norfolk, the Wellingtons of 524 Squadron and the Avengers of 855 (Fleet Air Arm) Squadron. During moonlit nights these aircraft would roam along the Dutch coast on patrols called Rovers, taking off singly at set intervals and seeking 'targets of opportunity'. On dark nights, they would sometimes adopt more involved tactics, known as Operation Gilbeys. These were combined bombing and torpedo attacks, and the method had been worked out as early as January 1944, based on experiments carried out by the Torbeaus of 254 Squadron at North Coates.

The tactics of Operation Gilbey involved the extensive use of flares. The Beaufighter could carry only four flares but the Wellingtons could carry as many as seventy as well as a load of 500 lb medium-capacity bombs. The Wellingtons, equipped with Gee radar and ASV (anti-surface vessel) radar, would hunt along the Dutch coast and try to locate a convoy, the crews sometimes having prior knowledge of the German intentions and the probable location of the enemy vessels. Once a Wellington had spotted a convoy, it would send a sighting report and the calculated wind velocity to Headquarters, and take up a position ten miles on the seaward bow of the convoy. There would be Torbeaus on patrol and these would be directed by Headquarters to this position while the Wellington would switch on its Rooster radar, a device that would enable the Torbeaus to home on to it. Once the Torbeaus were close to the Wellington, the aircraft would drop a stick of flares to show the direction in which the convoy was sailing. It would then fly towards the convoy, dropping a stick of four flares upwind of the vessels, and turn in for a bombing run, whilst the Torbeaus were flying towards the target from the seaward side. As the torpedo bombers neared the convoy, the Wellington would drop a stick of twelve flares on the landward side, silhouetting the ships as the Torbeaus flew in at low level for the kill. Such plans did not always work out with precision in practice, but the squadrons involved had been able to pick off a number of German vessels at night during August and September. A very successful series of attacks in the area of the Scheldt on the night of 12/13 September resulted in the sinking of nine small ships and an incompletely built torpedo boat, the *T-61* of 2,566 tons.

In the afternoon of 2 October 1944, six crews of 489 Squadron at Langham were briefed to fly that night on a Rover patrol, taking off at five minute intervals from midnight and flying to the German Frisian Island of Borkum; then back to the west along the Dutch Frisian Islands, and finally down to the Hook of Holland. They were instructed to land at Manston in Kent, since it was expected that a warm front would close down Langham before they could return. It was a moonlit night, but the weather forecast was not good, and much low cloud was expected. Involved in the activities of the night, but all operating independently, were four Wellington Mark XIIIs of 524 Squadron, whilst the Fleet Air Arm pilots of 855 Squadron were putting six Grumman TBF Avengers into the air.

During the day, one of the New Zealand pilots of 489 Squadron had to report sick and, when the Commanding Officer asked for a volunteer replacement, Warrant Officer Douglas Mann stepped forward. Born twenty-five years before of Scottish parents in Greymouth, a town in the South Island of New Zealand, Douglas Mann had taken many years to reach an operational squadron, although he had attempted to join the RNZAF at the outbreak of war. He was a carpentry joiner by trade, lucky to find employment in the years of depression. At first, he had to bring himself up to the educational standard required by the RNZAF, and he did not enter the service until July 1941. He qualified as a pilot after training on Tiger Moths and Airspeed Oxfords and arrived in the UK in March 1942, passing through an Advanced Flying Unit at Ossington and then a General Reconnaissance course at Harrogate. He trained on Beauforts at Turnberry but near the end of the course the New Zealand Government decreed that their nationals could only serve on RNZAF squadrons, and the only one available was 489 Squadron, which was then equipped with Hampdens. Thus, Mann had to undergo a conversion course to Hampdens but by the time this was completed the regulation had been forgotten and he was able to volunteer for Beauforts, which he preferred, in the Middle East. He and his crew picked up a new Beaufort from the factory at Filton and flew it to Egypt, where he took a night torpedo course at Shalufa, near the Bitter Lakes. By now, it was September 1943, and still the fates were determined to delay Mann, for the Beaufort was declared obsolete. Back to the UK he went, converted on to Beaufighters at East Fortune, and crewed up with a young English navigator called Donald Kennedy. The two men finally arrived at 489 Squadron in April 1944, over four years after Douglas Mann had tried to join the RNZAF.

Donald Kennedy was twenty-one years old, born in Southport and working as a booking clerk before volunteering for the RAFVR in May 1941. He began training as a pilot but it was regretfully decided that his chances of longevity would be improved if he remustered as a wireless operator/air gunner. He passed his courses at Blackpool and Yatesbury and a chance to train as a navigator arose. He trained as a navigator at Hamilton, Ontario and then passed his General Reconnaissance course at Prince Edward Island. He finally met Mann at East Fortune and, since there was a shortage of trained navigator/wireless operators in 489 Squadron, accompanied him to join the New Zealanders.

Beaufighter 'E' was scheduled to be the second to take off, a few minutes after midnight. By October, Mann and Kennedy were experienced flyers with twenty-eight operational sorties to their credit, and the take-off drill had become a familiar routine. Mann went through the pre-flight checks and ran up his engines. All seemed to be well, apart from one small detail. He was not a big man and his Sutton harness seemed to be loose. This consisted of four straps around his body, clipping in to the quick-release lock at his diaphragm, and they were not tight enough, even at the last eyelet holes. Mann hesitated for a moment but he was a meticulous airman, and he motioned for one of the ground crew to come up and help him. In a Torbeau, the torpedo slung in the bomb-bay prevented entry through the bottom hatches. The unlucky airman had to climb up to the top of the fuselage and drop through the hatch behind Mann, passing dangerously behind the rush of air from a whizzing propeller. With the 1,772 hp Hercules sleeve-valve engines of the Beaufighter TFX, there was a strong possibility of oiling up the plugs and cylinders if the engines were run below 1,500 rpm, so that Mann could not throttle back as much as he would have liked. However, the airman negotiated this hazard and dropped through the top hatch. He adjusted the straps at the rear of Mann's seat.

'They're *too* tight now,' said Mann, wriggling uncomfortably and somewhat impatiently in his bucket seat.

'OK, I'll slacken them off a bit,' said the long-suffering airman.

'We're too close to take-off time. Let it go,' replied Mann. He was getting worried at the delay, for take-off times and the intervals along the patrol route were intended to be exact. That decision was to save his life.

The airman clambered back to the tarmac. Mann taxied out for a normal take-off, followed by a climbing turn to port. Kennedy gave him the course for Borkum, just over an hour's flying time away. The pilot continued to climb to 1,000 feet, the height at which they would fly until they reached the target area, when they would drop down until Mann could see the sea reasonably clearly, usually around 150 feet.

The flight out was uneventful until they reached the convoy route off the island of Borkum. Suddenly a red light was directed at the Torbeau, about half a mile ahead. It would invite suspicion to alter course abruptly. Mann switched on his navigation lights in the manner of a friendly aircraft, but eased his left rudder bar forward a fraction. The ruse succeeded, for no shots were fired as they flew past, but Mann was curious to know what type of vessel was signalling at him. He continued north for about two miles, then turned and hunted south again, in and out of low cloud. When they finally spotted the German, the mysterious vessel proved to be a *Marinefährprahm*, or naval ferry barge. The RAF called these vessels tank-landing craft; they were 280 tons and about 163 feet long, quite dangerous with their armament of at least one 88 mm and one 37 mm guns and two 20 mm cannon. The Germans found them especially useful in the waterways of Holland, where they were sometimes converted into artillery vessels. However, the draught of just under nine feet was unlikely to be deep enough for a torpedo. Mann turned as quickly as he dared and began his westward patrol along the Dutch Frisian islands.

After this incident, the Beaufighter was about ten minutes late on patrol. Reaching the long flat island of Ameland, Mann said to Kennedy:

'Don, aren't we a bit too far south? We're flying over sand dunes with the coastline just to starboard.'

'We're OK on this course, Duggie,' replied Kennedy. 'The convoy route's close to the shore here and we're heading for the route off the next island of Terschelling.'

It was then that Mann saw the convoy, in a break in the low cloud, about four miles away over his starboard wing. A stream of tracer came from it, not directed at him but at some other aircraft nearer to it.

There were two German convoys off the Dutch coast that night. By 01.30 hours, they were close to each other off the Dutch Frisian islands. It seems certain that the one Mann spotted consisted of three more *Marinefährprahme*. These had left Terschelling at 19.30 hours the previous evening and were headed for Cuxhaven, probably expecting to be joined by the one that Mann had encountered off Borkum. Their numbers were *MFP 840*, *MFP 841* and *MFP 921*. Escorting them were four M-class minesweepers of the 38th Flotilla – the so-called Group Tams, named after the senior officer, Oberleutnant zur See Tams; these were *M-3824*, *M-3827*, *M-3828* and *M-3832*, all converted Dutch vessels armed with 37 mm guns and machine guns. The war diary of this Group records that they were attacked off Ameland at 0138 hours by a torpedo-carrying aircraft but that the torpedo missed. This was probably a Torbeau flown by Flying Officer K. Marsh, one of Mann's comrades on 489 Squadron, who reported that he attacked a convoy at that position and time; Mann followed Marsh a few minutes later and was probably assumed by the Germans to be the same aircraft.

'We'd better attack before this weather closes in completely,' said Mann. 'Make sure there's a flare in the 'chute, Don.' The Torbeaus were required to mark an attack with a flare, for the benefit of other aircraft.

Mann turned north and pushed forward his throttles, bringing his rpms up to 2,400 at plus 6 lb boost, flying at 220 knots. He brought his Torbeau down to thirty feet, as a protection against night fighters, for he reasoned that the signals from the German vessel a few minutes before indicated that Ju 88s or even FW 190s were in the locality. At low level, Mann had an advantage over night fighters, for his Torbeau was equipped with a radio altimeter, an enormous boon in this form of operational work. The normal altimeter worked on the aneroid principle and was accurate enough when set to the correct barometric pressure at sea level, but the pressure was known only at home and not over enemy coastal waters. The radio altimeter was a device that consisted of a transmitter, a receiver and an aerial; the signals that bounced back from the sea recorded the height with the remarkable accuracy of plus or minus five per cent. With this, Mann was able to adjust his aneroid barometer. The radio altimeters made in the UK in the early part of the war had proved unreliable, but in June 1944 Coastal Command had installed the Type AYB, a very efficient type made in the USA.

The Torbeau continued north for about five miles before Mann turned east and then south to make his torpedo drop from the seaward side of the convoy. What happened then cannot be related with complete accuracy.* The bright moon was by now completely obscured by a thick layer of low cloud, and visibility had become very poor. Sometimes Mann could hardly see ahead at all. In retrospect, it might be said that he should have abandoned his attack,

---

*   Unfortunately, the war diary of Group Tams is very brief, and the more detailed reports of the minesweepers have been lost.

but it is often difficult to tell in wartime where resolution ends and foolhardiness begins. He suddenly saw something directly in front of him, a long and thin object that looked like a mast or a balloon cable, and he made a sharp climbing turn to port. There was a bone-jarring crash on his starboard wing, as though it had been struck by a giant.

It may never be known what the Beaufighter hit. The damage could have been caused by the nearby explosion of a 37 mm shell or a direct hit from a cannon shell, but since the crew saw nothing this seems unlikely. It is far more probable that the aircraft hit a balloon cable, for these were usually flown by the German vessels. Whatever the cause, the Beaufighter immediately tried to roll over to starboard on to its back, and Mann had to fight to stay in the air. He applied full port rudder and bank with both trims wound hard over, put both engines in fine pitch, throttling his port engine right back and giving his starboard engine full revolutions and boost. The Beaufighter was shaking badly and nearing its stalling speed, but Mann could hold it for a few minutes. Through a gap in the clouds he saw a vic of three M-class minesweepers and he jettisoned his torpedo in their direction. There was no hope of a hit, however, for they were at least 1,500 yards away and at the wrong angle for an attack; it is unlikely that the Germans were ever aware of the torpedo.

'Look at the petrol!' shouted Kennedy.

Whatever had hit the Beaufighter had ruptured a fuel tank in the starboard wing, and a long stream of petrol was pouring out. Mann was still wrestling with the controls and was now at about 100 feet with the dangerously low airspeed of 100 knots. He could not avoid the minesweepers and flew directly over them with the white stream spewing out behind, clearly visible. Following the minesweepers was an R-boat, and all four vessels opened fire. A tremendous barrage of light flak converged on the Beaufighter, long arcs of orange sparks. It is astonishing that the Beaufighter was not destroyed. To Mann, the flak seemed to glow with an incandescent light as it passed through the petrol vapour, and he hoped desperately that none of the guns was firing incendiaries. He knew that he was now in a hopeless position, for the Beaufighter was barely flying, and the only option was to ditch.

'Get ready hatch, we're going in!' he called. Kennedy jettisoned his cupola by pulling the release lever on the port side of the fuselage and then strapped himself into his swivel seat, facing backwards. Mann remembered that the wind was westerly and that he should turn into it to starboard – the only way he could turn. He pushed down the nose of his juddering Beaufighter, managing to build up speed to 125 knots, and turned. There was a heavy sea running and he could see that he was approaching the troughs at right angles, but ditching was only a few seconds away. He jettisoned his top hatch and reached for the flap lever, but suddenly thought of the words of a lecture he had attended at Shalufa in Egypt, eighteen months before:

'If you're ditching in a Beaufighter and you suspect that you've got wing damage, don't use your flaps! If one comes down and the other doesn't, she'll roll on her back!'

Mann left the flap lever alone and approached the water at his high speed, trying to put the Beaufighter down as gently as possible. There was an unbearable deceleration and his body was rammed forward. His forehead smashed against the gunsight, which he had not been able to remove in the few seconds available. There was a brilliant white flash and he lost consciousness.

When Mann came to, after only a few seconds, the water was up to his waist. Groggily, he unclipped the over-tight Sutton harness that had saved his life when hitting the water at nearly 125 knots, and levered himself out of the top hatch. At the last moment, he reached in and pulled out his pilot's K type dinghy, an instinctive action that stemmed from his training. Looking around, he could see that Kennedy was already in the round L type dinghy, having clambered uninjured out of his top hatch a few moments before. This dinghy had opened automatically from the trailing edge of the port wing, activated by an immersion switch. Mann slithered down on to the wing and jumped into the water, swimming the few yards to join his navigator. He hauled himself up by the handling rope and got his feet inside the dinghy. To his dismay, one of his feet went straight through the fabric in the well of the dinghy.

It is possible that the L type dinghy had been damaged by flak, but it is also possible that the cord attaching the dinghy to the wing had torn part of the fabric, something that often happened if the crew were not quick enough to cut the line before the heavy aircraft began to sink. The waterlogged dinghy drifted away from the sturdy Beaufighter, which gurgled and disappeared below the waves. As it did so, the flame float came up from the flare chute, and ignited.

'That's all we need!' the two men said to each other, as a long squirt of red machine gun fire came in their direction, fortunately wide of the dinghy. There was a heavy swell and the dinghy was tossing up and down, whilst the two men sat around the rim with their feet in the water of the well. Mann leant over the side and was violently sick, noting grimly that there was enough light to see that blood was mixed with the vomit. His diaphragm was extremely sore, badly bruised from the impact of the quick-release box of his harness, and he thought he might have suffered internal damage. Blood was also streaming from the cut above his eye from the collision with the reflector sight. Both men were wet through and beginning to feel very cold. They were badly shocked and frightened, and out of their element in the heaving sea.

More ships began to pass them, a straggling convoy that seemed to continue for almost two hours. This must have been the second German convoy, number 1291, also eastbound and consisting of four merchant vessels of around 1,500 tons apiece, with fifteen escort vessels. It had been attacked repeatedly by the Avengers and the Wellingtons whilst off Terschelling. One merchant vessel in tow, an unfinished hull of 1,923 tons, had been set on fire and was to sink the following day, whilst one Wellington had been shot down.

Mann and Kennedy began to take stock of themselves. Kennedy was uninjured but Mann was slightly injured, so far as they could tell. They had their rations from the L type, water, food, paddles and signals. They were not wearing flying jackets but only their normal blue battledress and trousers, with Mae West lifejackets and ordinary black shoes. The Beaufighter was a warm aircraft to the point of being uncomfortable, the hot air ducts being positioned to keep the breech blocks of the cannon warm and not out of any consideration for the crew. The men of the Strike Wings did not swaddle themselves with the warm flying clothing worn by the crews of high-flying aircraft. They were cold and wet, but they must see what the morning would bring.

At first light the following morning, at around 06.00 hours, low cloud and rain passed over them. It was the remains of the 'occluded front' that had passed over their base in the night, and it brought a howling wind. The sea rose and fell, and the dinghy teetered on the tops of the waves and was then sucked down into the troughs. The two men were out of sight of land and hung on in sheer terror, wondering if they could possibly survive. For hours they clung to the handling rope around the rim of the dinghy whilst they were buffeted by a 35 knot gale, until the middle of the morning when the wind began to die down.

'We've got the K type,' said Mann. 'I'll blow it up.' They tied the smaller dinghy to the edge of the larger dinghy and both sat in it, their feet in the waterlogged well of the L type. At this point, they discovered a heart-breaking catastrophe – they had lost their rations through the hole in the floor. They were down to the little that they could find in the K type and their Mae Wests, a tin of water apiece and some Horlicks tablets. They decided to ration themselves to a mouthful of water three times a day accompanied by two tablets.

In the afternoon, what seemed like salvation appeared in the shape of two Thunderbolts streaking over the sea towards them. Mann fired a three-star signal light from the K type. The Americans saw them, dropped a smoke float and began to circle.

'The air/sea rescue boys will be out soon with airborne lifeboats or Lindholmes,' the two men said to each other in relief. There were special squadrons trained and equipped for this purpose, stationed at Langham and Bircham Newton. A lifeboat, dropped by a cluster of five parachutes, had its own engine and emergency equipment; it could take them right away from the enemy coast, with a range of about eighty miles. The Lindholme dinghy was a less attractive alternative in their present predicament; it had a large central dinghy with four smaller ones attached to it, all containing supplies. They waited eagerly for the reassuring sight of a Warwick or a Hudson, with an escort of Mustangs. Nothing appeared.

We now know that the two men were extremely unlucky following the sighting by the Thunderbolts. The USAAF were engaged on flying during daylight across the North Sea to Germany and one of their Fortresses had ditched not far from Mann and Kennedy, between Terschelling and Vlieland. A Hudson of 279 Squadron set out from Bircham Newton to this position and successfully dropped an airborne lifeboat. It seems probable that the two sighting reports were assumed to have been the same, although they were some fifteen miles apart.*

Night came and brought a sick disappointment and increased misery. The wind veered and began to blow steadily from the

---

*   Mann was told later that the RAF had sent a W/T message to the Germans requesting
them to rescue the Beaufighter men but that the Germans had preferred to leave them
in the sea as bait. The author can find no evidence of this.

north-east, bringing an icy blast from Scandinavia. The cold penetrated to the men's very bones and almost destroyed their ability to
think. They were acutely depressed and wet through. Spray was
breaking over them as they huddled together and gazed into the
blackness, suffering the slow torture of the damned. They spoke little,
for there was nothing that they could say or do to help themselves,
although Mann once said:

'Better not go to sleep, Don, or you'll never wake up.'

A grey dawn followed. There was a slight improvement in the
weather by mid-morning, but the watery sun of early October in
those latitudes gave out no real heat. This was the day that they saw
the lighthouse. Kennedy thought that it might be Terschelling, but
Mann recognized it as Ameland. The RAF provided an excellent
series of wall maps called Lighthouse Recognition Charts on which
were drawn, very delicately and accurately from photographs, the
lighthouses and their adjacent buildings around the European
coasts.* Ameland lighthouse stood near the western tip of the
island; it was a circular iron tower with brown and white horizontal
bands, 181 feet high. To calculate visibility distance in miles at sea,
one takes the square root of the height in feet and multiplies it by
1.15, so that theoretically the very tip of Ameland lighthouse, which
stood at 187 feet above sea level, could be seen from a distance of
just over fifteen miles. It is probable that the lighthouse was no
more than five miles away when the dinghies drifted past it, for the
two men could see most of its length.

The sight raised the spirits of the two men sufficiently for them to
formulate a plan: they would paddle towards the island and get
ashore at night, then carry the dinghy across and paddle to the
mainland, where they would try to contact the Dutch Resistance.
They paddled all day but their efforts proved fruitless; they were
simply wasting what little strength remained in their bodies. Of
course, dinghies drift with the wind. During the war it was
calculated that the L type and K type dinghies without drogues drifted at a speed of one knot in a wind speed of twenty miles an hour.
The original wind that affected the two airmen must have pushed
them to the north-east, but the bitter north-easterly wind had
driven them back again, past the point where they had ditched two
nights before. Now that same wind was preventing them paddling

---

*   Some of these beautiful charts may be seen by appointment at the RAF Museum. The
author has been instrumental in arranging for them to be photographed by the
National Maritime at Greenwich.

ashore, sending them out into the wastes of the North Sea. Towards nightfall, they gave up in exhaustion and despair.

The fiendish wind blew all that night and in the morning the lighthouse had disappeared. The two men stared out over the water, overcome by helplessness and loneliness. During the night, they had blown the whistles attached to their battledresses, but no help had come to them. In their lifejackets they had found a total of about £30 in Dutch and Belgian currencies – a small fortune in 1944 – and Mann thought how useless this money was to them. They would have given all they possessed, or were ever likely to possess, for a warm meal and warm clothes, or even a glass of water.

It was now 5 October and the RAF had assumed that the two men were dead, although messages to that effect were not sent to their relatives. No searches were made for them, although air/sea rescue aircraft, protected by Mustangs, were roaming the North Sea on the lookout for downed American fliers. No one sighted Mann and Kennedy as they drifted away from shore, their water exhausted and only the resilience of their bodies keeping them alive. If the temperature had dropped to below freezing point, they could not have survived more than another hour or so, but it remained high enough to keep them just alive. The day passed and another dreadful night followed. Then there was another day and night, and still they lived, although by now they were barely aware of anything except the pain of the intense cold and the craving in their starved and dehydrated bodies.

During the early morning of 7 October, a Strike Wing flew over them, at fifty feet. The Beaufighters and Mustangs came across the horizon, headed for the Dutch coast, and were upon them and then gone in a few seconds. The two men were sufficiently roused from their torpor to wave frantically, but evidently no one saw the little dinghies in the waves. By coincidence, however, help did come, half an hour later. Two Warwicks of 280 Squadron from Langham, escorted by eight Mustangs, were searching in the area for American crews who were reported to have ditched. At 09.15 hours, they spotted Mann and Kennedy. Warwick BV341, piloted by a Canadian called Pilot Officer L. Hagg, and Warwick BV382, piloted by Flying Officer L. Harvey, orbited the two dinghies, which they reported as 'two K types tied together'.

The two survivors were now some fifty miles west of the position where they had ditched. Pilot Officer Hagg flew over them at a height of 700 feet and at an airspeed of 120 knots. The lifeboat detached itself from the belly of the Warwick, and the parachutes opened; it floated down and landed in the sea with a splash, about 300 yards from the dinghies. According to the official records 'the survivors made no attempt to reach it'. The fact was, of course, that by now they were almost incapable of movement, and only barely aware of what was being done to help them. Mann, who was normally a strong swimmer, looked out across the sea at the lifeboat and sank back when he realized that he did not have the strength to reach it. The two Warwicks circled for nearly an hour, the crews watching the dinghies intently until they realized that the two occupants must be too weak or injured to help themselves. The lifeboat drifted away. Then Flying Officer Harvey came down low and carefully dropped a Lindholme dinghy. The two Warwicks continued circling but after a few minutes Hagg was called away to another search, whilst Taylor remained, his crew watching for any sign of movement.

Mann looked at the Lindholme dinghy, a hundred yards away. In his weakened condition, it would be an almost impossible feat of strength to reach it, but he knew that he must make the attempt for neither of them could last another night. There was a rope in the L type dinghy, and he uncoiled it, tying one end to Kennedy and the other to his Mae West. He detached the K type, sat in it and began to paddle. The sea was fairly calm, with the waves breaking only rarely, but for Mann the effort was almost beyond his last feeble reserves of strength. The journey may have lasted only fifteen minutes but to him it was an eternity, and he was gasping and near collapse when he reached the Lindholme. All the while, the crew in the Warwick were willing him on, the F24 camera clicking and winding as they took a remarkable series of pictures. Mann slithered into the Lindholme and lashed his little dinghy to the side. He and Kennedy began to pull on their rope, hauling the L type to salvation. Kennedy slid over into the Lindholme, tipping over the L type as he did so, and the two men had reached an uncomfortable haven.

The Lindholme carried survival suits and they gradually wriggled their way into these. Their new home was in the centre of a line of four containers, each connected to the other by seventy yards of rope made bouyant by Kapok floats, a string that was 280 yards long overall. They hauled in the containers and allowed themselves a full tin of water apiece, followed by a tin of condensed milk which they thought might bring back some of their strength. All this time the Warwick circled, remaining in position until forced to return to Langham at 15.00 hours. Before leaving, the crew dropped delayed action flame floats.

At 18.23 hours another Warwick found them, flown by Pilot Office K. Pull and guided by the flame floats. The Lindholme had drifted eight miles in six hours. It was nearly dark by now but the crew dropped a second lifeboat. The survivors saw it come down and glimpsed it in the distance. At one point, Mann got out of his survival suit and contemplated swimming to it, but it was too far away for him in his exhausted condition. They fired off red star signal cartridges in an attempt to see the lifeboat in the dark, and the crew of the Warwick dropped illuminating cartridges, but without success. The night enveloped them and when dawn broke the lifeboat had drifted out of their sight.

There was a form of uncanny and malignant ill-luck dogging the two men. Normally, the rescue aircraft would have been out to spot them the next morning, but two things happened to prevent this. Firstly, the Lindholme dinghy, which was a J type, began to drift quickly, at a speed of about 1½ knots, and by the next morning was well away from the position where it was dropped, driven south-east by a freshening wind. Secondly, one of the Warwicks of 280 Squadron was shot down on the day that Mann and Kennedy were spotted, and rescue efforts the next day were concentrated on finding this crew. This Warwick was flown by Flying Officer George Chesher and was shot down by two German fighters about thirty-five miles north-east of the Torbeau survivors. Chesher ditched successfully and the six-man crew got into their dinghy. The following day, the Warwicks hunted for their lost comrades and found them, dropping an airborne lifeboat which the crew boarded and set off for the English coast and their ultimate rescue by a high-speed launch.

Meanwhile, Mann and Kennedy were almost comatose. Their feet had ached intolerably for about seven hours after their entry into the sleeping bags and then had become completely numb. During the following day they drifted past a mine, horned and deadly, and they looked at it with indifference. Night came and then the eighth day afloat dawned. Once again, they were alone in an empty sea under an empty sky, drifting steadily south-east, although the wind was beginning to back and slacken. Of the two men, Mann was the worse; his strength seemed to have ebbed away until he was almost incapable of movement, but Kennedy still had a

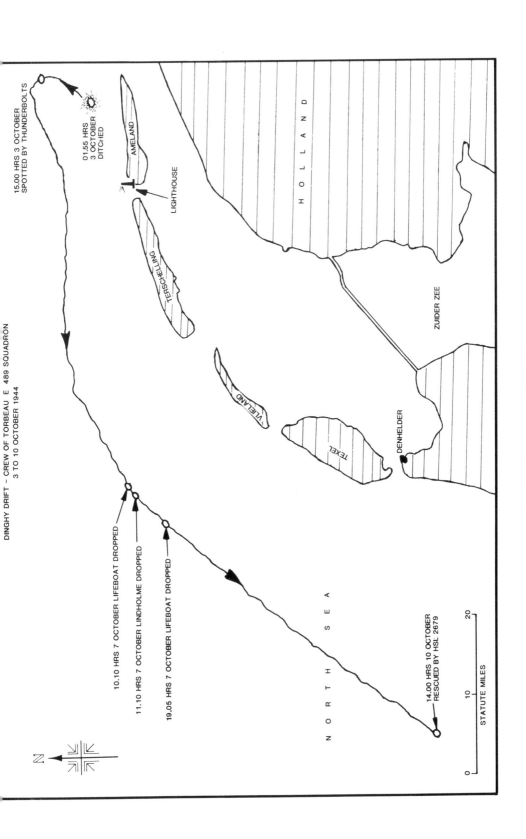

DINGHY DRIFT – CREW OF TORBEAU E 489 SQUADRON
3 TO 10 OCTOBER 1944

15.00 HRS 3 OCTOBER
SPOTTED BY THUNDERBOLTS

01.55 HRS
3 OCTOBER
DITCHED

AMELAND

LIGHTHOUSE

TERSCHELLING

HOLLAND

ZUIDER ZEE

VLIELAND

TEXEL

DENHELDER

10.10 HRS 7 OCTOBER LIFEBOAT DROPPED

11.10 HRS 7 OCTOBER LINDHOLME DROPPED

19.05 HRS 7 OCTOBER LIFEBOAT DROPPED

N O R T H   S E A

14.00 HRS 10 OCTOBER
RESCUED BY HSL 2679

N

0   10   20

STATUTE MILES

tiny reserve of strength. Another day passed and yet another
night.

On 10 October, Flying Officer David Ross was the duty officer at
Number 24 Air Sea Rescue Marine Craft Unit at Gorleston-on-Sea,
a little port just south of Great Yarmouth. His vessel was *HSL 2679*,
a high-speed launch of 68 feet in length called a Type III Hants and
Dorset built by the British Power Boat Company at Hythe. Ross
worked for a busy unit, one that had already rescued 292 lives in the
North Sea since January of that year. The sea was his element, for he
had been born in Findochty in Banffshire, the 35-year-old son of a
Scots fisherman who had been killed in action in the Royal Navy in
1917. Ross had joined the RAF in August 1938 and risen through
the ranks to his present position, a taciturn Scotsman who was good
at his job. Today his task was to steer to a position fifty-five sea miles
west of Den Helder and await further orders. The sea had mod-
erated and the wind had relented until it was no more than five
knots, blowing from the north-west, but there was still a heavy
swell. The high-speed launch would remain in position in case an
urgent signal came over the W/T or the R/T, one that would
galvanize the crew into an immediate and well-drilled efficiency.
That signal was called a Crash Call.
    The call came at precisely midday, from one of the Mustangs
escorting a Hudson of 279 Squadron, an air/sea rescue squadron
based at Bircham Newton.
    'Uncle leader to Teamwork. Vector 130 degrees thirty miles.
Dinghy with two occupants.'
    'Teamwork to Uncle leader. Roger. Wilco. Will you please orbit
dinghy?' replied Ross.
    They found an empty lifeboat first, an hour and a half later, and
then set off for the dinghy, guided by the Mustang circling
overhead. Mann and Kennedy had seen the Mustang two hours
before. They had one signal cartridge left, a device with a trigger
which one held up and fired off three red stars. Mann was unable to
make even this small effort, but Kennedy roused himself and the
signal was seen. The position given by the Mustang pilot was eleven
miles incorrect, for he had no real navigation aids, but Ross was
able to aim for the circling aircraft.
    The two men were too weak to help themselves in any way. The
crew of the launch tied a gear made of rope around them and gently
lifted them over the side. They were carried down into a warm sick

bay. A medical orderly stripped the stinking clothes off their emaciated bodies and wrapped them in warm blankets. He handed to each man a mug of sweet and steaming tea. That tea was like ambrosia; never in their lives, either before or after, did the survivors taste anything so superb.

Ross returned to the empty lifeboat and tried to take it in tow but he could make no progress in the heavy swell and had to cast it loose, to be sunk by gunfire from the Mustang. He arrived back at Gorleston-on-Sea at 18.30 hours and the two survivors were taken to a naval hospital at Great Yarmouth. Telegrams were sent to their homes:

GOOD NEWS DON PICKED UP AND PROGRESSING SATISFACTORILY=RAF LANGHAM

PLEASED TO INFORM YOU THAT YOUR HUSBAND WARRANT OFFICER DOUGLAS HAIG MANN PREVIOUSLY REPORTED MISSING ON AIR OPERA-TIONS HAS NOW BEEN RECLASSIFIED AS SAFE STOP THE PRIME MINISTER ON BEHALF OF THE GOVERNMENT DESIRES ME TO CONVEY TO YOU HIS SIN-CERE WISHES THAT THIS NEWS WILL SERVE TO RELIEVE YOUR ANXIETY LET-TER FOLLOWING +

F JONES MINISTER OF DEFENCE

The medical condition that was afflicting Mann and Kennedy was chronic immersion hypothermia. They were not frost-bitten, for if the temperature had reached freezing point they would not have lasted another hour. In one sense, they had now passed through a very critical time – the rescue itself. During the war, survivors who had suffered prolonged exposure at sea often died at the point of rescue; they would collapse back into the sea when climbing up the sides of rescue ships, or succumb to heart attacks, for physiological reasons that are still not fully explained. The best treatment was to immerse them in a hand-hot bath, if possible, and then cut the clothes off them; once they felt warm, they were wrapped in blankets in a warm bunk. Alcohol was found to be harmful, for it cooled the body again.

The main problem remaining with the two men was a non-freezing cold injury known as 'immersion foot'. Their feet were swollen up to the knees; the skin was mottled, pale and sensitive to the touch, softened by the continual soaking in water during an ordeal that had lasted for nearly eight days. As the circulation returned, their feet began to hurt badly; it was many weeks before they approached normality.

After a week of partial recovery in hospital, the two men were

7 October 1944. Douglas Mann (centre) in the 'K type' dinghy leaves Donald Kennedy in the 'I type' (bottom left) and paddles to the Lindholme (top left).

7 October 1944. The exhausted Douglas Mann nears the Lindholme dinghy.

10 October 1944. The survivors in the Lindholme dinghy (Douglas Mann far right, Donald Kennedy centre right) with the 'K type' dinghy attached. They have been adrift for over a week and are too weak to show any animation to the watching crew of *HSL 2679*.

(*Facing page, bottom left*) Warrant Officer Donald Kennedy, photographed 1945. (*Bottom right*): Flying Officer Douglas Mann, photographed in 1945.

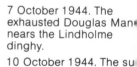

(*Below*): A high-speed launch of the 'Hants and Dorset' type, similar to *HSL 2679*. (*Right*): Flying Officer David Ross, photographed in Ischia in 1945.

sent to the Air Ministry in London to relate their story and to be re-categorized medically. They were told that their operational flying was at an end. Kennedy was sent on leave and then to South Wales as a briefing officer. After demobilization, he rejoined the RAF in 1946 and served for another twenty-two years.

Mann was advised to go back to New Zealand, but he was stubbornly determined to return to his squadron, in spite of his appalling experience and the dangers of operational flying; he was an intensely patriotic man who was proud of his squadron and who felt that he could not leave the unfinished business of the war to his comrades. He was turned down twice by the medical board, but he went on leave to stay with friends at Harrogate where he borrowed a bicycle and pedalled around the Yorkshire lanes until his feet were sufficiently restored to satisfy the examiners. He reported back to 489 Squadron to the acclamation of his comrades, although the RAF tried to charge him £4.50 for his service bicycle which someone had stolen in his absence. He resumed flying operationally; he was commissioned, and awarded a DFC in May 1945. Not surprisingly, he suffered heart trouble in later life, a condition which he combated with his usual courage. He died soon after approving the draft manuscript for this chapter.

CHAPTER ELEVEN

Mosquitoes and Tsetses

'There is in true beauty, as in courage, something which
narrow souls cannot dare to admire.'
William Congreve (1670–1729)

The Mosquito was a beautiful aeroplane. Few wartime airmen
would deny the truth of that rather hackneyed statement. The aircraft was considered one of the two most elegant of the war, the
other being the Spitfire. It also flew beautifully, a delight to control
from the pilot's seat. But was it a better or more suitable aircraft
than the Beaufighter for the work of attacking enemy shipping convoys? Put the question to a group of ex-aircrews of the Strike Wings
and one has a discussion that could last several hours without the
possibility of resolving the arguments.

The version of the Mosquito employed by Coastal Command as
a strike aircraft, from October 1943, was the Fighter/Bomber
Mark VI. In dimensions, this aircraft was slightly smaller than the
Beaufighter TFX, with a wing span of 54′2″, a length of 40′6″ and a
height of 15′3″. The engines were almost as powerful as those of a
Beaufighter, two Merlin 25s of 1,635 hp against the Hercules XVIIs
of 1,772 hp each. Surprisingly, the wooden Mosquito weighed little
less than the larger and metal Beaufighter, 14,300 lb empty against
15,600 lb, and 22,300 lb loaded against 25,200 lb. The Mosquito,
apart from a variant which will be discussed later, carried four .303
machine guns in the nose and four 20 mm cannon in front of the
bomb bay. It could also carry 2,000 lb of bombs, two 500 lb in the
bomb bay and two 500 lb under the wings. At first, this bomb load
often consisted of depth charges, for the Mosquito was employed
on anti-submarine work. Three months after the Mosquito squadrons began to coalesce into a Strike Wing, the bombing method of
attack was discontinued and eight rocket rails were installed under
the wings. The Mosquito could also carry drop-tanks, the four
machine guns being removed on these occasions, giving an extra
450 miles to a range which was otherwise the same as the
Beaufighter.

The major difference between the two aircraft lay in their handling qualities. The Beaufighter TFX, with its dorsal fin extension
and blunt engines rated at sea level with single-stage super-
chargers, had the handling qualities of a medium bomber; the pilot
not only needed to use the strength in his hands and arms but also
experienced a slight inbuilt delay with the controls. But the Mosquito handled more like a fighter. Apart from a slight tendency to
swing to the left on take-off, this superb aircraft had no vices. The
controls were light and responsive; it was even possible to loop and
roll the aircraft, although such aerobatics were not permitted on
operational squadrons. The streamlined engines and exquisite
aerodynamic shape of the Mosquito gave it the added speed of 20
knots or more over the Beaufighter at sea level; it was the fastest
twin-engined and piston-driven aircraft of the war – an Arab steed
by comparison with the warhorse of the Beaufighter.

Thus the Mosquito was unquestionably the better aircraft in
combat with enemy single-engined fighters. Pursued by Me 109s or
FW 190s, the Beaufighter pilot rammed his throttles wide open,
then corkscrewed and side-slipped violently in the hope of deflect-
ing the aim of his adversary, heading for friendly cloud if the
weather conditions permitted. The Mosquito pilot acted in the
same way, but with far more chance of success. The German
fighters flew at roughly the same speed as the Mosquito and thus
could not hope to catch it unless aided by the extra momentum of a
dive. Moreover, the German fighter pilots had far more respect for
this agile aircraft; they knew that if they were outmanoeuvred by a
Mosquito, a well-aimed burst from its enormous fire-power would
blast them out of the sky.

However, the aircrews of the Strike Wings faced enemy fighters
only occasionally, when the Beaufighters usually came off worse
unless protected by long-range Spitfires or Mustangs. On the other
hand, they were certain to fly into concentrated and murderous flak
whenever they attacked an enemy convoy, which was their main
raison d'être. Some pilots who had experience of flying in both
Beaufighters and Mosquitoes preferred the former aircraft in such
attacks. The all-metal Beaufighter was considered a much more
robust aircraft than the Mosquito, even though flak splinters would
punch holes in a metal airframe just as easily as through a wooden
airframe. If hit in their fuel supplies, both aircraft would burn with
the same degree of intensity, for the magnesium alloy of the
Beaufighter flared as fiercely as wood once it had melted. What

counted most, however, was the difference in the engines. The Bristol Hercules XVII engines of the Beaufighter TFX were radial and air-cooled; inelegant they might be, but they seemed to absorb flak damage with phenomenal success. On the other hand, the streamlined Merlin engines of the Mosquito VI were water-cooled, the water mixed with glycol, with numerous pipes and tubes under the nacelles. A single piece of flak in one of those engines and the perturbed crew might witness the unwelcome sight of glycol streaming from the trailing edge of the wing. A few minutes later, the over-heated engine would seize up or have to be closed down. Perhaps the other engine would go the same way shortly afterwards, if also damaged.

Every pilot of Coastal Command had to nerve himself for a possible ditching, and here the Beaufighter had another advantage. The stressed skin of the Beaufighter acted like a skid on the water, giving the crew a vital few seconds to scramble clear before the heavy aircraft sank. The wooden ply of the Mosquito, with little tensile strength, could easily rip off on contact with the water, leaving a gaping hole so that the aircraft would dive straight below the waves. There were instances of successful ditchings in Mosquitoes, but the Pilot's Notes recommended baling out rather than ditching.

The first Mosquito Strike Wing was formed at Portreath in Cornwall during early June 1944. Only two squadrons were involved. One was 235 Squadron, commanded by Wing Commander J.V. Yonge, a squadron that had operated on Beaufighters since December 1941, from bases in Scotland over the Norwegian coast, and from bases in Cornwall over the Bay of Biscay and the Western Approaches. 235 Beaufighter had been based at Portreath since August 1943, converting to Mosquito VIs at the time of D-Day. The other was 248 Squadron, commanded by Wing Commander A.D. Phillips, which had been based in South Wales or Cornwall since September 1942, flying long-range fighter patrols over the Bay of Biscay and the Western Approaches. 248 Squadron was the more experienced on Mosquitoes, having converted from Beaufighters to this aircraft in January 1944.

There was a special detachment in 248 Squadron which flew a modified form of Mosquito VI known as the Mosquito XVIII, one of the most interesting aircraft of the War. In this Mosquito, the four cannon were removed, being replaced by an anti-tank gun. This gun was an automatic loader, devised by the Molins Machine

Company, and fired six-pound shells of 57 mm calibre. It had been abandoned by the Army in favour of a seventeen-pounder anti-tank gun when the Germans introduced tanks with heavier armour, such as the Tiger. The surplus six-pounder guns were tested in Mosquitoes in the latter part of 1943, the intention being that they should be used for anti-submarine work. The tests proved successful, both at the butts and in the air. The big and accurate gun was mounted in the bomb bay with its muzzle protruding from the fuselage underneath the nose. It fired a magazine of twenty-five rounds at the rate of about two shells per second. There was little feeling of recoil within the Mosquito, but one strange effect was that the crews in nearby aircraft could sometimes hear the noise of the explosions, in the same way that they could sometimes hear or feel the shock of flak bursts near them. When fitted with the Molins gun, the Mosquito was able to retain its four machine guns and could carry either drop-tanks or two 500 lb wing bombs. This Mosquito XVIII was called the Tsetse, representing its more powerful sting. The special detachment of 248 Squadron usually consisted of three or four Tsetses, and it proved successful. On 25 March 1944, *U-976* was sunk in the Bay of Biscay by two Tsetses.

During June and July of 1944, the Portreath Wing flew on several strikes. There were usually about eighteen aircraft on these attacks, which were not escorted by single-engined fighters. They were flown against targets on the west coast of France, the area over which the Beaufighters of the Davidstow Moor Wing were operating. The Mosquitoes usually carried bombs or depth charges, for their main function was to hunt for the U-boats that were operating from the French ports and which were beginning to slip away to Norway as the Allied armies advanced. The Mosquitoes were not fitted with rocket rails at this stage. However, the new Wing sometimes attacked merchant ships as well as destroyers and escorts, and scored some successes. At the same time, more crews were lost than in the previous months, for they were now flying in far more dangerous circumstances. On 4 July, the commanding officer of 248 Squadron, Wing Commander A. D. Phillips, was killed; in turn, he had taken over from Wing Commander O.J.M. Barron, who was lost during the previous April.

On 5 July, Wing Commander G.D. 'Bill' Sise took over command of 248 Squadron. Sise had flown in the Torbeaus of 254 Squadron from North Coates for over a year, and was one of the most highly regarded men in the Strike Wings. He was a New

(*Above*): The cockpit of a Mosquito. The pilot's seat on the left and the navigator's seat on the right have been removed to make room to photograph the instruments.

(*Right*): Rocket-firing practice in a Mosquito. The arrows point to the firing range.

The normal armament of the Mosquito VIs of the Banff Strike Wing was four .303 Browning machine guns in the nose and four 20mm Hispano-Suiza in the bomb bay. Eight rocket rails were usually fitted under the wings.

(*Left*): Loading the ammunition boxes of the four Browning .303s in the nose of a Mosquito. (*Right*): In some of the Mosquitoes of 248 Squadron, the four 20mm cannon were replaced with a version of the six-pounder anti-tank gun. These were the Mosquito XVIII, only about twenty-seven of which were produced; originally they were called Tsetses.

Zealander of twenty-seven years of age who had joined the RNZAF on the outbreak of war. Already, he had been awarded both the DSO and the DFC for his skilful and determined flying in 254 Squadron. He was a popular choice to command 248 Squadron. Moreover, he was highly experienced in the tactics of the Strike Wings, having helped in their formulation during the early days at North Coates. He was to become one of the prime movers in the creation of the Mosquito Strike Wing and to make many contributions towards its success.

Following the destruction of the German warships, merchant vessels and escorts around the coasts of France, the squadrons of the Strike Wings began to move to northern bases in the UK. By September 1944, the Allies had advanced into Belgium and part of Holland. Fighting had begun on the territory of the Reich itself. In that month, Sweden closed her Baltic harbours to Germany, but her iron ore still flowed south via Narvik and the German ports. War supplies were still shipped northwards from Germany to Norway. Henceforth, the work of the Strike Wings was concentrated on the coasts of Norway, Denmark, Germany and Holland.

The two Mosquito squadrons of the Portreath Wing arrived at Banff in north-east Scotland during mid-September. Meanwhile, the Davidstow Moor Wing, consisting of the Beaufighters of 144 and 404 Squadrons, had moved to Strubby in Lincolnshire, arriving on 1 July; after operating from this base, these two squadrons also moved to Banff, arriving just before the Mosquito squadrons. This mixed force of Beaufighters and Mosquitoes formed the new Banff Wing of Coastal Command. The renowned station was commanded by Group Captain the Hon J.W. Max Aitken, who was the son of Lord Beaverbrook, the newspaper proprietor and former Minister of Aircraft Production. Max Aitken, who was thirty-four years of age, had flown in the Battle of Britain and then as a night fighter pilot; he had been awarded the DSO and DFC.

There was a flight from another squadron at Banff. This was a section of 333 Squadron of the Royal Norwegian Air Force, commanded by Commander F. Lambrechts, a dual-purpose squadron that was partly equipped with Mosquito VIs operating from Banff and partly with Catalina flying boats based at Sullom Voe in the Shetlands. Although 333 Squadron did not, strictly speaking, form part of the Banff Wing, its Mosquito section was an invaluable adjunct to it. The skilled and experienced Norwegian pilots and navigators were familiar with the complex coastline of their home country; their reconnaissance reports became essential to the operations of the Beaufighter and Mosquito Wing. Later, the courageous and reliable Norwegians adopted the practice of sending two of their Mosquitoes to act as guides or 'outriders' to the main force, a system that contributed to many successes. The men of the Banff Wing had a great respect for their Norwegian comrades.

The mixture of Mosquitoes and Beaufighters often operated together from Banff in September and October of 1944. Long-range Mustangs were seldom available to escort the twin-engined aircraft; the faster and more manoeuvrable Mosquitoes acted as fighter cover to the Beaufighters. The crews found that conditions off the Norwegian coast differed radically from those over the French coast and the southern North Sea. The convoys were small and infrequent, usually consisting of only two or three merchant vessels creeping down the Leads, heavily escorted by three times their number of flak-ships and minesweepers. It was a rarity to find any of these convoys during daylight, for they were anchored in fjords during these hours and sailed only in the lengthening nights of a northern autumn. Distances were so vast along the maze of islands and fjords that even the hard-working Norwegians of 333 Squadron were unable to cover the entire area on their daily reconnaissance flights. A convoy sheltered by precipitous cliffs had usually moved to another hiding place by the next day. Only a few isolated vessels were found and either sunk or damaged during those early weeks.

There was one chink in the armour of the German defences. The convoys were often still at sea during the early morning, for the Germans realized that the Strike Wings could not fly in accurate and compact formations at night, so that there were a couple of hours sailing time available after 'first light' whilst the aircraft were flying over the North Sea. But the Banff Wing decided to try a system that had been perfected at North Coates during the previous August.

At 04.15 hours on 9 October, an air-sea rescue Warwick of 281 Squadron took off in darkness from Banff, laden with marine markers, flame floats and drift lights. Nearly two hours later, this aircraft had fashioned an ingenious form of floating aerodrome lights almost six miles in diameter, about 100 miles west of Stavanger. Half an hour after the Warwick, eight Mosquitoes of 235 Squadron armed with cannon, began taking off singly for this destination. Eight Beaufighters of 404 Squadron, armed with cannon and rockets, were on the same course. Six Beaufighters of 144

Squadron, armed with cannon, also took off, together with another four armed with torpedoes. At 06.20 hours, the first aircraft of the Strike Wing began to circle the brilliantly lit rendezvous of floating lights. Dawn began to appear in the sky. Half an hour later, the Wing was heading in close formation for Egersund, the stretch where convoys were without the protection of the Leads. The dying lights that they left behind were called the Drem system, after the air establishment where it had been devised.

The formation was led by the ubiquitous Wing Commander Tony Gadd, who was rarely away from the scene of action and had now taken over command of 144 Squadron from David Lumsden. At 07.10 hours, the Wing pounced on a convoy and sank the *Rudolf Oldendorff*, a German freighter of 1,953 tons, as well as the escorting submarine-hunter *UJ.1711* of 485 tons. The Norwegian freighter *Sarp* of 1,116 tons was badly damaged. The German gunners put up a spirited defence, in spite of their astonishment at encountering a fully-fledged 'Tommi' striking force at that hour of the morning, but the sequence of cannon, rockets and torpedoes smothered their fire. Three aircraft were damaged, but all returned.

Later in October, some of the squadrons of the Strike Wings moved bases yet again. 143 Squadron flew up to Banff from North Coates; this much-travelled squadron had converted to Mosquito VIs and was commanded by another New Zealander in the RAF, Wing Commander E.H. McHardy. The aircraft of all three Mosquito squadrons had been fitted with rocket rails and the pilots were trained in this weapon at a range near the aerodrome at Tain. Thus the Banff Wing became an all-Mosquito Wing, and remained so until the end of the war. Meanwhile, the two Beaufighter squadrons at Banff moved to Dallachy, in the adjoining county of Morayshire. Here they were joined by the Australians of 455 Squadron and the New Zealanders of 489 Squadron, who had moved north from their base at Langham. These four Beaufighter squadrons, three from the Dominions and one from the UK, formed yet another Strike Wing – the Dallachy Wing.

Only 236 and 254 Squadrons remained at their original base of North Coates, where they continued to hunt in their Beaufighters along the Dutch, German and south-west Norwegian coasts for enemy shipping. Apart from frequent detachments to other aerodromes, North Coates remained the base for these two squadrons of the first Strike Wing until the end of the war. By October 1944, the tactics evolved at North Coates were being used by nine battle-hardened squadrons of Coastal Command. These formed three Strike Wings, the most devastating anti-shipping force employed by the Allies in north-west Europe.

As the nights lengthened, the Drem system lost some of its value off Norway, for the enemy convoys had already reached their anchorages by dawn. Only one method of attack was possible – to strike at the vessels moored in the shelters of harbours or fjords. A typical strike of this nature was made by the Banff Wing on 5 December. Thirty-three Mosquitoes took off at around 11.50 hours, led by Bill Sise. There were fourteen of 248, ten of 143, eight of 235 and one from the RAF Film Unit. This formation included four Mosquito XVIIIs of 248 Squadron, each fitted with a six-pounder gun. The system of outriders had not yet been introduced at Banff; the whole formation was engaged on an armed patrol, hunting a series of targets discovered in the fjords by previous reconnaissance, the most important being a large ship seen in Volde fjord.

At 13.45 hours, the Mosquito Wing flew over Nord Gulen, a broad fjord stretching inland near the port of Florø. Here, they spotted four large merchant vessels moored at the head of the fjord, protected by clusters of flak-ships and a couple of large tugs. Sise took a long look at these unexpected targets. They seemed likely prospects, but he had been ordered to hunt in adjacent fjords. Nevertheless, in case he decided not to return, he thought that the Jerries should have a taste of Mosquito medicine. He ordered two Tsetses to give the vessels a couple of squirts. Flying Officer W.G. Woodcock dived, firing fifteen six-pounder shells, whilst Flying Officer W.N. Cosman fired another six. Both reported hits on the superstructure of merchant vessels, and rejoined the main formation.

The vessels in Nord Gulen formed part of two convoys, one headed north and one south, coincidentally having arrived at the same daytime anchorage. All four merchant vessels were German. They were the *Ostland* of 5,273 tons, the *Tucuman* of 4,621 tons, the *Magdalena* of 3,283 tons and the *Helene Russ* of 993 tons. Although the latter was the smallest, she was in some ways the most impor-tant, for she was an ammunition ship loaded with supplies for Ger-man garrisons. Protecting them were seven flak-ships of the 51st and 53rd Vorpostenflotille, *Vp 5102*, *Vp 5109*, Vp 5111, *Vp 5305*,

Vp 5306, *Vp 5308* and *Vp 5310*. There were also two armed tugs, the *Aasenfjord* and the *Fairplay X*. The Kriegsmarine officers had been alerted by the sight of reconnaissance aircraft earlier in the day and their *Vorpostenboote* had closed up to the shelter of steep cliffs. The merchant vessels had also moved closer to the sides of the fjord but the mooring facilities were inadequate for the larger vessels and they were positioned further out in the waters.

The vessels put up a wall of fire and thought that they had driven off the Mosquitoes, but Bill Sise was intent on investigating the primary potential target. He led the Wing north-east and took a look in nearby Orse fjord, where he could see only a coaster of about 1,500 tons. He found the main target in Volde fjord, a modern vessel of over 6,000 tons, together with a coaster of about 400 tons, but these were tucked up against the side of a narrow part of the fjord and impossible to attack through the low cloud that was scudding over the mountains. Sise decided to return to Nord Gulen.

On the short return flight to the target, Sise addressed each vic of Mosquitoes over the R/T, quoting their colour codes and detailing the sequence of attack. His calm voice and confident manner were, as usual, immensely reassuring to the crews, even those who had already seen plenty of action.

At the controls of 'V' of 248 Squadron, 21-year-old Warrant Officer W.G.S. Parfitt was flying on his forty-fourth operational sortie. Like many other wartime entrants in the UK, Parfitt had trained in Canada. In May 1943, he had joined 235 Squadron at Leuchars and had flown on nine operational sorties in Beaufighters. Whilst at Portreath in January 1944, he had transferred to 248 Squadron, where he converted to Mosquitoes. His worst experience had been on 11 July 1944 when he had been flying in the anti-flak section of a combined attack made by seventeen Mosquitoes of 235 and 248 Squadrons on shipping in the harbour of Camaret-sur-Mer in Brest Estuary, under the leadership of Bill Sise. It had been at last light and not only did the fiery streaks of tracer look more terrifying than in daylight but they found both his engines. The starboard extinguisher had done its work but he had flown back to Portreath with port engine streaming smoke, making a skilful landing with the single starboard engine. Although the experience had been very alarming, Bill Parfitt had gained confidence in the Mosquito, which he regarded as the 'Rolls Royce of the air'.

In Mosquito 'X' of 248 Squadron, Flying Officer Gilbert E.E. 'Geep' Peckover sat beside his pilot, Flight Lieutenant H.H.K. 'Alec' Gunnis, a Scotsman from Alloa in Clackmannanshire. Peckover, nearly twenty-two years of age, had joined the RAFVR in June 1941 and had trained as an observer/wireless operator in England. In November 1942, he had joined 252 Squadron in the Middle East and then completed a full tour of operations on Beaufighters. Returning to the UK, he had been posted to 248 Squadron in August 1944. He also liked the Mosquito, preferring it to the Beaufighter. It was a bit of a squeeze to get into the entry hatch in the starboard side, but once installed beside the pilot, he had a splendid view forwards and to the sides. All the Mosquitoes were fitted with wireless sets, and Gee was installed in a few of them. Peckover soon learned to cope with the wireless and the navigation from his cramped position. He usually tuned into the local German radio wavelength on the approach to a target; sometimes the programme would suddenly stop and three cuckoo-like sounds would be broadcast, followed by an incomprehensible stream of German, presumably giving warnings of a forthcoming attack.

The Mosquito Wing returned to Nord Gulen only twenty-five minutes after the two Tsetses had made their first token attack. Sise gave the order and led in the first wave, for it was impossible to attack together in the confined space. The Tsetses were amongst the first to go in; they needed a clear field as they pumped out their six-pounder shells. Then the rocket-firing Mosquitoes followed. Bill Parfitt dived from 1,200 feet, his airspeed indicator showing 360 knots. He felt the Mosquito jolt as it flew through the barrage of heavier 88 mm and 37 mm flak thrown up from the ships and the shore, but he kept his sight on the *Magdalena*, the most westerly ship in the fjord. The Mosquito juddered as he opened fire with his cannon, the splashes straddling the target. Then he released his salvo of eight rockets, flew over the target and broke away to port, heading westwards out to sea. To his port, a Mosquito was on fire, losing height. A few minutes later, it crashed in the sea and the pilot, Flight Lieutenant L.N. Collins, and the navigator, Flying Officer R.H. Hurn, lost their lives.

'Geep' Peckover picked up and aimed his heavy camera as Gunnis dived north-west over the mountain to the target. The flak was fierce, but he hoped for the best. Some of the ships were firing rockets, the missiles hurtling into the air. He glanced right and left, to see how the other boys were doing. The four cannon thudded beneath him and eight rocket streaks converged to their target, the *Helene Russ*. There seemed to be a forest of masts as Gunnis pulled out low over the fjord and headed west. Some of the ships were exploding and smoke was pouring out of others.

The flak-ships fired a total of about 200 exploding shells of 88 mm calibre, 250 of 40 mm and 1,000 of 37 mm, together with 7,000 cannon shells of 20 mm calibre. They also fired about 80 sticks of rockets. This was apart from the fire from the merchant vessels and the shore, which is not recorded. The escort vessels were completely unharmed. Tucked under the cliffs, they were so well protected that all the Mosquito pilots had aimed at the vessels moored towards the middle of the fjord. The *Magdalena* and the *Helene Russ* were both hit by cannon shells and rockets, some of the latter below the waterline; they were ablaze when the Mosquitoes left. The *Tucuman* and the *Ostland* were hit above the waterline, but were less seriously damaged. The tug *Aasenfjord* was so badly hit that her wooden superstructure was totally destroyed, but she did not sink. Six sailors were killed on these vessels, and fourteen wounded. The captain of the *Helene Russ* was amongst the wounded.

The flak-ships slipped their moorings and went to help the merchant vessels, bringing medical personnel and first aid equipment. The crew of the *Helene Russ* abandoned ship, for ammunition was exploding in all directions. Some of the crew of *Vp 5306* boar-

The flash of light as a six-pounder shell fired by a Tsetse streaks to the German *Wartheland* in Eidfjord on 12 December 1944. The vessel sank.

5 December 1944. Attack on shipping in Nordgulen fjord by the Banff Strike Wing. Camera gun films from Mosquito 'E' of 235 Squadron, flown by Flight Lieutenant Mayhew.

1. (*Top left*): Banking over the cliffs at the landward end of the fjord.
2. (*Bottom left*): Straightening up and diving on the target.

(*Above left*): Flight Lieutenant 'Geep' Peckover. (*Above right*): Warrant Officer Bill Parfitt.

3. *(Top right)*: Firing the cannon and rockets. The vessel on the right, the *Ostland*, appears to be firing 'parachute-assisted cable' rockets.

4. (*Centre right*): The rockets strike the target, the ammunition ship *Helene Russ*. The intense return fire cannot be seen in such photographs.

ded the blazing and sinking ammunition ship, whilst all the other vessels moved away from the danger zone. The German seamen battled for ten hours, plugging the underwater holes and putting out the fires. Then a pump steamer arrived to help the seamen. After another two hours, the rescue had succeeded and the *Helene Russ* was out of danger. Had they been in the open sea, it is almost certain that the ammunition ship and probably three other vessels would have sunk.

The men of the Kriegsmarine were never lacking in courage. Nevertheless, they were called upon to account for the fact that all their ships had escaped damage whilst all their charges had been badly hit. The *Vorpostenboote* commandants issued orders to ensure that in future all merchant ships moored close to steep cliffs in 'protected areas', where suitable mooring rings would be provided.

The German seamen reported that three Mosquitoes were shot down during the attack and that three more left the scene on fire. The harbour master at Florø said that three Mosquitoes crashed in the sea after leaving the fjord. As usual, these statements were wildly inaccurate. Six Mosquitoes were hit but only Collins failed to return. One damaged aircraft landed at Wick. Two landed at Sumburgh, but one of these, flown by Flying Officer R. Gilchrist of 143 Squadron, came in on one engine and overshot, hitting a brick wall; Gilchrist was killed and his navigator, Flying Officer Knight, sustained cuts.

Ten minutes after the Banff Wing attacked the ships in Nord Gulen, fifteen Beaufighters from the Dallachy Wing flew near the same target and saw the burning vessels. The Germans thought that these were single-engined fighters and that they could not face their flak, but the Beaufighters were heading north for another target. Fifteen minutes later, they attacked two German ships in Orsten fjord and sank both of them; they were the *Radbord* of 4,354 tons and the *Albert Janus* of 2,275 tons. One Beaufighter was lost whilst another ditched off Sumburgh, the crew being rescued.

The turn of the year saw the Strike Wings at peak strength, equipped with magnificent aircraft flown by aircrews who were probably the most highly trained of any wartime air force. In the last four months of the War, they would sink nearly 90,000 tons of shipping, the highest rate achieved during the entire conflict.

CHAPTER TWELVE

Black Friday

And on a Friday fil al this meschaunce.
Geoffrey Chaucer (c.1343–1400)

Spike Holly looked in astonishment at his navigator's seat of Beaufighter 'Y', serial NE743, of 144 Squadron. There was a small hole in the right part of the back, punched through by a sliver from one of the cannon shells fired by the FW 190. Pulling up his shirt, Holly sat down on the seat. The hole matched exactly the scar on his body, underneath the right armpit. Part of a propeller blade stood near the seat, against the wall of the barn. His wife would be surprised when she saw these, but she had gone into the farm. The two Norwegians were grinning at him, relishing the moment.

'Which one would you like?' asked Arne Hopen. 'You can take either home with you as a souvenir.'

'Do you mean it?' said Holly. 'I think I'd really like the seat. How on earth did you find them?'

'A skin-diving team has been down into the waters of the fjord,' replied Hopen. 'And they've fished up some bits of your Beaufighter.'

'Well, they certainly bring back a few memories,' said Holly. 'It's all a long time ago.'

The date was 19 June 1979, over thirty-four years since that disastrous day when Henrik and Arne Hopen had dragged him, wounded and semi-conscious, from the icy waters of Hoydals fjord. It had been the worst day in the history of the Strike Wings. 9 February 1945. Black Friday, they called it, those who managed to get back to Dallachy.

In early 1945 the Banff and the Dallachy Wings were still striking again and again at merchant vessels and their escorts off the coast of Norway, sometimes attacking the same targets. The fighting was as bitter and as bloody as at any stage of the war. Torpedoes were rarely used by then, especially in the confined Norwegian waters; the main weapons were the 20 mm cannon and the 25 lb rocket

(*Above*): The navigator's seat of Beaufighter TFX, letter 'Y' serial NE743, recovered from Høydals fjord in 1979 after ditching on 9 February 1945.

(*Top right*): The aerodrome at Dallachy in Morayshire in 1945.

(*Bottom right*): February 1945. A typical briefing at Dallachy.

warhead. Ship after ship was sunk, aircraft after aircraft was shot down, but the balance of advantage in this grim struggle moved steadily in favour of the Strike Wings.

Faced with mounting losses, the Germans were forced to improve their defensive measures. For many months, they had moved their convoys only at night, but the Wings were attacking them in their anchorages in the fjords. They began to shelter them deeper into the fjords, where steep cliffs towered over the narrow approaches and gun platforms could be built to intensify the barrage put up by the ships' gunners. Yet the Strike Wings continued to attack. The system they adopted was to employ aircraft as 'outriders'. These aircraft, usually two in number, would detach themselves from the main formation and fly inland, parallel to the general line of the coast. Thus they would cross over fjord after fjord, reporting over the R/T to the strike leader on the vessels that they could see tucked away in the heads of the fjords. The strike leader would then bring his formation inland and try to attack over the cliffs from the land towards the sea. The tactics were usually successful, most attacks taking another toll of enemy shipping. The aircrews began to learn by heart the names of the merchant vessels remaining to the Germans. Accurate silhouettes of these vessels were displayed in the intelligence libraries of the RAF stations, to be eagerly crossed off after each sinking.

Black Friday, 9 February 1945, began with a morning reconnaissance over Norway by two Beaufighters of 489 Squadron. Armed with cannon only and flown by Warrant Officer J. Brightwell and Flight Sergeant R. Priest, the two aircraft made landfall at Utvar lighthouse, at the entrance of Sogne fjord. Then they began their highly dangerous and unescorted sortie over enemy territory. They turned north-east and saw a merchant vessel of about 1,500 tons in Stong fjord. Continuing northwards, they saw something startling in the narrow Førde fjord, east of Vevring: a Narvik class destroyer of about 2,300 tons, a minesweeper and two flak-ships. Further north, in the waters of Nord Gulen, they saw an inviting target: five merchant vessels, the largest being about 5,000 tons and the others around 2,500 tons. After spotting two more minesweepers and another flak-ship near Bremanger, further along their course, the two New Zealand pilots turned west towards Dallachy, their navigators busy with their W/T keys, reporting their discoveries. They landed at 13.25 hours.

At Dallachy, the staff in the Operations Room studied the

reports sent back by the two reconnaissance Beaufighters. The Dallachy Wing was on standby, waiting to attack during the short daylight hours of a northern winter. There were three potential targets. The single merchant vessel in Stong fjord certainly did not justify sending out the Wing. The five merchant vessels in Nord Gulen were an obvious choice – natural targets in a good position for a Wing attack. But then there was that Narvik class destroyer; it was in a very awkward position under those high cliffs, and it would be heavily defended, but it had to be the one. There was, in effect, no choice at all. As Air Vice Marshal A.B. Ellwood, the Senior Air Staff Officer of Coastal Command, said on 8 November 1944 in a lecture given at the Royal United Services Institute:

'As the branch of the Royal Air Force specially created and trained to take part in maritime warfare, Coastal Command works under the operational control of the Admiralty.'

Four days after that lecture, the *Tirpitz* – the largest and most powerful battleship in the world when she was built – was sunk in Tromsö fjord by high-flying Lancasters of Bomber Command. Germany had only two major and seaworthy warships left, other than destroyers. These were the cruisers *Prinz Eugen* and the *Nürnberg*, both hard at work in the Baltic helping to cover the fighting retreat of the German army all the way from Leningrad. But there were still some German destroyers in Norway, moving southwards down the coast now that they were no longer needed to provide escorts for the *Tirpitz*, coming within range of the Strike Wings. The Admiralty gave orders of priority for targets. Destroyers were 'Class I'. Merchant vessels came further down the list.

Of course, the Admiralty gave little thought to the aerial tactics in issuing this perfectly reasonable list of priorities. Few of the senior officers knew much about RAF air operations, and there was no love lost between the two branches of the armed services. Naval officers could admire the courage of aircrews, for this was a quality that they possessed in abundance themselves – even if some of the wartime entrants into the RAF seemed to betray their inferiority with their stupid slang and their long hair, plastered with Brylcreem. What smarted at the Admiralty was the way in which the RAF had been given priority for its equipment, at the expense of the Navy and its air support. That fellow Arthur Harris, who had the ear of Churchill, had collared half the country's war production for bombing Germany, at a time when the outcome of the Battle of the Atlantic was in doubt. The Admiralty gave Coastal Command its orders. How the airmen carried them out was their business. After all, the RAF had demonstrated that it could sink destroyers, when they put paid to *Z-24* and *T-24* at Le Verdon on 24 August, under six months before. They could do the same again.

At 13.55 hours on 9 February, thirty-two Beaufighters of the Dallachy Wing formed up to fly towards Norway. There were eleven of 455 and eleven of 404, armed with cannon and 25 lb rockets, together with nine of 144 and one of 489, armed with cannon and machine guns. The single aircraft from 489 and one of 144 were acting as outriders. The formation made rendezvous over Peterhead with ten Mustangs of 65 Squadron. The two outriders flew ahead, whilst two air/sea rescue Warwicks of 279 Squadron brought up the rear.

The Wing was led by Wing Commander Colin Milson, an Australian who had flown in Beauforts in the Mediterranean before joining 455 Squadron. After much operational experience as a Flight Commander, he had taken over command of the squadron from Jack Davenport during the previous November. He wore the ribbons of the DSO as well as the DFC and bar. Milson had also acquired Davenport's English navigator, Flying Officer Ralph E. Jones, a 35-year-old ex-civil servant born in Dulwich. Jones had passed his wireless course at Cranwell and then trained as a navigator in Canada, before joining 455 Squadron in August 1943. His age and prematurely grey hair were such that the younger spirits in the Australian squadron disrespectfully addressed him as 'Gramp' or even 'Snow White'. By 1945, however, he had flown on many dangerous operational sorties and had been awarded the DFC. Neither Milson nor Jones relished the task ahead of them. Both had proven records of courage, but they saw little point in squandering lives on what threatened to be a suicidal attack, especially when the war was so obviously drawing to a close. Nevertheless, they had their orders and they would carry them out to the best of their ability.

Beaufighter 'Y' of 144 Squadron was flown by Pilot Officer Percival C. Smith and navigated by Pilot Officer F.S. 'Spike' Holly, another very experienced crew. Their squadron was still commanded by the redoubtable Tony Gadd, who had been awarded a bar to his DFC only three days before, but Gadd had not been ordered to fly on this particular strike. 'Smithy' was twenty-six years of age, a man who had joined the army just before the outbreak of war,

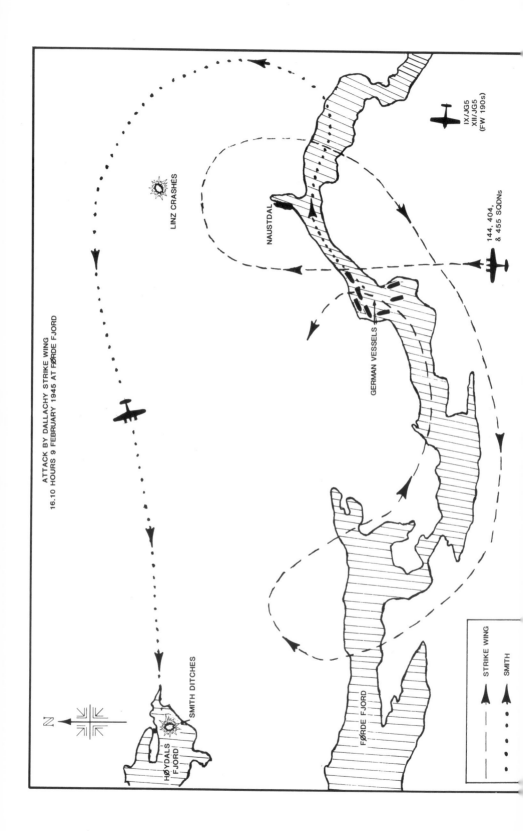

ATTACK BY DALLACHY STRIKE WING
16.10 HOURS 9 FEBRUARY 1945 AT FØRDE FJORD

N

HØYDALS
FJORD

SMITH DITCHES

LINZ CRASHES

NAUSTDAL

IX/JG5
XII/JG5
(FW 190s)

144, 404,
& 455 SODNs

GERMAN VESSELS

FØRDE FJORD

STRIKE WING
SMITH

transferring to the RAF in June 1941. Training followed, first in South Africa and then back in the UK. He crewed up with Holly during operational training at Catfoss. Holly, who was twenty-three years of age, had followed the normal pattern of many Beaufighter navigators by training at Cranwell and then in Canada. The two men took their torpedo training together at Castle Kennedy, near Stranraer, before joining 144 Squadron in August 1943, just after the squadron returned from the Mediterranean. They had each flown on over thirty-five sorties. Unlike Bomber Command, which set thirty flights over Germany or their equivalent over other territories as the norm for an operational tour, the practice varied in Coastal Command, which could never quite make up its mind as to what constituted an operational tour on strike aircraft.* However, Smith and Holly had been told that their tour would last eighteen months; this meant that they would be 'tour-expired' in five days' time, and they expected this to be their last operational flight. They were quite correct in that belief, but not in the way that they hoped.

Milson led the main formation with his eleven Beaufighters of 455 Squadron. Jones made landfall neatly at the entrance of the broad Sogne fjord. The Beaufighters flew inland, to sweep northwards towards the little town of Naustdal on the narrow Førde fjord, near where their target lay hidden. Then they would make their attack over the cliffs, towards the sea and home. With any luck, this would be a surprise attack and they would minimise their losses. The outriders went further ahead, scouring the waters of other fjords in case the destroyer had changed position. The Canadians of 404 Squadron were on the port side of the Australians, whilst the British of 144 Squadron were on the starboard. Smith was on the outer extremity of 144, leading a vic of three. The Mustangs followed the main formation.

As they neared Forde fjord, shore batteries opened up on them, the heavy flak bursting mainly around the Canadians. Førde fjord lies east-west, and at this stretch is shaped like a letter 'S' on its back, with steep cliffs on both sides. The destroyer – which was Z-33, a warship of 2,603 tons, equipped with five 105 mm and six 37 mm guns as well as eight 20 mm cannon – was tucked behind a cliff on

* When the author flew in strike aircraft of Coastal Command in 1941, the crews flew until they failed to return or were considered exhausted, the latter point usually being reached at around 200 hours. Of course, flying to the enemy coast involved much shorter but more frequent sorties than those of Bomber Command.

the southern side, shielded from the line of approach of the Wing. The formation flew straight over the fjord, and Milson wheeled the Beaufighters to starboard, then circling round to attempt an attack towards the sea. Once again, the destroyer proved to be shielded by the cliff. There was only one way to get at her and that was by running the gauntlet, flying eastwards up the waters of the fjord. Milson headed towards the mouth of the fjord, turned the formation once more, and gave the order to attack. Heavy flak from the thoroughly alerted Germans followed them around.

Leadership is the quality that counts most in a squadron. Milson went in first. On either side of the fjord, the shore batteries blazed at the diving Beaufighter, depressing their gun barrels to below the horizontal as Milson streaked over the waters. In front of Z-33, two M-class minesweepers opened fire, as well as a *Sperrbrecher* and several flak-ships. These were spread in an arc around the destroyer, which also opened fire. Behind Milson, the other Beaufighters jockeyed for position to follow him into the narrow valley of fire.

Smith knew that he should be one of the first in, for he was in the anti-flak section. He turned, banked, and cut corners to try to find a way through the milling aircraft. The flak was so intense that, as one pilot said long afterwards, 'It looked as though you could have put your wheels down and taxied on top of it'. Yet the Beaufighter pilots competed with each other in trying to find a way into this fiery furnace. Eventually, Smith found a clear patch of air, and dived. Out of the corner of his eye, he could see a squadron of single-engined fighters approaching from the south-east. There seemed to be about eight of them, in close formation. Smith wondered if they were the Mustang escorts. Then he concentrated on the target ahead. It was 16.10 hours.

The Ninth and Twelfth Staffeln (Squadrons) of Jagdgeschwader 5 (5th Fighter Group) were based on the airstrip at Herdla, near Bergen, about sixty-five miles to the south of Førde fjord. In their remote and frozen base, the Germans called their Group the Eismeerjäger, the Polar Sea hunter. They were equipped with the FW 190, the compact and agile little fighter that was armed with four 20 mm cannon and two 13 mm machine guns. Their most notable pilot was Leutnant Rudi Linz; he was the commander of the Twelfth Staffel, came from Ilmenau in Thuringia, and was just five days short of his twenty-eighth birthday. Linz was a fighter ace who had been credited with sixty-nine aerial victories, mostly on the Russian front but including a few British. He was probably the most formidable fighter pilot in Norway. At 15.50 hours, the two fighter squadrons were scrambled to attack the Dallachy Strike Wing and their Mustang escorts. Twenty minutes later, they came to the confused mass of flak and aircraft near Naustdal.

Astonishingly, most of the Beaufighters seem to have passed through the crossfire of flak in the fjord, although many were hit and some aircrew were wounded. Milson came through unscathed. The third aircraft into the fjord was flown by Flying Officer Harold R. Spink of 455 Squadron, an experienced ex-flying instructor from New South Wales, who was on his first operational flight. As he dived, Spink could see shells explode along his starboard wing towards him. Then he fired his rockets. A fraction of a second later, a final shell tore great holes in the side of his cockpit, spraying splinters into his chest and right arm. Nevertheless, he cleared the target. Then he saw the FW 190s and climbed into cloud. Almost immediately, ice began to form on the leading edges of the wings. He pushed the control column forward with his left arm, wondering about the condition of his navigator and whether he should try to make for Sweden, or ditch the Beaufighter, or head back towards Dallachy.

Smith aimed at an M-class minesweeper, made a good attack, and believes that his Beaufighter was not hit at that stage. Hits were seen on all the enemy vessels, including a large red explosion on the bridge of *Z-33*, but none was sunk. In Smith's Beaufighter, Holly heard the familiar thudding of the cannon and watched the coloured tracer streaming past the wings. He picked up his camera to photograph the chaotic scene from the rear as they sped north-eastwards away from the targets. He could pick out the white church at Naustdal. A fighter was coming up on their tail, very near and slightly on their port side. For a fraction of a second, Holly thought that he was looking at a Mustang and he wondered what it was doing so close to them. But this fighter had a radial engine. He dropped his camera, flicked up his intercom switch and shouted urgently:

'One-ninety, hundred yards astern!'

The next series of events happened in a few seconds. Holly swung over his .303 Browning machine gun. This was mounted on a pivot, fastened to one side of the cupola when not in use. It was belt-fed from the port side and was fired through two sliding doors. It had only a limited traverse, for a wider angle would cause the ammunition to jam in the breech. Holly had never trained as an air gunner, but he had fired a Browning at the butts on the ground and had occasionally loosed off a few rounds at ships after their attacks. Fortunately for him, a deflection shot which required much training and experience was not required. The FW 190 was flying straight towards them, a mere hundred yards away. The most successful fighter pilots were those with the courage to close right up to their targets and then let rip with a killing burst. Holly fired. The radial engine of the FW 190 was close enough to look like a dartboard. At that range, Holly could not miss. At the same time, the German pilot fired. Some of the cannon shells exploded inside the navigator's compartment, entering the port side of the fuselage. The splinters severed Holly's ammunition belt and put his Browning out of action; they cut his intercom cord to Smith; and they sprayed into his legs just above his knees, one entering his stomach whilst another grazed his body underneath the right armpit and passed through the back of the seat. Holly's seat belt, his parachute harness and release box saved him receiving the type of injury that fighting men most dread, but the shock of the splinters smashed him backwards into his seat and knocked him unconscious. The FW 190 did not fire again, but drifted off to port.

As Smith reacted to Holly's warning, he saw another Beaufighter smoking and diving lower, disappearing under his port wing. This was probably 'O' of 455 Squadron, flown by Flight Lieutenant R.C. McColl. Further up the fjord, the waters were completely icebound. McColl made a belly-landing, skidding to rest on the ice; he and his navigator, Warrant Officer L.L. MacDonald, were fortunate to survive. They ended the war as POWs. But Smith had no opportunity to look back at this other Beaufighter. The same burst that wounded Holly put a cannon shell into his cockpit. Something whipped below his right arm, without wounding him, and passed through the front of the Beaufighter. At the same time, his port engine was hit, with immediate loss of power. His intercom went dead and he had no idea what had happened to Holly behind the armoured doors. It flashed through his mind that the FW 190 might have shot down the Beaufighter on his port, before spraying his aircraft. He had intended to turn in this direction, to make his escape northwards from the fjord, over a wooded slope that he had noticed was lower than the rest, but the FW 190 was probably still on that side.

He dived even lower over the fjord, hoping that the German would not dare to follow him at that height. But he could stay down for only a few seconds before smashing into the cliffs. He was now fighting the controls of a sluggish aircraft, trying to keep it in the air, following the remainder of the S-shaped fjord inland. He had passed the town of Naustdal, on the north side of the fjord, and had turned south-east, but was running out of space. There was a slope ahead, on the east side of the curved fjord. It was covered with snowy trees, two of them in line and higher than the rest. He managed to pull up the nose of the Beaufighter slightly, knowing that he could not clear the tree-tops but hoping that he would not hit the main trunks.

The crashing, rushing, tearing noise brought Holly back to consciousness. He could see the branches of the trees whipping the Beaufighter and knew that he was going to die. In a split second, the Beaufighter would smash into the forest and burn up. He slipped back into unconsciousness.

The incredible Beaufighter tore through the tree-tops and continued to fly. At the top of the wooded rise, Smith swept round to port, the direction of the sea and home. Fortunately, there was lower ground in front. The controls were now so sluggish that he had no option but to put down the nose to pick up airspeed and prevent stalling. He could see flak coming up at the other Beaufighters. It was impossible to get home. The aircraft was trying to sink lower, and he did not know what condition Spike was in. He had better try to put it down somewhere.

There was another fjord ahead, just to the north of Førde fjord. He noticed a rock shelving into the water at a shallow angle and wondered if he could ditch in the fjord in front of it. Perhaps the Beaufighter would come to rest on the rock just underneath the water and not sink completely. This was a forlorn hope but it entered Smith's mind, for he knew that Holly was as poor a swimmer as himself. A man could expect to survive in that icy water for only a few minutes. Smith put the Beaufighter down in the fjord, grazing a tree and the rock, making a good ditching in spite of the dead engine. The water poured into the aircraft immediately. Only a miracle could now save their lives.

Whilst Smith was trying desperately to find a way out of the cliffs of Førde fjord, other aircraft were crashing, either from the effects of flak or the aerial battle that followed the attack. In addition to the two aircraft flown by Smith and McColl, seven Beaufighters were shot down. 455 Squadron lost another Beaufighter; both Warrant Officer Donald E. Mutimer and Pilot Officer John D. Blackshaw were killed in a crash near the destroyer. All the other Beaufighters were lost by 404 Squadron. Flying Officer J.R. Savard, the Canadian pilot of Beaufighter 'O' survived to become a POW, but his English navigator, Flying Officer Jeffrey Middleton, was killed. The crews of all the other aircraft were Canadians and all lost their lives: Flying Officer H. Smook and Warrant Officer A.M. Duckworth in 'Q'; Pilot Officer W.J. Jackson and Pilot Officer W.E. Blunderfield in 'V'; Flying Officer P.R. Myrick and Pilot Officer C.G. Berges in 'W'; Flying Officer H.C. Lynch and Flying Officer C.W. Knight in 'C'; and Flying Officer C. Smerneos and Flying Officer N.D. Cochrane in 'F'. It was a staggering blow to the Canadian squadron that had fought so well for the Allies.

No 65 Squadron lost one Mustang. This was flown by Warrant Officer Cecil C. Caesar, who lost his life by the guns fired by Unteroffizier Heinz Orlowski of the 9th Staffel. But the Mustangs and the rear guns of the Beaufighters took their toll of the FW 190s. The Germans lost five aircraft. Leutnant Wolfgang Koch escaped by parachute. Unteroffizier Herbert Schäfer and Unterroffizier Heinz Orlowski were both wounded. Two pilots were reported missing and were later found to have been killed; they were Feldwebel Otto Liebfred and the air ace, Leutnant Rudi Linz.

Twenty-three Beaufighters turned to make their way back to Dallachy, the appearance of many bearing witness to the tragedy. Amongst them was Harold Spink in 'X' of 455 Squadron. His navigator, Flying Officer Lloyd R. Clifford of the RAAF, was wounded in the leg but came forward to help his pilot. As the navigator entered the cockpit, he slipped and fell over, for hydraulic oil from a punctured pipe had covered the floor. The flak burst had also wrecked the fuel mechanism of the starboard tanks, so that the petrol cocks to that engine were useless. The engine was in fully fine pitch, racing furiously, but flak had destroyed the control mechanism. There was a deafening roar from the desynchronized engines through the gaping holes in the cockpit, so loud that it was impossible for the two men to hear each other. The intercom had been severed. The only way that they could communicate was by pointing to letters on the pilot's panel, in particular to a notice that concerned the dihedral tailplane which

(Right): 9 February 1945.
Førde fjord looking inland.
The destroyer Z-33 is
under attack in the
foreground. Beyond, the
ice is thickening, under-
neath towering cliffs.
Taken from Beaufighter 'T'
of 404 Squadron, flown by
Flying Officer H.P. Flynn.

(Below): 9 February 1945.
Beaufighter TFX, letter
'O' serial NF831 of 144
Squadron, flown by Flight
Sergeant S.A. Butler at
Dallachy.

announced 'Warning. Modified Tailplane'.

Clifford broke open the first aid box and applied a tourniquet to Spink's arm, which was streaming with blood. He also gave his pilot a single injection of morphine. The two men decided to head for home. They tried to find another Beaufighter on which they could formate, but for once the sky was empty. Somehow, they brought the Beaufighter all the way across the North Sea to Scotland, gradually correcting an initially wide navigation error, for Clifford could not return to his table. It was dark when they reached Dallachy. Red Very lights were fired at them from the aerodrome, warning them not to land. But the Beaufighter was almost out of fuel. Clifford fired a warning Very light and Spink came into land, putting down his undercarriage. Then he realized that his hydraulics were useless and that he would belly-land on the runway. He made another circuit, helped by Clifford, heading for the grass alongside the runway.

The starboard engine, which had been showing a cylinder head temperature of 360°, about 180° above the permitted maximum, began to flame. They tried to pump down the undercarriage, but the warning light remained on. The Beaufighter skidded on its belly along the grass. Spink pressed the fire extinguisher button. He was hoisted out of the top hatch and taken to a long recovery in hospital. Both Spink and Clifford were awarded DFCs.

Dallachy was a scene of wrecked and damaged aircraft. In 'Q' of 455, the tailplane was hit by flak whilst one tyre was shot away, but Flying Officer C. Thomson made a successful belly landing. Flying Officer W. G. Herbert landed 'F' of 455 with an elevator shot away and a shell hole in a fuel tank. One aircraft of 404 was badly damaged by an FW190, but the crew brought it home. Three of 144 were shot up but all landed safely. The men and women at Dallachy were appalled at the scale of their losses.

The Hopen family lived in their remote farmhouse near the eastern end of Høydals fjord, where they earned their living by mixed farming and trapping salmon. Henrik Hopen, who was fifty-two years of age, had spent several years with his wife Frida in the USA before returning to his native country. Their son Arne was aged seventeen, a candidate for forced labour under the Germans. This family of hardy Norwegians were patriots, strongly in favour of the Allied cause.

At about 14.15 hours on 9 February 1945, Frida was in the

(above): November 1944.
Flying Officer Ralph Jones
(left) with his skipper, Wing
Commander Jack
Davenport.

(right): November 1944.
Wing Commander Jack
Davenport (left) talks to his
successor, Wing Comman-
der Colin Milson.

Flying Officer Lloyd R.
Clifford (left) Flying Officer
Harold R. Spink (right).

February 1945. A
crashed Beaufighter at
Dallachy after the strike on
Forde fjord.

farmhouse when she heard the roar of an approaching aircraft. Looking out, she could tell at once that it was in difficulties, for there was a strange note to the engines whilst it was losing height. Then it sheared off the top of a pine tree on a small hill to the west of the farmhouse and disappeared out of view in the direction of the fjord. Frida rushed outside, down to where her husband and son were working, calling out to them. They ran up a hill and looked out over the fjord. There was a twin-engined aircraft in the water, sinking rapidly. The two men did not waste an instant. They tore down to their little jetty, where each jumped into a rowing boat and pulled with all their strength to the site of the sunken Beaufighter. They knew that anyone in that icy water would die of immersion hypothermia within minutes.

Smith wrenched open his top hatch and hoisted himself up. In training, his flying gear and Mae West had always snagged in the narrow emergency exit, but on this occasion he shot straight through. Freezing water covered him and he inflated his lifejacket, but he could see no sign of the aircraft dinghy, which must have been hit by shells and gone down with the aircraft. Holly regained consciousness once more, to find the water rising round his feet. He released his seat belt and opened his cupola. The Beaufighter sank beneath him and he floated clear. He pulled the air bottle lever of his lifejacket but the rubber had been shredded by cannon fire and did not inflate; the kapok pads kept him afloat, however. The two men dog-paddled in the freezing water, trying to reach the shore. They tried to climb on a wheel that had somehow come to the surface from the sunken Beaufighter, but this proved impossible. Holly began to lose consciousness again. Then hands grabbed him and he could feel himself being pulled into a small wooden boat. The two airmen had been in the water for about ten minutes and were near death.

Smith could walk to the farm-house, but Henrik and Arne Hopen put their arms round Holly and half-carried him, bleeding and fainting, to warmth and safety. Smith stripped off his freezing clothes and swaddled himself in the blankets which Frida provided. He put his battledress in front of the fire to dry off. Henrik spoke to him in English but he could not reply properly, for his jaws were chattering and his body was shaking uncontrollably. Holly was put down gently on a sofa. The Norwegians took off his clothes carefully and tried to stop the bleeding from his wounds. Frida tore up a sheet and bandaged him as best she could.

1946. Flying Officer 'Spike' Holly (left) and Flying Officer P.C. Smith.

(*Left*): Henrik Hopen, sitting by his salmon trap, photographed after the War. (*Right*): Arne Hopen, photographed after the War.

Henrik explained to Smith that Holly had to have proper medical attention. He telephoned a doctor, but was told that the only access to the farm in the depths of winter was by boat, on a route that was watched over by the Germans. Henrik apologized to Smith, saying that there was no alternative but to notify the Germans if Holly's life was to be saved. What he did not tell the English pilot was that he had arms hidden underneath the jetty and that he was putting the lives of his family and himself in jeopardy by inviting their oppressors to the farm. Smith concealed some of their escape kit and waited. He did not stop shivering for two hours. Henrik telephoned Dr Yttri in the coastal town of Florø, telling him that he would have to come with the Germans.

During the night, the Germans came with a doctor. They took the two prisoners by boat to Florø, where Holly was put in sick quarters and Smith was locked up. The next night, they were taken by boat to Bergen. Holly was put on a couch in the saloon, in company with several German sailors who were also wounded, probably in the attack of two days before, but there was no animosity on either side. The Germans even gave cigarettes to the RAF men and allowed Smith to sit with Holly; they were, of course, fighting men and not prison guards or members of the Gestapo.

At Bergen, the two men parted. Holly was taken to a hospital where the cannon shell splinters were extracted, whilst Smith was sent on to Oslo. Holly followed on to Oslo a few days later and spent five weeks in hospital there. Meanwhile, Smith had joined up with the other POW survivors of Black Friday, Bob McColl and L.L. MacDonald of 455 Squadron, and Roger Savard of 404 Squadron; they were sent next to Aarhus in Denmark and then to Frankfurt and Bremen in Germany before ending up at Stalag Luft 1 near Barth on the Baltic coast. Holly joined them at the same POW camp. After liberation, each was flown back to the UK in Flying Fortresses. Smith was awarded a DFC.

After the war, Spike Holly was browsing in a book shop when he came across an old Baedeker guide to Norway. In this, he saw the place-name Hopen in Høydals fjord and wondered if this could be the home of the people who had saved his life. He took a chance, wrote to the address, and before long was reunited with the Norwegian family. He discovered that Arne Hopen had taken to the mountains to avoid forced labour and had escaped to England, where he served in the Royal Norwegian Navy during the last few weeks of the war. After many years of friendship with Spike Holly, Henrik Hopen died in 1971, but each year on 9 February the Hopen family receive a card from the UK.

The FW 190 flown by Rudi Linz, number 732183, crashed at Solheimsstølen, near the town of Naustdal, and burnt for hours. During the evening, a Norwegian went to the site on skis, and the body was brought down the following day. Linz had been seen by his comrades attacking a Beaufighter in that area; after having put the Beaufighter out of action, he was seen to have been hit by return fire. In 1982, the battle of Førde fjord was reconstructed by Per Nordeide, a local journalist, and Per Skaugstad, a skin-diving expert who is writing a book on the air war over Norway.* After having examined the British and German records, talked to survivors on both sides, and plotted the positions of crashed aircraft, the Norwegians decided that only one Beaufighter was in that position at that exact time. Spike Holly had shot down Rudi Linz.

---

*   *Fallen Airmen in Norway 1939–45: Their Aircraft and Fate.* (in preparation).

CHAPTER THIRTEEN

Retribution

Feldmarschall Wilhelm Keitel:
'Was konnen wir tun?' (What shall we do now?)
Feldmarschall Gerd von Rundstedt:
'Frieden schliessen, ihr Narren! Was denn sonst?' (Make peace, you fools! What else can you do?)
Conversation reported in June 1944

There was no relaxation of effort by the Strike Wings during the last few months of the war. Almost every day, the Banff and Dallachy Wings went out in force to Norwegian waters. Sometimes, elements of these two Wings operated together, whilst on other occasions they would attack the same targets on successive strikes. The North Coates Wing found fewer targets off Holland; they hunted for the last of the midget U-boats in which Hitler had placed such vain hopes, the two-man *Seehund* and the one-man *Biber* and *Molch*. Sometimes, the North Coates and Dallachy Wings cruised along the coasts of Germany itself. Although the Luftwaffe fighters were still dangerous, more Mustang escorts were available. Sinkings multiplied, especially in the Norwegian fjords. On 30 March, the Banff Wing swept into Oslo fjord itself and sank five merchant vessels in a single murderous attack.

The three Strike Wings entered the final period of ascendancy over their enemy. So few merchant vessels remained available to the Germans that the aircrews could almost memorise their names. Some of these were damaged, repaired, and put into service again. In spite of their terrible losses, the Germans kept a trickle of their coastal traffic in operation. Troops were withdrawn by ship from Norway to help stiffen their crumbling forces on the eastern and western fronts. Their flak still remained effective, pouring up from ship and shore, and many Allied aircraft were lost. Although their war machine was disintegrating around them, the German fighting men continued to defend themselves with desperate courage.

Whilst the Germans were losing the fight in the North Sea, conditions became even more disastrous for them in the Baltic. In September 1944, Sweden closed her harbours to German ships.

Meanwhile, the Russians advanced steadily along the southern shores of the Baltic, their numbers reinforced by troops released from the war against Finland, which had concluded an armistice with Russia in that month. By October, Russian forces entered Prussia and threatened the U-boat training bases in the area around Danzig. At the same time, Bomber Command increased its minelaying campaign in the Baltic; by now, the Kriegsmarine was desperately short of minesweepers, so that the magnetic mines of the RAF took an enormous toll of enemy shipping. As the Russians continued their advance, the surviving German ships and U-boats began to stream westwards towards the Kiel canal, some of them bringing anguished refugees from eastern Germany. The Baltic, which might have been called the German Sea since the beginning of the war, now became a death-trap for the Kriegsmarine and the German merchant ships.

There were over seventy U-boats bottled up in the Baltic, operational boats as well as training boats. By April 1945, these were compelled to seek new bases in Norway, where they could try to continue the fight. But to reach these safer ports, the U-boats had to run the gauntlet, through the narrow and shallow channels around the numerous islands to the east of the Danish peninsula. First they had to pass through the Fehmarn Straits, near the German port of Lübeck, then thread through the passage of the Great Belt, before reaching the broader waters of the Kattegat. Then once again the waters narrowed, near the Swedish port of Göteborg, before the U-boats could attain the deeper waters of the Skaggerak and the relative safety of the Norwegian ports. The narrow waters of this passage had been sown thickly with aerial mines. It was less perilous to attempt the journey on the surface than to risk being blown apart by a mine under water. At least a minesweeper could precede them, although little air cover could be expected from the Luftwaffe.

Meanwhile, the movements of the U-boats were being monitored by the Tracking Room in the Citadel. Coastal Command awaited the arrival of their ancient enemy with almost pleasurable anticipation. A U-boat was still a prime target, something to be killed without mercy, like a vicious shark. Most RAF aircrews carried in their minds a vision of British sailors suffocating and drowning in oily or burning seas, whilst the vital contents of their torpedoed vessels lay at the bottom of the Atlantic. Now was the time for retribution.

In the late afternoon of 9 April, the Banff Strike Wing was on patrol, approaching the Kattegat. There were twelve Mosquitoes from 143, nine from 235 and nine from 248 Squadron. Two Mosquitoes from 333 Squadron acted as outriders whilst, unusually, there was also a Mosquito from the RAF Film Unit. Almost all these aircraft were fitted with eight rockets apiece in addition to the usual four cannon, and each was carrying two 100-gallon drop-tanks. The Wing Leader was Squadron Leader H. H. K. Gunnis of 248 Squadron. The formation had picked up a Mustang escort over Peterhead and had flown into the Skaggerak, where they spotted three innocent-looking fishing boats. They turned south into the Kattegat, looking for victims.

A few minutes later, Gunnis saw two wakes to starboard and turned the formation to approach them from out of the sun. The Mosquitoes were at 2,500 feet when Gunnis ordered the twelve aircraft of 143 squadron to dive on the vessels; there was no point in expending all the rockets if the targets proved insufficiently important.

'They're U-boats!' called Squadron Leader D. L. Pritchard of 143 Squadron, as his Mosquitoes split into two sections to attack each target. By this time, Gunnis and the Mosquitoes of 248 Squadron had over-flown the target, but the Wing Leader immediately ordered the nine aircraft of 235 Squadron, which were further behind, to dive into the attack.

One will never know why the U-boats remained on the surface, for there were no survivors. In the lead was *U-804*, a type IX U-boat of 1,144 tons, commanded by Leutnant zur See Herbert Meyer; she was fitted with *Schnorkel* and had completed two war cruises. Slightly behind her was *U-1065*, a type VII U-boat of 769 tons, commanded by Leutnant zur See Panitz; she was on her initial cruise. Both boats were making about fifteen knots, headed north for Horten in Oslo fjord.

No 143 Squadron fired their cannon and over seventy rockets at the two U-boats, which almost disappeared in spray and thick smoke. 235 Squadron delivered a similar attack immediately afterwards. *U-804*, which had been firing at the attackers, suddenly sank but reappeared about ten seconds later, her bows raised slightly out of the water. Behind her, *U-1065* swung abruptly to starboard; there was an explosion and she turned on her side before sinking, leaving on oily patch of brilliant greens and reds, in which bodies as well as yellow dinghies could be seen. Then 248 Squadron swept down to join in the attack. As the additional Mosquitoes reached the target area, *U-804* exploded. There was a violent flash and a sheet of flame, followed by a great mushroom of grey and white smoke. Debris was hurled high into the air, damaging four of the attackers. The Mosquito of the RAF Film Unit caught the full effect of the blast; it was thrown upwards and on to its back, before spinning down to explode in the sea. Three damaged Mosquitoes announced that they were 'going to Brighton', the code message for an aircraft in difficulties making for Sweden; they all landed safely in that neutral country.

Meanwhile, another Mosquito was trying to find the formation. This was flown by Flying Officer E.J. Rendell of 235 Squadron, who had turned away from the Wing ninety minutes earlier to escort another of his squadron which had reported engine failure. When the other pilot told him that he felt he could reach Banff safely, Rendell tried to re-join his Wing. Cutting a corner, he had flown clean past it. At precisely the same time that the Wing was sinking the two U-boats, Rendell came across a third, about twenty miles to the southeast. This was *U-843*, another type IX of 1,144 tons, commanded by Leutnant zur See Herwatz. She was a blockade runner, returning from her third cruise to Djakarta in Indonesia. Unlike the other two, she was headed towards Kiel instead of away from it, having made a call at Bergen in Norway. Rendell attacked out of the sun, scoring at least two underwater hits with his rockets. *U-843* tried evasive action but did not submerge. Again, Rendell dived down, firing his cannon at the conning tower and hull. He then circled round and made a third and last attack. Smoke began to pour from the U-boat. Although Rendell could not prove his success at the time, he had sunk *U-843* when she was almost at the end of her long voyage. In the three U-boats, 144 German submariners were killed.

On 19 April, another convoy of U-boats was spotted by the Banff Wing when flying over the southern waters of the Kattegat. On this occasion, there were ten Mosquitoes of 235 Squadron, four of 143 and five of 248, accompanied by two outriders of 333 Squadron and an escort of Mustangs. The formation was led by Wing Commander A.H. 'Junior' Simmonds, the 27-year-old commanding officer of 235 Squadron, a pilot who had flown operationally almost continuously throughout the war, first on Vildebeests, then on Beauforts, next on Beaufighters, and finally on Mosquitoes.* Simmonds

*   See *Torpedo Airmen*, by the author, for an account of some of the operational flying of A.H. Simmonds.

saw several inviting targets, which he did not attack for he had been told to hunt for U-boats. Then he saw four U-boats in line astern, each about 200 yards apart. They were led by an M-class minesweeper and headed towards Norway. He gave the order to attack, at 16.30 hours.

As the Mosquitoes dived from 3,000 feet, across the sun, the leading U-boat submerged. The minesweeper and the second and fourth U-boats received the brunt of the attack. The second U-boat turned to port in a vain attempt to escape the stream of cannon fire and rockets. Evidently she was too badly hit to submerge, for she began to smoke whilst about ten dinghies appeared around her. This was *U-251*, commanded by Leutnant zur See Seck, a type VIIC of 769 tons that had completed nine war cruises; her luck ran out that day, for she was destroyed with her crew of thirty-nine. The third U-boat was *U-2502*, a type XXI of 1,621 tons, commanded by Leutnant zur See Franke; she was only lightly damaged. The fourth U-boat was seen to have a damaged conning tower and to be emitting black smoke before she submerged. This was *U-2335*, a prefabricated boat of 232 tons, commanded by Leutnant zur See Bethin, on her first operational cruise; she managed to reach Kristiansand, in spite of extensive damage. The minesweeper was left covered in thick black smoke, but she did not sink. One of the Mosquitoes was so badly hit by flak that the pilot had to make for Sweden. Another was hit on the journey home over Denmark and made a belly landing in the country whilst another Mosquito shot up a column of German troops nearby.

The Banff Wing encountered an unusual enemy on 21 April, two days after the attack on the four U-boats. Forty-two Mosquitoes, consisting of sixteen of 143, eleven of 235, eleven of 248 and four of 333, crossed the west coast of Denmark in the late afternoon headed for the Kattegat; they were escorted by twenty-four Mustangs. This large formation was led by Wing Commander Christopher N. Foxley-Norris, a 28-year-old officer who had also flown continuously during the war, on Lysanders in France, on Hurricanes in the Battle of Britain, and on Beaufighters in Britain and in the Mediterranean. On their return to the UK, the Beaufighter crews of his 603 Squadron had been invited by Max Aitken to convert to Mosquitoes and join the Banff Wing. Foxley-Norris took command of 143 Squadron – one of his old squadrons – when Wing Commander J.M. Maurice, the well-liked and remarkable Frenchman whose real name was Max Guedj, was

April 1945. Attack by
Mosquitoes of the Banff
Wing on U-boats in the
Kattegat.

April 1945. Another
attack by Mosquitoes of
the Banff Wing on U-boats
in the Kattegat.

May 1945. Attack by
Mosquitoes of the Banff
Wing on U-boats in the
Kattegat.

killed over Norway in February 1945.

There was mist and rain over the Kattegat, and only a few small vessels could be seen, not justifying an attack. The Wing then flew back over the Danish peninsula and hunted without success for targets in enemy coastal waters on the North Sea. At 19.38 hours, the frustrated pilots set course for base. Twelve minutes later, the Mustangs parted company with the Mosquitoes. It seemed to have been another of those uneventful patrols.

About half an hour later, when nearly half-way across the North Sea on their peaceful journey home, the Mosquito pilots saw another formation of aircraft, flying south, at right angles to their westerly course. They could see eighteen aircraft at 100 feet, in six vics of three in line astern. As the pilots approached, flying through the mist at about 200 feet, they could see that the strangers were a force of Ju 88s and Ju 188s, with a few He 111s. Some of them were carrying torpedoes. Luftwaffe records for the period are fragmentary, but the aircraft almost certainly formed part of the bomber group KG26 which was based in Denmark and at that time was making a series of attacks on Convoy JW66 which left the Clyde on 16 April bound for Russia, with an escort of warships. Foxley-Norris gave the order to attack. In a few moments the air was full of a gyrating mass of agile Mosquitoes chasing their slower, lighter armed and less manoeuvrable opponents. The result was a foregone conclusion. The Mosquito pilots saw nine German aircraft break up, spin down in flames and smoke, or crash into the sea. There was return fire, but no casualties were suffered by the Mosquitoes. The remaining Germans scattered. Long after the war, in 1969, Foxley-Norris met a German Colonel, Hans Geisemann, who told him that only two of the German aircraft managed to return to make belly landings at their base in Norway. Apparently, the unfortunate crews were inexperienced; certainly they were no match for the well-trained British pilots in their superb Mosquitoes.

During April, 404 Squadron converted to Mosquitoes and the Canadians switched from the Dallachy Wing to the Banff Wing. On 2 May at 08.55 hours, thirty-three Mosquitoes of this larger Banff Wing, led by Squadron Leader A. G. Deck and escorted by twenty-four Mustangs, found two more U-boats on the surface in the Kattegat. Five miles to the north-west was an M-class minesweeper. The Wing attacked and sank *U-2359*, a type XXIII of 235 tons, commanded by Leutnant zur See Bischoff on her initial cruise to Horten in Oslo fjord; some of the U-boat men were seen to escape into their

(*above*): 3 May 1945.
Attack by the Dallachy
Wing on three vessels
moored alongside each
other in Nakskov harbour,
Denmark. The foremost
vessel, the *Java* of 8,681
tons, sank. The two behind
were damaged. (*Right*):
The effect of a 25lb rocket
on a merchant vessel,
showing a small entry hole
in the side of the cabin
and a much larger exit
hole in the deck. This is a
'dry hit', above the
waterline. A hit below the
waterline, called a 'wet hit',
was far more dangerous
for the vessel.

dinghies, but twelve went down with the boat, which sank in a patch of oil, wreckage and bubbles. The Wing also damaged the second U-boat, another type XXIII. The minesweeper, *M-293* of 637 tons, was left burning furiously and later sank. One damaged Mosquito headed for the sanctuary of Sweden after the attack.

In the last week of the war, the North Coates Wing also scored a series of successes against trapped U-boats. Only 236 and 254 Squadrons were now left in this Wing – the original two that had developed the tactics from such shaky beginnings in November 1942. The crews of both squadrons still flew the magnificent Beaufighter TFX, although during April 254 Squadron had been given a few Mosquito VIs and XVIIIs, the latter carrying the six-pounder gun. Wing Commander D. G. Hall had taken command of 236 Squadron after Bill Tacon was shot down and taken prisoner on 12 September 1944, whilst Wing Commander Dave L. Cartridge had taken over 254 Squadron from Paddy Burns later in the same month.

In the afternoon of 3 May, twelve rocket-firing Beaufighters of 236 and seventeen Beaufighters of 254, armed only with cannon, entered the Kattegat on a patrol that bore the name Penetration and Withdrawal. They were led by Wing Commander E.P.W. 'Jock' Hutton, the Wing Commander Flying at North Coates, and escorted by Mustangs. At 17.20 hours at the northern end of the Great Belt they found *U-2524*, a type XXI U-boat of 1,621 tons. She was headed towards Norway on her initial cruise, commanded by Leutnant zur See Witzendorff. Eleven Beaufighters attacked. *U-2524* seemed to explode before she sank, but most of the crew survived by jumping into the water, only two being killed.

The North Coates Wing then rampaged down the Great Belt, finding a myriad of targets. The avenging Beaufighters attacked no less than fifteen vessels in succession, raking them with cannon and rocket fire. Seven vessels were either sunk or seriously damaged. Amongst these was the two-funnel liner *Der Deutsche*, a vessel of 11,453 tons, 490 feet long, built in 1924. Two 25 lb solid-shot rockets hit the liner below the waterline, so that she flooded and heeled over at an angle of thirteen degrees. She was beached in the Fehmarn belt, later to be re-floated. The liner was escorted by three minesweepers which put up intense light and heavy flak. On this attack, the North Coates Wing suffered its last casualties of the war, when 'X' of 254 Squadron was shot down near the liner and Flight Sergeant J.E. Scott and Flight Sergeant M.K. Farrington lost their lives. The rest of the Beaufighters landed at B86 at Helmond in south-east Holland, to re-fuel, re-arm and find sleeping quarters for the night.

During the mid-afternoon of the following day, twenty-two Beaufighters took off from their temporary base in Holland and flew back towards the Kattegat in search of further targets. They were escorted by Mustangs and led by Squadron Leader Stan R. Hyland, one of the Flight Commanders of 236 Squadron. Once more, they attacked a succession of targets, including a destroyer, with no casualties to the Beaufighter crews. Finally, they found four U-boats on the surface at the north end of the Little Belt, and sank them all. They were *U-2503*, a type XXI of 1,621 tons, commanded by Leutnant zur See Wächter; *U-2338*, a type XXIII of 232 tons, commanded by Leutnant zur See Mumm; and *U-393*, another type VIIC of 769 tons, commanded by Leutnant zur See Herrle. All these U-boats were headed to Norway from Kiel. They were sufficiently close to the shore for most of the crews to reach safety, but it is known that at least twenty-seven men lost their lives. A few damaged Beaufighters returned to Holland, whilst the remainder headed back to North Coates.

It was the last attack of the war for the North Coates Wing. On the same day, the Banff Wing also struck into the Kattegat, sinking one vessel and damaging two more. The previous day, the Dallachy Wing had attacked three vessels moored in Nakskov harbour, in the Danish island of Lolland; after the war, several of their 25 lb rockets were found to have passed clean through one vessel and damaged another.

The fighting was over for the Strike Wings.

CHAPTER FOURTEEN

The Reckoning

> Would that I could discover truth as easily as I can dis-
> cover falsehood.
>
> *Cicero (106–43 BC)*

The events related in this book do not constitute a full account of
every major attack made by the Strike Wings. They do, however,
illustrate aspects of the work of the crews who flew in the
Beaufighters and Mosquitoes during the periods that 143, 144, 235,
236, 248, 254, 404, 455 and 489 Squadrons formed part of these
Wings. The sorties selected have been researched with the aid of
British and German records, but the narrative could not have been
written without the first-hand accounts of several airmen who flew
in these squadrons and who have helped the author with their vivid
recollections of these dramatic events. Some of these men were
rewarded with decorations for bravery; some went on to reach very
high rank and distinction in the post-war RAF. But there are
numerous airmen, equally brave, who flew in the Strike Wings and
are not mentioned at all in the narrative. The author estimates that
about 700 airmen, pilots and navigators, flew in the nine squadrons
during the periods covered by this brief history. Of these, some 450
airmen lost their lives, almost 65% of the total. This ratio of loss is
about the same as that of Bomber Command during the war. The
Strike Wings also lost about 250 aircraft by enemy action, whilst
many more were damaged beyond repair. Terrible though these
human losses were, they were less grim than the casualties suffered
by the crews who flew in Coastal Command's strike aircraft in the
earlier days of the war, when the chance of survival was probably
under 20%; this was probably the highest casualty rate of any
branch of the armed services.

How do the losses of the Strike Wings compare with the losses
suffered by their German targets? One is able to make an assessment of the material losses with some accuracy. The targets of the
Strike Wings were entirely strategic, so that the results can be
measured in terms of German-controlled ships known to have

sunk. These are listed in Appendix III. In so far as wartime records were accurate – and the author is reasonably confident that the list gives the true picture – one can compare the German losses with those of the Strike Wings.

The Strike Wings sank 300,055 tons of enemy shipping and naval escorts. They seriously damaged another 118,137 tons of shipping, plus an unlisted but considerable number of escort vessels that managed to limp into harbour in their damaged state. In the period covered by this history, November 1942 to May 1945, the total tonnage of German shipping sunk by direct air attack was about 450,000 tons; thus the Strike Wings destroyed about two-thirds of this total; in addition, the surprising total of about 415,000 tons was sunk by aerial minelaying; some of these losses occurred in the Baltic Sea from mines dropped by Bomber Command, outside the normal area of operations of the Strike Wings.

Most of the vessels sunk by the Strike Wings differed markedly from those sunk by U-boats. An E-boat of 92 tons, a flak-ship of 450 tons, a *Sperrbrecher* of 1,500 tons or a well-armed merchant vessel of 3,000 tons, were far tougher and more dangerous targets than unarmed merchant vessels sailing in Allied convoys, even though the latter were defended by destroyers and corvettes. The Allies sank a far greater proportion of the shipping available to the Germans than the ratio of loss inflicted on Allied shipping by U-boats. By the end of the war, Allied attacks resulted in the almost complete destruction of German-controlled shipping. The Strike Wings were the most potent single force in this achievement; they sank 215 enemy vessels and damaged numerous others. One cannot estimate reliably the casualties of enemy seamen in these vessels, but from the sample of about thirty attacks examined in detail by the author, an average of at least four seamen were lost for every airman.

Apart from the balance sheet of losses of Allied men and aircraft against German seamen and ships, the question remains as to whether the losses impaired the German wartime economy. There is no doubt that the attacks caused considerable alarm to the Germans. For instance, the sinkings of merchant vessels off the Norwegian coast in 1944 reached such a pitch that Hitler discussed the possibility of building a new railway system through the Norwegian mountains, the idea being that such a route could be more easily defended. Slave labourers were sent to Norway, but the scheme was not completed. In September 1944, the Swedish government closed all her Baltic harbours to German shipping, whilst permitting the iron ore trade to continue through the Norwegian route until the end of the year. By this time, the Swedes had lost 100,000 tons of merchant shipping, although their skippers still referred to their highly profitable trade with Germany as the 'gold run'. The real reason for the suspension of this trade may not have been concern at the shipping losses. The Swedish government probably thought that it would be imprudent to continue trading with a partner who was obviously beaten militarily; profitable relations could be restored with the advent of peace and a programme of rebuilding a shattered country.

One of the astonishing revelations of the German economy from early 1942 to the end of 1944 is that the output of aircraft, tanks, weapons, munitions etc. rose steadily during this period. This was, of course, the result of the work of Albert Speer, who took over as Minister of Armaments and Munitions in February 1942. He achieved this success by brilliant organization, by diverting sections of the economy from domestic to war production, and by the use of millions of foreign workers and slave labourers. Even the massive attacks by Bomber Command and the USAAF failed to cause more than temporary setbacks in this war production. It was not until most of the occupied territories and part of Germany itself were over-run by the Allied armies that this enormous war machine began to grind to a halt. Germany's large stocks of iron ore were one of the factors that enabled her to continue until this stage was reached. The squadrons of the Strike Wings were too few and too late to topple the colossus by cutting its vital lifeline to Sweden.

Nevertheless, it can now be seen that the Strike Wings were achieving a remarkable economic success. After the war, two teams of researchers descended on Germany, each bent on discovering the effects of the Allied bombing offensive on her economy. By far the larger of these two teams was the United States Strategic Bombing Survey (USSBS), employing about a thousand personnel, which soon released a voluminous series of reports. The smaller team was the British Bombing Survey Unit (BBSU), with Professor Solly Zuckerman as the scientific advisor. The BBSU also produced a series of reports, but these were not generally released for many years, presumably because the contents were considered unpalatable to the war-weary public and the relatives of those who had lost their lives on the bombing offensive.

Both the American and British teams reached similar conclu
sions. They discovered that the policy of 'area bombing' of German
towns was far less injurious to the German war economy than had
been generally believed. About 500,000 Germans were killed whilst
160,000 Allied airmen lost their lives. But, as Sir Henry Tizard – the
eminent scientist who was largely responsible for the installation of
the British radar chain – said after the war:

> Experience has shown that a nation, with toughness and a will to
> work, can stand far more punishment in the form of bombard-
> ment of cities and homes than most people thought possible
> before the trial. No one now thinks that it would have been pos-
> sible to defeat Germany by bombing alone. The actual effort in
> man-power and resources that was expended in bombing Ger-
> many was greater than the value in manpower of the damage
> caused.

However, when the BBSU turned to examine the work of the Strike
Wings, the experts came to a totally different conclusion. In the
prosaic language of scientists and economists, 'man-months' (the
average amount of labour expended by a man in a month) were
used as the unit of measurement for comparison of the German
losses with those sustained by the Strike Wings. Taking the German
losses first, it was discovered that a considerable amount of time
was lost in forming shipping convoys and providing escort protection. The average size of merchant vessel sunk by the Strike Wings
was taken as 3,000 tons, giving a cost to the Germans:

Cost of vessel	6,000 man-months
Cost of cargo	400 man-months
Cost of delays to shipping	1,400 man-months
Cost of delays to cargo	800 man-months

Total   8,600

Turning to the losses sustained by the North Coates Strike Wing
from April 1943 to August 1943, it was calculated that in order to
sink a merchant vessel of an average size of 3,000 tons, 120 aircraft
sorties needed to be flown, whilst an average of 1.9 Beaufighters was
lost. The cost of this effort to the Allies was:

Cost of aircraft	1,440 man-months
Cost of aircrew training ⎤	1,560 man-months
Cost of petrol and armament ⎟	
Cost of maintenance ⎦	

Total   3,000

There was thus a 'gain factor' in favour of the North Coates Wing of nearly three to one, according to these calculations. This favourable ratio improved further as the war progressed and the Strike Wings gained more ascendancy over the enemy. Examining the Mosquitoes of the Banff Wing from March 1945 to May 1945, the BBSU calculated that there was a 'gain factor' of nearly four to one in favour of the Banff Wing.

The only conclusion that can be drawn from these findings is that it would have been far more advantageous for the Allied war effort if resources had been diverted from Bomber Command to Coastal Command. After the war, the highly respected physicist, Professor P.M.S. Blackett – who was Director of Operational Research at the Admiralty during the war – expressed the opinion that if the Allied air effort had been used more intelligently, the war could have been over half a year or even a year earlier. This does not imply that the higher echelons of Coastal Command possessed superior qualities. It simply means that the targets of Bomber Command were often of less strategic importance than those of Coastal Command. Those at Group and Command Headquarters were, in the opinion of the author, lamentably slow in recognizing the correct anti-shipping tactics for their strike aircraft. Indeed, it is doubtful if these tactics would have been developed at all without the impetus from pilots at Squadron and Flight Commander level, who had to devise the methods by bitter experience in a hail of enemy fire.

The BBSU also examined the effectiveness of the aerial weapons used in anti-shipping operations. They discovered that the weapon which caused the maximum damage to ships was the magnetic mine. This is not surprising, since it contained about 1,000 lb of explosive. Provided the mine, which rested on the sea bed, exploded within about ninety feet of the vessel, severe shock was caused. Whipping of the hull took place, with fractures of castings and buckling of plates; often seacocks in engine rooms were wrenched off their seatings. This damage resulted in flooding, usually followed by sinkings or groundings. Tankers absorbed damage best, sub-divided into watertight compartments.

Torpedoes were also found to have caused considerable damage. Structurally, a torpedo hit would blow a bigger hole in a vessel than a mine, but the shock damage was usually severe only locally; nevertheless, this would almost certainly cause a freighter of average size to sink if far from land, but tankers might survive a hit.

The team found that the 25 lb rocket projectile was the best anti-shipping weapon for its size; underwater hits caused sinkings, whilst hits on the superstructure could destroy machinery and impair the crew's morale. But if the vessel managed to reach safety, the entry and exit holes of the 25 lb warhead could be easily patched over. The 60 lb warhead was generally less effective as a sinking weapon, but it sometimes set ships on fire; this type of warhead was found to have sunk two U-boats that were hit when surfaced.

Five hundred pound medium-capacity bombs were found to be at their most effective if fitted with a short delay, such as 0.04 seconds. Oddly enough, a near miss with these bombs could sometimes prove more damaging than a direct hit, causing severe structural damage and shock, even to destroyers and large merchant vessels. Some of these bombs were timed to burst in the air; they caused little damage to the ships but the flak gunners seemed to hate them more than other weapons.

Twenty mm cannon fire was not intended to sink vessels, but it is known that one small coaster was sunk by five waterline hits with the armour-piercing version of this weapon. Of course, cannon fire was intended primarily for anti-personnel work, and investigations in the course of researching this book have demonstrated its effectiveness.

There is one major effect of the Strike Wings which the BBSU could not assess but which is known to have been considerable. They were largely responsible for bringing the Luftwaffe fighters back to battle with Allied fighter aircraft in 1943. After 20 April 1943, the date when Wing Commander Wheeler led the first successful attack of the North Coates Wing, Germany was compelled to apportion more fighter squadrons to protect her coastal traffic, at the expense of other fighting fronts. Prior to this date, the Allies had experienced difficulty in enticing German fighters to combat outside the confines of the occupied territories. Germany was able to produce large numbers of fighter aircraft, but was falling behind technically by comparison with the USA and the UK. Moreover, the number of experienced pilots available to the Luftwaffe was dwindling steadily, as well as supplies of aviation fuel. The Strike Wings helped to accelerate the downfall of the Luftwaffe.

What then of the men who fought in these coastal battles? The German seamen and their Luftwaffe escorts fought with extreme ferocity until the last hours of the war, when even the most fanatical and blinkered must have known that their defeat was inevitable. Perhaps they did so because they thought their cause was just; love of Fatherland and Führer, patriotism, duty and obedience may have inspired them to fight until the last moment. Perhaps, as some would contend, they did so because they feared the vengeance – even annihilation – that the Allies would wreak upon their people when the full horror of the atrocities that their countrymen had committed came to light. Whatever the reason, noble or ignoble, they fought very effectively until the Strike Wings ceased attacking on 4 May 1945.

The veterans of the Strike Wings who are still alive today are in their late-middle or old age. Those that the author has interviewed seem modest men, not given to recounting their experiences outside the circle of their old Service friends. Nevertheless, most are quietly proud of their achievements. The North Coates Wing, comprising 143, 236 and 254 Squadrons, holds a well-attended annual reunion. 144 Squadron also holds an annual gathering, as does 248 Squadron. There is a 455 Squadron Association in Australia. These men are not plagued with doubts about the wisdom of their operations, for they were never ordered to attack civilian targets; they could see the enemy face to face, and exchanged fire with him. In so far as any conflict can be 'clean', this was the war fought by the Strike Wings.

How these men managed to continue flying when their squadrons suffered such heavy losses may puzzle a younger generation. One has to remember, however, that the more senior were professional airmen, whilst the wartime entrants had all volunteered for aircrew as an alternative to some less dangerous branch of the armed services, often before they had reached their 'call-up' age. All were highly trained patriots, fully aware of the risks that they had to take. They had faith in their squadrons, their Wings, their aircraft and their tactics; sacrifices were inevitable but acceptable. When the new tactics were introduced into the North Coates Wing in April 1943, the loss-rate on anti-shipping attacks in daylight dropped from twenty to about three per cent; the average to the end of the war was roughly four per cent. These figures refer to attacks – not to sorties, some of which did not result in attacks for various reasons.

It was considered that the highest loss that could be borne for continued operations of this type was seven per cent, a figure that was reached only for very short periods by squadrons of the Strike Wings. In fact, a much higher percentage seemed to be acceptable amongst aircrews if they thought that their targets were sufficiently important. For a period in the summer of 1943, when Dönitz ordered his U-boats to remain on the surface and fight it out with aircraft instead of submerging, Coastal Command crews hurled themselves at these hated enemies and suffered losses of twenty per cent without hesitation.

Of course, the men in the Strike Wings were not without fear. Most of them knew this insidious enemy but learned how to control its effects, using their fear as an instrument to help in their survival. A few may have thought themselves invulnerable; for them, it seemed unnatural as well as unfair to be killed at such an early age – it would always be the other fellow who would be lost. Others, perhaps more rational and deep-thinking, considered the chances of survival and decided that the odds were weighted impossibly against them. Nevertheless, most carried on. One such man was Flying Officer Ernest Raymond Davey, a 22-year-old pilot from London, Ontario, serving in 404 (RCAF) Squadron; he went back to his room one day and wrote a simple but moving poem:

> Almighty and all-present power,
>   Short is the prayer I make to Thee;
> I do not ask in battle hour
>   For any shield to cover me.
> The vast unalterable way,
>   From which the stars do not depart,
> May not be turned aside to stay
>   The bullet flying to my heart.
> I ask no help to strike my foe;
>   I seek no petty victory here.
> The enemy I hate, I know
>   To Thee is dear.
> But this I pray: be at my side
>   When death is drawing through the sky;
> Almighty God who also died,
>   Teach me the way that I should die.

Ernest Davey was killed on 2 October 1944. It is for men such as him, the men of the Strike Wings, that this book has been written.

Appendix I

Main Locations of the Strike Wings

NORTH COATES (November '42 to May '45)

Squadron	Commanding Officer	From	To	Aircraft	From	To
236	W/Cdr HD Frazer	November '42	November '42	Beaufighter VIC	June '42	July '43
	W/Cdr HNG Wheeler	November '42	September '43	Beaufighter TFX	July '43	May '45
	W/Cdr WH Cliff	September '43	March '44			
	W/Cdr PDF Mitchell	March '44	August '44			
	W/Cdr EW Tacon	August '44	September '44			
	W/Cdr DG Hall	September '44	May '45			
254	W/Cdr REX Mack	November '42	April '43	Beaufighter VIC	June '42	October '43
	W/Cdr CS Cooper	April '43	September '43	Beaufighter XI	October '43	January '44
	W/Cdr AWD Miller	September '43	January '44	Beaufighter TFX	January '44	May '45
	W/Cdr RE Burns	January '44	September '45			
	W/Cdr DL Cartridge	September '44	May '45			
143	W/Cdr WOV Bennett	December '42	June '43	Beaufighter IIF	December '42	March '43
	W/Cdr RN Lambert	June '43	August '43	Beaufighter XIC	March '43	August '43
	W/Cdr EH McHardy	February '44	October '44	Beaufighter TFX	February '44	October '44

WICK (October '43 to May '44)

144	W/Cdr DOF Lumsden	October '43	May '44	Beaufighter TFX	October '43	May '44
404	W/Cdr CA Willis	October '43	May '44	Beaufighter TFX	October '44	May '44

Squadron	Commanding Officer	From	To	Aircraft	From	To
LEUCHARS (March '44 to April '44)						
455	W/Cdr JN Davenport	March '44	April '44	Beaufighter TFX	March '44	April '44
489	W/Cdr JS Dinsdale	March '44	April '44	Beaufighter TFX	March '44	April '44
LANGHAM (April '44 to October '44)						
455	W/Cdr JN Davenport	April '44	October '44	Beaufighter TFX	April '44	October '44
489	W/Cdr JS Dinsdale	April '44	August '44	Beaufighter TFX	April '44	October '44
	W/Cdr LA Robertson	August '44	October '44			
DAVIDSTOW MOOR (May '44 to July '44)						
144	W/Cdr DOF Lumsden	May '44	July '44	Beaufighter TFX	May '44	July '44
404	W/Cdr AK Gatward	May '44	July '44	Beaufighter TFX	May '44	July '44
STRUBBY (July '44 to September '44)						
144	W/Cdr DOF Lumsden	July '44	August '44	Beaufighter TFX	July '44	September '44
	W/Cdr A Gadd	August '44	September '44			
404	W/Cdr AK Gatward	July '44	August '44	Beaufighter TFX	July '44	September '44
	W/Cdr EW Pierce	August '44	September '44			
PORTREATH (June '44 to September '44)						
235	W/Cdr JV Yonge	June '44	September '44	Mosquito VI	June '44	September '44
248	W/Cdr AD Phillips	June '44	September '44	Mosquito VI and Mosquito XVIII	June '44	September '44
	W/Cdr GD Sise	July '44	September '44			

Squadron	Commanding Officer	From	To	Aircraft	From	To
BANFF (September '44 to May '45)						
143	W/Cdr EH McHardy	October '44	December '44	Mosquito VI	October '44	May '45
	W/Cdr JM Maurice	December '44	February '45			
	W/Cdr CN Foxley-Norris	February '45	May '45			
235	W/Cdr JV Yonge	September '44	October '44-	Mosquito VI	September '44	May '45
	W/Cdr RA Atkinson	October '44	December '44			
	W/Cdr AH Simmonds	December '44	May '45			
248	W/Cdr GD Sise	September '44	March '45	Mosquito VI and Mosquito XVIII	September '44	May '45
144	W/Cdr RK Orrock	March '45	March '45	Beaufighter TFX	September '44	October '44
	W/Cdr HN Jackson-Smith	March '45	May '45			
404	W/Cdr A Gadd	September '44	October '44	Beaufighter TFX	September '44	October '44
	W/Cdr EW Pierce	September '44	October '44	Mosquito VI	March '45	May '45
DALLACHY (October '44 to May '45)						
144	W/Cdr A Gadd	October '44	May '45	Beaufighter TFX	October '44	May '45
404	W/Cdr EW Pierce	October '44	March '45	Beaufighter TFX	October '44	March '45
455	W/Cdr CG Milson	October '44	May '45	Beaufighter TFX	October '44	May '45
489	W/Cdr LA Robertson	October '44	February '45	Beaufighter TFX	October '44	May '45
	W/Cdr DH Hammond	February '45	May '45			

Notes

1. The above dates refer only to the periods when the squadrons formed part of the Strike Wings, e.g. the period when 143 Squadron was based in Cornwall from August '43 to February '44 for special duties is not included.

2. The dates and places do not include the numerous occasions when elements of the squadrons were detached to other aerodromes for short periods or for special strikes, e.g. to Predannack, Manston or Sumburgh.

3. The normal complement of a squadron was 20 pilots, 20 navigators and 20 aircraft.

Appendix II

Kriegsmarine (German Navy) Vessels attacked by the Strike Wings

Zerstörer
=Destroyer.

Z-class. 3,605 tons. 5/150mm guns, 6/37mm guns, 7/20mm guns. Speed 38 knots.

Torpedoboot
=Torpedo boat.

T-class. 2,566 tons. 4/127mm guns, 4/37mm guns, 16/20mm guns. Speed 35 knots.

Torpedoboot
=Torpedo boat.

Elbing class. 1,754 tons. 4/105mm guns, 4/37mm guns, 7/20mm guns. Speed 33 knots.

Schnellboot
=E-boat.

Motor torpedo boat 90 tons. 1/37mm gun, 3/20mm guns. Speed 35-40 knots.

Räumboot
=R-boat.

Small motor minesweeper. 125 tons. 1/37mm gun, 2 machine guns. Speed 18-20 knots.

Minensuchboot
=M-class.

Minesweeper or escort vessel. 600-750 tons. 2/105mm guns, 3/37mm guns, 2 machine guns. Speed 17 knots.

Sperrbrecher
=Mine clearance.

Ex-merchant vessel specially strengthened. 1,000-8,000 tons. Heavily armed with 88mm guns, 37mm guns, 20mm guns and machine guns.

Artillerieträger
=A-boat.

Gun barge. 300-400 tons. 2/88mm guns, 2/75mm guns, 1/37mm gun, 4/86mm rockets. Speed 9 knots.

KriegsUjäger =UJ-boat.	Ex-trawler. Used for anti-submarine.	
Vorpostenboot =Vp-boat.	Ex-trawler. Used for convoy escort.	These converted vessels were usually 150-750 tons and could carry 88mm guns, 20mm guns, and machine guns. The RAF called them flak ships.
Fischdampfer. Walboot.	Ex-trawler. Used for convoy escort. Ex-trawler. Used for convoy escort.	
Kriegsfischkutter =KFK-boat.	Ex-drifter	These converted vessels were usually up to 150 tons. Used as auxiliary minesweepers, harbour defence and local escort duties. Carried 20mm guns and machine guns. The RAF called them small flak-ships.
Motorfischkutter =MFK-boat.	Ex-drifter.	

Unterseeboot =U-boat.

Type XXI	1,621 tons surfaced,	1,819 tons submerged.
Type XVIII	1,482 tons surfaced,	1,652 tons submerged.
Type IXC	1,120 tons surfaced,	1,232 tons submerged.
Type VIIC	769 tons surfaced,	871 tons submerged.
Type XXIII	234 tons surfaced,	258 tons submerged.

Seehund	Midget submarine.	15 tons.	Two-man.
Molch	Midget submarine.	10 tons.	One-man.
Biber	Midget submarine.	6½ tons.	One-man.

Appendix III

Vessels Sunk or Damaged by The Strike Wings

Date	Name	Description	Flag	Tonnage sunk	Tonnage damaged	Squadrons	Location
20 Nov '42	Indus – BS4	Naval tug	Dutch	449		236,254	Hook Holland
18 Apl '43	Hoegh Carrier	Merchant vessel	Norwegian	4906		143,236,254	Texel
29 Apl '43	Aludra	Merchant vessel	Dutch	4930		143,236,254	Terschelling
	Narvik	Merchant vessel	Swedish	4251		143,236,254	Terschelling
	Auguste Kämpf – Vp807	Flak ship	German	385		143,236,254	Terschelling
17 May '43	Kyphissia	Merchant vessel	German	2964		143,236,254	Texel
	M.414	Minesweeper	German	637		143,236,254	Texel
	Hermann Hindrichs – Vp1102	Flak ship	German	523		143,236,254	Texel
1 Jun '43	U-418	Type VIIC U-Boat	German	769		236	West of Brest
13 Jun '43	Stadt Emden	Merchant vessel	German	5180		143,236,254	Den Helder
	Mähren – Vp1108	Flak ship	German	487		143,236,254	Den Helder
2 Aug '43	Fortuna	Merchant vessel	German	2700		143,236,254	Texel
	Arctur – Vp1108	Flak ship	German	314		143,236,254	Texel
25 Sep '43	Neubau 553 – Vp316	Flak ship	German	550		236,254	Den Helder
19 Oct '43	Strassburg	Liner	German		i7000	236,254	Ymuiden
5 Nov '43	S.74	E-boat	German	92		254	Texel
22 Nov '43	Arcturus	Merchant vessel	Norwegian	1651		144,404	Stadlandet
	Gol	Merchant vessel	Norwegian		985	144,404	Stadlandet
	Kari Louise	Merchant vessel	Norwegian		800	144,404	Stadlandet
23 Nov '43	Weissenburg	Tanker	German	6316		236,254	Texel

Date	Name	Description	Flag	Tonnage sunk	Tonnage damaged	Squadrons	Location
18 Dec '43	Pietro Orseolo	Merchant vessel	Italian	6344		248,254	Concarneau
22 Dec '43	U-1062	Type VIIF U-boat	German		1084	144,404	South Norway
14 Jan '44	Wittekind	Merchant vessel	German	4029		144,404	Lister
	Entrerios	Merchant vessel	German	5179		144,404	Lister
	Maurita	Merchant vessel	Norwegian		1569	144,404	Lister
20 Jan '44	Emsland	Merchant vessel	German	5170		144,404	Stadlandet
1 Feb '44	Valencia	Merchant vessel	German	3096		144,404	Stadlandet
	Unitas III – UJ1702	Submarine chaser	German	341		144,404	Stadlandet
21 Feb '44	R131	R-boat	German	150		143,236,254	Texel
1 Mar '44	Maasburg	Merchant vessel	Dutch	6415		143,236,254	Texel
5 Mar '44	Unitas IV – UJ1703	Submarine chaser	German	341		455,489	S.W. Norway
5 Mar '44	Diana	Merchant vessel	Swedish	1878		254,415	Borkum
6 Mar '44	Rabe	Merchant vessel	German	994		455,489	Stavanger
Mar '44	Ryfylke	Merchant vessel	Norwegian	898		455,489	Lister
29 Mar '44	Hermann Schulte	Merchant vessel	German	1305		143,236,254	Juist
	Christel Vinnen	Merchant vessel	German	1894		143,236,254	Juist
30 Mar '44	Monte Rosa	Liner	German		13882	144,404	South Norway
7 Apl '44	Cornouaille	Merchant vessel	German		3324	144,404	Stadlandet
18 Apl '44	Vooruit – Vp1223	Flak ship	German	165		143,236,254	Borkum
	Augusta – Vp1236	Flak ship	German	177		143,236,254	Borkum
19 Apl '44	Notre Dame – Vp1237	Flak ship	German	482		143,236	Ameland
	Hast 2	Buoy layer	German	566		143,236	Ameland
20 Apl '44	Condor – Sperrbrecher 102	Mine destructor ship	German	889		143,236,254	Borkum
	Storfors	Merchant vessel	Swedish	898		143,236,254	Borkum
26 Apl '44	Luise Leonhardt	Merchant vessel	German	4816		143,236,254	Schiermonnikoog

Date	Name	Description	Flag	Tonnage sunk	Tonnage damaged	Squadrons	Location
26 Apr '44	Lasbek	Merchant vessel	German	2159		143,236,254	Schiermonnikoog
6 May '44	Eduard Geiss	Merchant vessel	German	1456		143,236	Borkum
14 May '44	Vesta	Merchant vessel	Dutch	1854		455,489	Borkum
	M.435	Minesweeper	German	637		455,489	Borkum
6 Jun '44	Z.32	Destroyer	German		2603	144,404	Belle Ile
	Z.24	Destroyer	German		2603	144,404	Belle Ile
	ZHI	Destroyer	Dutch		1204	144,404	Belle Ile
8 Jun '44	Elbe	Harbour defence	German	150		143,236	Cherbourg
	Johanna	Harbour defence	German	150		143,236	Cherbourg
13 Jun '44	R97	R-boat	German	125		143,236	Boulogne
	S178	E-boat	German	92		143,236	Boulogne
	S179	E-boat	German	92		143,236	Boulogne
	S189	E-boat	German	92		143,236	Boulogne
15 Jun '44	Coburg – Schiff 49	Experimental vessel	Dutch	7900		236,254, 455,489	Shiermonnikoog
	Gustav Nachtigal	Depot ship	Belgian	3500		236,254, 455,489	Shiermonnikoog
	M.103	Minesweeper	German	772		236,254, 455,489	Shiermonnikoog
23 Jun '44	R79	R-boat	German	125		143,236	Boulogne
29 Jun '44	AFP8	Gun barge	German	280		143,236	Le Treport
30 Jun '44	FV439 – UJ1408	Submarine chaser	German	530		235,248,404	Biscay
4 Jul '44	AFP99	Gun barge	German	280		143,236	Boulogne
5 Jul '44	Heinrich Onnen – Vp1256	Flak ship	German	274		236,254	Texel
	RIII	R-boat	German	125		236,254	Texel
5 Jul '44	512	Air sea rescue	German	50		143,236	Boulogne

Date	Name	Description	Flag	Tonnage sunk	Tonnage damaged	Squadrons	Location
6 Jul '44	Ernst Brockelmann	Merchant vessel	German		1900	144,404, 455,489	Norderney
	Stadt Riga	Merchant vessel	German	3002		144,404, 455,489	Norderney
8 Jul '44	Tannhauser	Merchant vessel	German	1923		144,404, 236,254	Heligoland
	Sif	Merchant vessel	Swedish	1437		144,404, 236,254	Heligoland
	Miranda	Merchant vessel	German	736		144,404, 236,254	Heligoland
	M.264	Minesweeper	German	637		144,404, 236,254	Heligoland
	555	Air sea rescue	German	58		144,404, 236,254	Heligoland
15 Jul '44	Mars – Vp621	Flak ship	German	268		235,248	Belle Ile
15 Jul '44	Irania	Tanker	Norwegian		2184	144,455,489	The Naze
18 Jul '44	R139	R-boat	German	150		144,236, 254,404	Juist
21 Jul '44	Orient	Merchant vessel	Finnish	4160		144,404, 455,489	Wangeroog
	M.307	Minesweeper	German	637		144,404 455,489	Wangeroog
22 Jul '44	Falkand – Vp810	Flak ship	German	314		236,254	Wangeroog
	Amtsgerichtsrat Pilsche – Vp812	Flak ship	German	386		236,254	Wangeroog
6 Aug '44	Jupiter – Sans Pareil	Fast escort ship	French	1500		236,254	Ile de Yeu
8 Aug '44	M.366	Minesweeper	German	637		236,254	Bourgeneuf
8 Aug '44	M.367	Minesweeper	German	637		236,254	Bourgeneuf
8 Aug '44	M.428	Minesweeper	German	637		236,254	Bourgeneuf

Date	Name	Description	Flag	Tonnage sunk	Tonnage damaged	Squadrons	Location
8 Aug '44	M.438	Minesweeper	German	637		236,254	Bourgeneuf
8 Aug '44	Vim	Merchant vessel	Norwegian	1221		254,455,489	Egersund
	Carsten Russ	Merchant vessel	German		994	254,455,489	Egersund
10 Aug '44	Santos	Merchant vessel	German	5943		455,489	Heligoland
12 Aug '44	Sauerland – Sperrbrecher 7	Mine destructor ship	German	7087		236,404	La Pallice
	Germania – Vp410	Flak ship	German	427		236,404	La Pallice
	M.370	Minesweeper	German	637		235,248	Gironde
	Mari Therese – M.4204	Minesweeper	German	288		235,248	Gironde
13 Aug '44	Schwanheim – Sperrbrecher 5	Mine destructor ship	German	5339		236,404	Royan
	Magdeburg – Sperrbrecher 6	Mine destructor ship	German	6128		236,404	Royan
13 Aug '44	M.383	Minesweeper	German	637		254,455,489	Heligoland
	Preussen	Flak ship	German	425		254,455,489	Heligoland
14 Aug '44	Schwarzes Meer	Tanker	German		3371	235,248	Le Verdon
14 Aug '44	Le Leroux	Harbour defence	French	55		236,404	Arachon Bay
20 Aug '44	August Bösch – Vp409	Flak ship	German	401		236,404	Sables d'Olonne
	Jean Marthe – M.4214	Minesweeper	German	156		236,404	Sables d'Olonne
21 Aug '44	M.292	Minesweeper	German	637		235,248	Le Verdon
24 Aug '44	Z.24	Destroyer	German	2603		236,404	Le Verdon
	T.24	Torpedo boat	German	1294		236,404	Le Verdon
25 Aug '44	M.347	Minesweeper	German	637		144,254,445, 489	Schiermonnikoog

Date	Name	Description	Flag	Tonnage sunk	Tonnage damaged	Squadrons	Location
27 Aug '44	Otto	Merchant vessel	German	154		248	St Nazaire
29 Aug '44	Hermes – Sperrbrecher 26	Mine destructor ship	German	2503		144,254,455,489	Heligoland
	Valeria – Sperrbrecher 176	Mine destructor ship	German	1450		144,254,455,489	Heligoland
	Mewa VIII – Vp1269	Flak ship	German	112		144,254,455,489	Heligoland
1 Sep '44	Tilly	Minelayer	German	146		254	Ymuiden
6 Sep '44	Rosafred	Merchant vessel	Swedish	1496		455,489	Wangeroog
	Breda	Merchant vessel	Norwegian	1261		455,489	Wangeroog
	Emil	Lightship	German	400		455,489	Wangeroog
8 Sep '44	Hengelo	Merchant vessel	Dutch	195		236,254,455,489	S.W. Norway
11 Sep '44	M.426	Minesweeper	German	637		236,254,455,489	South Norway
	M.462	Minesweeper	German	637		236,254,455,489	South Norway
11 Sep '44 and	T.61	Torpedo boat	German	1931		143,524,855	West Frisian Is.
12 Sep '44	Gooland	Dredger	Dutch	239		143,524,855	West Frisian Is.
	AFP.49	Gun barge	German	280		143,524,855	West Frisian Is.
	AFP.59	Gun barge	German	280		143,524,855	West Frisian Is.
	MFP.185	Landing craft	German	200		143,524,855	West Frisian Is.
	MFP.186	Landing craft	German	200		143,524,855	West Frisian Is.
	MFP.	Landing craft	German	200		143,524,855	West Frisian Is.
	MFP.	Landing craft	German	200		143,524,855	West Frisian Is.
	KFK.279 – M.3246	Minesweeper	German	150		143,524,855	West Frisian Is.
	Den Helder	Harbour defence	Dutch	150		143,524,855	West Frisian Is.
13 Sep '44	FV203	Harbour defence	Dutch	60		143,524,855	West Frisian Is.

Date	Name	Description	Flag	Tonnage sunk	Tonnage damaged	Squadrons	Location
14 Sep '44	Sülldorf – Vp1608	Flak ship	German	264		144,404,235,248	Christiansand
	Iris	Merchant vessel	German		3323	144,404,235,248	Christiansand
17 Sep '44	Friedrich Suthmeier – Vp1202	Flak ship	German	194		143,236,254	Heligoland
	Juno – Vp1201	Flak ship	German	210		143,236,254	Heligoland
19 Sep '44	Lynx	Merchant vessel	Norwegian	1367		144,235,404	Askevold
	Tyrifjord	Merchant vessel	Norwegian	3080		144,235,404	Askevold
21 Sep '44	Vangsnes	Merchant vessel	Norwegian	191		144,404,235,248	Lister
	Hygia	Merchant vessel	Norwegian	104		144,404,235,248	Lister
	Fishing vessel		Norwegian	75		144,404,235,248	Lister
24 Sep '44	Biber – V5502	Harbour defence	German	168		248	Hjeltefjord
	Storesund	Merchant vessel	Norwegian		563	248	Hjeltefjord
25 Sep '44	M.471	Minesweeper	German	637		143,236,254,455,489	Den Helder
	Jannetje – Vs.423	Harbour defence	Dutch	107		143,236,254,455,489	Den Helder
28 Sep '44	Dragoner NK.02	Harbour defence	German	80		248	South Norway
4 Oct '44	Wachtel NY922	Merchant vessel	German	992		143,855	Hook Holland
9 Oct '44	Rudolf Oldendorff	Merchant vessel	German	1953		144,235,404	Egersund
	Sarp	Merchant vessel	Norwegian		1116	144,235,404	Egersund
	O.N. Anderson – UJ.1711	Submarine chaser	German	485		144,235,404	Egersund
15 Oct '44	Inger Johanne	Tanker	Norwegian	1202		144,235,248,404	Christiansand

Date	Name	Description	Flag	Tonnage sunk	Tonnage damaged	Squadrons	Location
15 Oct '44	Mosel – Vp1605	Flak ship	German	426		144,235,248,404	Christiansand
15 Oct '44	Europa	Harbour defence	Dutch	339		236,254,455	Wangeroog
	KFK.93	Harbour defence	German	110		236,254,455	Wangeroog
	Margaret – LAT.15	Light gun barge	German	200		236,254,455	Wangeroog
21 Oct '44	Eckenheim	Merchant vessel	German	1923		235,248,404	Haugesund
	Vestra	Merchant vessel	Norwegian	1432		235,248,404	Haugesund
23 Oct '44	Zick – V5506	Harbour vessel	Norwegian	220		235,248	Hjeltefjord
	Biri	Merchant vessel	Norwegian		940	235,248	Hjeltefjord
8 Nov '44	Aquila	Merchant vessel	German	3495		144,404,455,333	Midtgulen
	Helga Ferdinand	Merchant vessel	German	2566		144,404,455,333	Midtgulen
	Framnaes	Merchant vessel	Norwegian		307	144,404,455,333	Midtgulen
13 Nov '44	Rosenburg I	Merchant vessel	Norwegian		1964	144,235,248	Rekefjord
	R32	R-boat	German	110		144,235,248	Rekefjord
	529	Air sea rescue	German	75		144,235,248	Rekefjord
14 Nov '44	Sardinien	Trawler	Norwegian	177		143,235,248	Sognefjord
	Gula	Merchant vessel	Norwegian		264	143,235,248	Sognefjord
21 Nov '44	Flamingo	Harbour defence	German	165		236	Weser
	Lumne	Harbour defence	German	169		236	Weser
25 Nov '44	AFP.4	Gun barge	German	280		254	Borkum
27 Nov '44	Jersbek	Merchant vessel	German	5740		404,489	Sulafjord
	Fidelitas	Merchant vessel	Italian		2804	404,489	Sulafjord
5 Dec '44	Radbord	Merchant vessel	German	4354		455,489	Orstenfjord
	Albert Janus	Merchant vessel	German	2275		455,489	Orstenfjord

Date	Name	Description	Flag	Tonnage sunk	Tonnage damaged	Squadrons	Location
25 Jan '45	Ilse Fritzen	Merchant vessel	German	5099		143,235,248	Eidgfjord
	Bjergfin	Merchant vessel	Norwegian	696		143,235,248	Maaloy
3 Feb '45	Tiefland	Merchant vessel	German		1923	143,235,248	Bergen
12 Feb '45	Sivas	Merchant vessel	German		3832	143,235	Flado
21 Feb '45	Ibis	Merchant vessel	Norwegian		1367	235	Lervik
	Gula	Merchant vessel	Norwegian		264	235	Lervik
	Austri	Merchant vessel	Norwegian	490		235	Lervik
26 Feb '45	Rogn	Tanker	Norwegian		835	404	Christiansand
7 Mar '45	MFP.	Gun barge	German	130		143,235,248, 333	East Skaggerak
	MFP.	Gun barge	German	130		143,235,248, 333	East Skaggerak
	MFP.	Gun barge	German	130		143,235,248, 333	East Skaggerak
	MFP.	Gun barge	German	130		143,235,248, 333	East Skaggerak
	Innsbruck Vp1610	Flak ship	German	256		143,235,248, 333	East Skaggerak
8 Mar '45	Phoenicia	Merchant vessel	German		4124	144,404,455, 489	Kiel Canal
	Heimdal	Merchant ferry	Danish		978	144,404,455, 489	Midgulen
17 Mar '45	Iris	Merchant vessel	German	3323		143,235,248, 333	Aalesund
	Remage	Merchant vessel	German	1830		143,235,248, 333	Aalesund
	Log	Merchant vessel	Norwegian	1684		143,235,248, 333	Aalesund
	Erna	Merchant vessel	German		865	143,235,248, 333	Aalesund

Date	Name	Description	Flag	Tonnage sunk	Tonnage damaged	Squadrons	Location
23 Mar '45	Lysaker	Merchant vessel	Norwegian	910		144,489	Stadlandet
23 Mar '45	Inga Essberger	Merchant vessel	German		1827	143	Aalesund
	Romssdale	Merchant vessel	Norwegian		138	143	Aalesund
23 Mar '45	Rotenfels	Merchant vessel	German		7854	235,333	Dalsfjord
24 Mar '45	Thetis	Merchant vessel	German	2788		144,404,455, 489	Egersund
	Sarp	Merchant vessel	Norwegian	1116		144,404,455, 489	Egersund
24 Mar '45	Biber	Midget submarine	German	6		254	Hook Holland
25 Mar '45	Seehund	Midget submarine	German	12		254	Hook Holland
30 Mar '45	Scharnhorn	Merchant vessel	German	2643		143,235,248, 333	Porsgrunn
	Gudrid Borgstad	Merchant vessel	Norwegian	1664		143,235,248, 333	Porsgrunn
	Svanefjell	Merchant vessel	Norwegian	1371		143,235,248, 333	Porsgrunn
	Gudrid	Merchant vessel	Norwegian	1305		143,235,248, 333	Porsgrunn
	Torafire	Merchant vessel	Norwegian	823		143,235,248, 333	Porsgrunn
2 Apl '45	Concordia	Merchant vessel	Norwegian	5154		143,235,248, 333	Sandefjord
	William Blumer	Merchant vessel	German	3604		143,235,248, 333	Sandefjord
	Espana	Merchant vessel	German		7465	143,235,248, 333	Sandefjord
	Kattegat	Merchant vessel	German		6031	143,235,248, 333	Sandefjord

Date	Name	Description	Flag	Tonnage sunk	Tonnage damaged	Squadrons	Location
2 Apl '45	Hektor	Merchant vessel	Norwegian		5742	143,235,248, 333	Sandefjord
	Belpamela	Merchant vessel	Norwegian		3165	143,235,248, 333	Sandefjord
4 Apl '45	Palmyra	Merchant vessel	German		3007	455,489	Feddefjord
5 Apl '45	Helmi Sohle	Flak ship	German	453		143,235,248, 333	Kattegat
	Fishing vessel		German	50		143,235,248, 333	Kattegat
7 Apl '45	Oldenburg	Merchant vessel	German		4595	144,455,489	Sognefjord
9 Apl '45	U-804	Type IXC U-boat	German	1144		143,235,248	Skaggerak
	U-843	Type IXC U-boat	German	1120		143,235,248	Skaggerak
	U-1065	Type VIIC U-boat	German	769		143,235,248	Skaggerak
9 to 13 Apl '45	Biber (4 vessels)	Midget submarines	German	24		236,254,119, 810	Scheldt
10 Apl '45	Seehund	Midget submarine	German	12		254	Ostend
11 Apl '45	M.2	Minesweeper	German	772		144,455,489	S.W. Norwegian
11 Apl '45	Dione	Merchant vessel	Norwegian	1620		143,235,248, 333	Porsgrunn
	Kalmar	Merchant vessel	German	964		143,235,248, 333	Porsgrunn
	Nordsjo	Merchant vessel	Norwegian	178		143,235,248, 333	Porsgrunn
	Traust	Merchant vessel	Norwegian	190		143,235,248, 333	Porsgrunn
	Helgoland	Merchant vessel	German		535	143,235,248, 333	Porsgrunn
	Skagen	Trawler	Swedish		219	143,235,248, 333	Porsgrunn

Date	Name	Description	Flag	Tonnage sunk	Tonnage damaged	Squadrons	Location
12 Apl '45	Seehund	Midget submarine	German	12		236,254	Hook Holland
	Seehund	Midget submarine	German	12		236,254	Hook Holland
19 Apl '45	U-251	Type VIIC U-boat	German	769		143,235,248, 333	Kattegat
	U-2335	Type XXIII U-boat	German		234	143,235,248, 333	Kattegat
22 Apl '45	Elmar	Merchant vessel	German	268		455,489	Maaloy
23 Apl '45	Ingerseks	Merchant vessel	Norwegian	4969		144,455,489	Sognefjord
2 May '45	M.293	Minesweeper	German	637		143,235,248, 404,333	Kattegat
	U-2359	Type XXIII U-boat	German	234		143,235,248, 404,333	Kattegat
	U-	Type XXIII U-boat	German		234	143,235,248, 404,333	Kattegat
3 May '45	U-2524	Type XXI U-boat	German	1621		236,254	The Belts
	Ramfoss	Merchant vessel	Norwegian		1165	236,254	The Belts
	Dorpat	Merchant vessel	German	3535		236,254	The Belts
	Inster	Merchant vessel	German	4747		236,254	The Belts
	Pallas	Merchant vessel	German	627		236,254	The Belts
	Greif – VS524	Small flak ship	German	50		236,254	The Belts
	Der Deutsche	Liner	German		11453	236,254	Kiel Bay
	Taifun	Tanker	German	6405		236,254	Kiel Bay
3 May '45	Java	Merchant vessel	Danish	8681		144,455	Kiel Bay
	Falstria	Merchant vessel	Danish		6992	144,455	Kiel Bay
	Jutlandia	Merchant vessel	Danish		8457	144,455	Kiel Bay
4 May '45	Wolfgang L.M. Russ	Merchant vessel	German	3750		143,235,248, 404,333	Aarhus
	Günther Russ	Merchant vessel	German		998	143,235,248, 404,333	Aarhus

Date	Name	Description	Flag	Tonnage sunk	Tonnage damaged	Squadrons	Location
4 May '45	Angamos	Merchant vessel	Danish		3540	143,235,248, 404,333	Aarhus
4 May '45	U-2503	Type XXI U-boat	German	1621		236,254	The Belts
	U-2338	Type XXIII U-boat	German	234		236,254	The Belts
	U-393	Type VIIC U-boat	German	769		236,254	The Belts
	U-236	Type VIIC U-boat	German	769		236,254	The Belts
		Totals		300,055	118,137		

Under Flags	Sunk	Damaged
German	157	32
Norwegian	35	20
French	2	–
Danish	1	4
Swedish	4	2
Dutch	12	1
Italian	2	–
Belgian	1	–
Finnish	1	–
	= 215	= 59

Notes: (1) This list does not include the numerous escort vessels damaged by the Strike Wings.

(2) Where squadrons other than the Strike Wings joined in the attacks, the squadron numbers are also included.

(3) This list is compiled from British and German records. Whilst these are the best records available, they were kept in wartime and cannot be considered reliable in every respect.

Bibliography and Sources

Books, articles and official publications:

A.P. 1721H. Pilot's Notes, Beaufighter TFX. HMSO, 1946.
A.P. 1730B. Prismatic Gun Sight, Type G.1. March, 1941.
A.P. 2019E. Pilot's Notes, Mosquito FBVI. HMSO, 1944.
Arnt, P. *Deutsche Sperrbrecher, 1914–45*. Stuttgart: Motorbuch Verlag, 1979.
Beaver, P. *E-Boats and Coastal Craft*. Cambridge: Patrick Stevens, 1980.
Beaver, P. *German Destroyers and Escorts*. Cambridge: Patrick Stevens, 1980.
Beesley, P. *Very Special Intelligence*: The Story of the Admiralty's Intelligence Centre, 1939–1945. London: Hamish Hamilton, 1977.
Bekker, C. *Hitler's Naval War*. London: MacDonald, 1974.
Bergel, H. *Flying Wartime Aircraft*. Newton Abbot: David & Charles, 1972.
Blackett, P.M.S. *Studies of War*. Edinburgh: Oliver & Boyd, 1962.
Brice, M. *Axis Blockade Runners of World War II*. London: Batsford, 1981.
Burns, R.E. *Anti-Shipping Strikes*. London: Aerospace, February 1979.
Churchill, W. *The Second World War*. London: Cassell, 1948–54.
Coastal Command Reviews, Monthly. November 1942 to June 1945. Unpublished.
Cocker, M. *Destroyers of the Royal Navy, 1893–1981*. London: Ian Allan, 1981.
Couhant, J.L. *French Warships of WW2*. London: Ian Allan, 1971.
E.B. 692. *British Rocket Stores*. London: Ministry of Supply, 1946.
Foxley-Norris, C. *A Lighter Shade of Blue*. London: Ian Allan, 1978.
Frankland, N. *The Bombing Offensive against Germany*. London: Faber, 1965.
Fuehrer Conferences on Naval Affairs. London: Admiralty, 1947–8.
Girbig, W. *Jagdgeschwader 5 'Eismeerjäger'*. Stuttgart: Motorbuch.

Golden, F. St. C. 'The Management of Rescued Shipwreck Survivors'. – Journal of the Royal Naval Medical Service. Summer, 1980.

Green, W. *Warplanes of the Third Reich*. London: MacDonald, 1970.

Gröner, E. *Die Deutschen Kriegsschiffe, 1915–1945*. Munich: Lehmanns, 1966.

Herington, J. *Australia in the War, 1939–45*. Canberra: Australian War Memorial, 1963.

Jones, G. *The Month of the Lost U-boats*. London: Kimber, 1977.

Keating, W.R. *The Role of Cold in Immersion Accidents*. Hypothermia Ashore and Afloat. Aberdeen: University Press, 1981.

Kostenuk, S. & Griffin, J. *RCAF Squadrons and Aircraft*. Toronto: Hakkert, 1977.

La Marina Italiana nella Seconda Guerra Mondial: I Violatori di Blocco. Rome, 1963.

Lawson, J.H.W. *The Story of 455(RAAF) Squadron*. Melbourne: Wilke, 1947.

Lenton, H.T. *German Warships of WW2*. London: MacDonald & Janes, 1975.

Lloyds War Losses, The Second World War, Vol. 3.

Memorandum on the Conduct of Anti-Shipping Operations. London: Coastal Command, 1945.

Mendlicott, W.N. *The Economic Blockade*. London: Longmans Green, 1959.

Milward, A. *The German Economy at War*. London: Athlone Press, 1965.

Norway Basic Handbook. London: Ministry of Economic Warfare, 1943.

Norway Volume II. Naval Intelligence Division. London: Admiralty, 1943.

Obermaier, E. *Die Ritterkreuzträger der Luftwaffe*. Mainz: Dieter Hoffman.

PAP No. 108. *Aircraft Torpedo Sight*. Beaufighter (Travelling Lamp Type), 1944.

Pawle, G. *The Secret War, 1939–45*. London: Harrap, 1956.

Peyton-Ward, D.V. *The RAF in Maritime War*. The Atlantic and Home Waters, Vols III, IV, V. July 1941 – May 1945. Unpublished.

Peyton-Ward, D.V. *U-boats 1939–45*. Individual Histories. Unpublished.

Phelan, K. & Brice, M.H. *Fast Attack Craft*. London: MacDonald & Janes, 1977.

Price, A. *Aircraft versus Submarine*. London: Kimber, 1973.

P-51 Mustang Combat Stories. North American Aviation Inc., 1945.

Rawlings, J.D.R. *Coastal, Support & Special Squadrons of the RAF and their Aircraft*. London: Janes, 1982.

RCAF Overseas. Toronto: Oxford University Press, 1944–45.

Richards, D. & Saunders, H. St.G. *The Royal Air Force 1939–45*. London: HMSO, 1953–54.

Robertson, B. *Aircraft Camouflage and Markings, 1907–54*. Marlow: Harleyford, 1956.

Roskill, S.W. *The War at Sea*. London: HMSO, 1954–61.

Rössler, E. *The U-boat*. London: Arms & Armour Press, 1981.

Sharp, C.M. & Bowyer, N.F.J. Mosquito. London: Faber, 1967.

Speer, A. *Inside the Third Reich*. Weidenfeld & Nicholson, 1970.

Stars and Stripes. *American Forces Newspaper*. January – August, 1944.

Thetford, O. *Aircraft of the Royal Air Force since 1918*. London: Putnam, 1979.

Thomson, H.L. *New Zealanders with the Royal Air Force, 1939–45*. Wellington: Owen, 1953.

Toynbee, A. & V.M. *The War and the Neutrals*. London: Oxford University Press, 1956.

United States Strategic Bombing Survey. The Effects of Strategic Bombing on German Transportation. Transportation Division. 1945.

Wallace, G.F. *The Guns of the Royal Air Force, 1939–45*. London: Kimber, 1972.

Webster, C. & Frankland, N. *The Strategic Offensive against Germany*. London: HMSO, 1961.

Zuckerman, S. *From Apes to Warlords*. London: Hamish Hamilton, 1978.

War Diaries etc. – Allied:

65 Squadron	AIR27	595	Public Record Office.
118 Squadron	AIR27	907	Public Record Office.
143 Squadron	AIR27	978	Public Record Office.
		979	
144 Squadron	AIR27	983	Public Record Office.
167 Squadron	AIR27	1092	Public Record Office.
183 Squadron	AIR27	1137	Public Record Office.
193 Squadron	AIR27	1157	Public Record Office.

War Diaries etc. – Allied: (*cont.*)

235 Squadron	AIR27	1444	Public Record Office.
236 Squadron	AIR27	1447	Public Record Office.
		1448	
		1449	
248 Squadron	AIR27	1496	Public Record Office.
		1497	
254 Squadron	AIR27	1515	Public Record Office.
		1516	
266 Squadron	AIR27	1559	Public Record Office.
279 Squadron	AIR27	1610	Public Record Office.
280 Squadron	AIR27	1612	Public Record Office.
316 Squadron	AIR27	1705	Public Record Office.
402 Squadron	AIR27	1777	Public Record Office.
404 Squadron	AIR27	1786	Public Record Office.
416 Squadron	AIR27	1815	Public Record Office.
455 Squadron	AIR27	1898	Public Record Office.
487 Squadron	AIR27	1935	Public Record Office.
489 Squadron	AIR27	1938	Public Record Office.
524 Squadron	AIR27	1997	Public Record Office.
611 Squadron	AIR27	2110	Public Record Office.
613 Squadron	AIR27	2117	Public Record Office.
16 Group	AIR25	303	Public Record Office.
16 Group Appendices	AIR25	367	Public Record Office.
24 Air Sea Rescue	AIR29	443	Public Record Office.
Combat Report:	AIR50	517	Public Record Office.
S.S. Shulemson			
British Bombing	AIR15	706	Public Record Office.
Survey			
RAF Banff	AIR28	49	Public Record Office.
RAF Coltishall	AIR28	168	Public Record Office.
HMS *Belfast*	ADM53	117015	Public Record Office.
HMS *Castletown*	ADM199	1407	Public Record Office.
HMS *Illustrious*	ADM53	117658	Public Record Office.
USS *Shad*	ADM1	14426	Public Record Office.

Headquarters 8th Fighter Command, USAAF.
Intelligence Summary No. 249.   Maxwell Air Base, USA.

War Diaries – German:

20 November 1942	13 Vorpostenflottille.
	II/391 2nd Gruppe of Jagdgeschwader 1.
18 April 1943	8 Vorpostenflottille.
22 June 1943	Befehlshaber der Sicherung der Nordsee.
	5 Sicherungsdivision.
	27 Minensuchflottille.

War Diaries – German: (*cont.*)

22 June 1943	6 Minensuchflottille.
	8 Vorpostenflottille.
	11 Vorpostenflottille.
	13 Vorpostenflottille.
	20 Vorpostenflottille.
2 August 1943	Befehlshaber der Sicherung der Nordsee.
	1 Sicherungsdivision.
	3 Sicherungsdivision.
	Admiral in der Niederlanden.
	8 Vorpostenflottille.
	11 Vorpostenflottille.
	13 Vorpostenflottille.
	III/391 3rd Gruppe of Jagdgeschwader 1.
4–18 December 1943	Marinegruppenkommando West.
	Befehlshaber der Sicherung West.
	3 Sicherungsdivision.
	24 Minensuchflottille.
26 January 1944	Marineoberkommando Norwegen.
	Admiral der norwegischen Westküste.
	17 UJ-Flottille.
	59 UJ-Flottille
19 May 1944	Marinegruppenkommando West.
	5 Torpedobootflottille.
	"Jaguar".
	3 Sicherungsdivision.
	24 Minensuchflottille.
	40 Minensuchflottille.
6–7 June 1944	8 Zerstörerflottille.
	"Z.24".
	"Z.32".
	"ZH.1".
15 June 1944	7 Minensuchflottille.
8 August 1944	Admiral der norwegischen Westküste.
	6 Küstensicherungsverband.
	"K.2".
	17 UJ-Flottille.
24 August 1944	Marinegruppenkommando West.
	Führer der Zerstörer.
	Befehlshaber der Sicherung West.
	1/Skl Part D.
2–3 October 1944	38 Minensuchflottille.
5 December 1944	Admiral der norwegischen Westküste.
	51 Vorpostenflottille.
	53 Vorpostenflottille.
	Kustensicherungsverborden norwegischen Westküste.

Index